SPIRITUAL LIVES

General Editor
Timothy Larsen

SPIRITUAL LIVES

General Editor
Timothy Larsen

The *Spiritual Lives* series features biographies of prominent men and women whose eminence is not primarily based on a specifically religious contribution. Each volume provides a general account of the figure's life and thought, while giving special attention to his or her religious contexts, convictions, doubts, objections, ideas, and actions. Many leading politicians, writers, musicians, philosophers, and scientists have engaged deeply with religion in significant and resonant ways that have often been overlooked or underexplored. Some of the volumes will even focus on men and women who were lifelong unbelievers, attending to how they navigated and resisted religious questions, assumptions, and settings. The books in this series will therefore recast important figures in fresh and thought-provoking ways.

George Eliot

Whole Soul

ILANA M. BLUMBERG

OXFORD
UNIVERSITY PRESS

Great Clarendon Street, Oxford, OX2 6DP,
United Kingdom

Oxford University Press is a department of the University of Oxford.
It furthers the University's objective of excellence in research, scholarship,
and education by publishing worldwide. Oxford is a registered trade mark of
Oxford University Press in the UK and in certain other countries

© Ilana M. Blumberg 2024

The moral rights of the author have been asserted

All rights reserved. No part of this publication may be reproduced, stored in
a retrieval system, or transmitted, in any form or by any means, without the
prior permission in writing of Oxford University Press, or as expressly permitted
by law, by licence or under terms agreed with the appropriate reprographics
rights organization. Enquiries concerning reproduction outside the scope of the
above should be sent to the Rights Department, Oxford University Press, at the
address above

You must not circulate this work in any other form
and you must impose this same condition on any acquirer

Published in the United States of America by Oxford University Press
198 Madison Avenue, New York, NY 10016, United States of America

British Library Cataloguing in Publication Data
Data available

Library of Congress Control Number: 2023942274

ISBN 978–0–19–284509–2

DOI: 10.1093/oso/9780192845092.001.0001

Printed and bound by
CPI Group (UK) Ltd, Croydon, CR0 4YY

Links to third party websites are provided by Oxford in good faith and
for information only. Oxford disclaims any responsibility for the materials
contained in any third party website referenced in this work.

To Priya, Shai, and Tzipora.
May you find what sustains you.

Contents

Preface ix
Acknowledgments xiii
List of Abbreviations xv

1. "Longing to See and Know Many Things," 1819–1840   1
2. "New Treasures," 1840–1842   16
3. "Giving Full Faith to Every Symbol," 1843–1849   32
4. "This Fuller Life," 1849–1854   49
5. "A Heathen and an Outlaw," 1854–1856   64
6. "We Mortals," 1856–1857   81
7. "A Divine Work to Be Done in Life," 1857   94
8. "Harvest Time," 1858–1859   110
9. "Pilgrims on Earth," 1859–1860   129
10. The "Soul's Own Warrant," 1860–1863   145
11. "A Heart without a Livery"? 1864–1869   162
12. "With Measured Wing," 1869–1872   179
13. "In Heaven or On Earth," 1873–1881   192

Works Cited 207
Index 213
List of other titles in Spiritual Lives series 231

Preface

George Eliot, born Mary Anne Evans, was the premier novelist of ideas in her era, unique in combining her extraordinary erudition across the fields of theology, philosophy, history, and the sciences, with great talent for storytelling that appealed to a broad Victorian audience. A little more than two hundred years after her birth, her works remain central to our understanding of Victorian literature and the period itself.

Like all major figures, George Eliot has come to stand for something beyond herself. Her life story lends itself to readers today as an inspiration.[1] For some, she stands as the woman writer who dared to defy social norms and, living unmarried with the man she loved, pseudonym in place, wrote her way to the summit of English literary history. Though she was too scandalous in her time to be buried in Westminster Abbey, a century after her death she was memorialized by a stone in Poets' Corner.

For many others, she stands as the modern writer who lost her early religious faith, broke with her family in order to live as a freethinker, and then invented secular humanism not through sermons but through ambitious, bestselling novels. Familiar ending: though she was too scandalous in her time to be buried in Westminster Abbey, a century after her death she was memorialized by a stone in Poets' Corner.

There is truth to these versions, especially the courageous, scandalous part.

But George Eliot's writings—her letters, essays, poetry, and novels—also alert us to a writer who was anxious about any form of forgetting the past, bruising one's roots, breaking loyalty to what had nurtured and raised one, individually and culturally. I am interested in this challenge, then: to understand how a writer who did, indeed, renounce Christian beliefs she had held sacred made sense of a cultural world and a historical moment that still, to her mind, absolutely demanded "religion," as she defined it in 1859: "something, clearly, that lies outside personal desires, that includes resignation for ourselves and active love for what is not ourselves."[2]

Part of my interest comes from the sense that the story we have told ourselves—we, modern readers, scholars of literature in the late twentieth and early twenty-first century—is too simple.[3] That no one who "loses faith," and then spends her entire adult life writing is simply rehearsing what she already knows to be true. Especially George Eliot, who repeatedly described her financial success as the freedom to write what she truly wanted and not merely another version of what had last pleased the crowd.

It is my intention in this book to re-encounter the George Eliot who could not separate her contemporary project of poetry and prose from the pressing, existential demand to see herself in continuity with the past and with some purchase on a future of fuller knowledge that could shape a better world; she also sought to see herself in relation to the people among whom she lived.

The England that surrounded her was by no means secular. Though some of the most famous Victorian stories we know concern intellectuals who confronted challenges to their religious faith (some remaining traditionally faithful, some adapting their faith, some abandoning or transforming it in successive considerations), nonetheless the dominant culture for most of George Eliot's readers was religiously vital. It was characterized, among other things, by massive amounts and kinds of religious publication (far outstripping scientific publication), highly attended sermons, increased church-building, and intense denominational rivalry. As the historian Frank M. Turner has demonstrated, divisions between what we today construe as "religious" and "secular" activities, forms of thinking, and social roles impair our ability to understand the mix of things in Victorian experience.[4] It may be easier for us to appreciate this mix if we consider that, two hundred years later, the worlds many readers of *this* book live in have not yielded decisively to secularism in terms of community-building, personal ethics, calendar, life rituals, valued texts, commercial markets, political affiliations, or expressions of national aims and ideals.

In returning to George Eliot's life and writings, recognizing that what we see in them is shaped, too, by what has and has not unfolded since their creation, we have the opportunity to see a great writer, a courageous woman, who kept turning and turning the materials of faith, representing the personal and social possibilities and liabilities of belief, affiliation, action. That she made something new, there is no doubt. In that spirit, here is a new story of George Eliot.

Notes

1. Evocative explorations of personal relations to Eliot's novels include Mary Gordon, "George Eliot, Dorothea and Me: Reading (and Rereading) *Middlemarch*," *New York Times*, May 8, 1994, https://www.nytimes.com/1994/05/08/books/george-eliot-dorothea-and-me-rereading-and-rereading-middlemarch.html; my own "Reading George Eliot in Jerusalem," *Lilith*, Spring 2013, https://lilith.org/articles/reading-george-eliot-in-jerusalem/; Rebecca Mead, *The Road to Middlemarch: My Life with George Eliot* (London: Granta, 2014); and *My Victorian Novel: Critical Essays in the Personal Voice*, ed. Annette R. Federico (Columbia: University of Missouri Press, 2020). Investigating George Eliot's life as an exploration of the philosophical questions posed by the public institution and the private reality of marriage, Clare Carlisle's *The Marriage Question: George Eliot's Double Life* (New York: Farrar, Straus and Giroux, 2023) also brings the life into conversation with readers' own contemporary relations to marriage.
2. George Eliot, *The Mill on the Floss*, ed. A. S. Byatt, New York and London: Penguin Classics, 1985, p. 386.
3. In 2006, Barbara Hardy summarized the relationship between Eliot's attitudes toward Christianity and her fiction as follows: "She was to base her novels on a secular morality and an understanding tolerance for religious faith. Her insistence on human love and duty is inseparable from her agnosticism, her emphasis in life and art grounded in Feuerbach's belief that Christianity is a supernaturalizing of natural affections"; *George Eliot: A Critic's Biography* (London and New York: Bloomsbury Academic Press, 2006), p. 7. I take Hardy's summary as representative of the ease with which even the best literary critics often settle the matter of Eliot's "secular" beliefs. Hardy's use of the term "secular morality" reflects the tendency among scholars to assume that such a description points to a clearly understood body of beliefs and ideals.
4. See Frank M. Turner, *Contesting Cultural Authority: Essays in Victorian Intellectual Life* (Cambridge: Cambridge University Press, 1993), esp. pp. 3–37. There is a growing body of post-secular literary history and interpretation, many texts of which I cite here. For a good introduction, see Lori Branch and Mark Knight, "Why the Postsecular Matters: Literary Studies and the Rise of the Novel," *Christianity & Literature* 67.3 (2018), pp. 493–510, who helpfully explain the "post" in "post-secular" as signifying not the end of the secular but the movement beyond an "unreflective assumption of secularization" that characterized much research in the humanities and social sciences in the second half of the twentieth century (p. 494). For the claim that Eliot represents a quintessentially secularist approach, see Michael Rectenwald, "Secularism," in *George Eliot in Context*, ed. Margaret Harris (Cambridge: Cambridge University Press, 2013), pp. 271–8.

Acknowledgments

George Eliot has occupied the center of my interest for almost thirty years. The wealth of scholarship on her novels and life, while overwhelming, is also a cause for much gratitude. I have included only a small portion of it here due to the constraints of space.

Amidst many outstanding scholars of multiple generations, I want to thank those who have shaped my appreciation of Eliot so deeply that I would know a different and impoverished Eliot had I not encountered her through their compelling and wise readings: Barbara Hardy, David Carroll, Rosemarie Bodenheimer, and Philip Davis. I have noted explicit instances of their influence, but their traces run throughout this book. It took restraint not to look back to their writings too often, in service of writing my own story, and so, paradoxically, they may appear less frequently than they should. I hope this book will inspire readers to turn to their accounts for themselves. Clare Carlisle's wonderful study came out only after this manuscript was completed but I am grateful to her for sending me a copy that was consequently all pleasure in the reading.

I want to acknowledge my dissertation advisor, the late Nina Auerbach, who told me in 1996 not to "moralize" George Eliot too readily and gave me a copy of her review essay "The Waning George Eliot," inscribed with the charge to "make GE wax again." Linda C. Dowling's unsurpassedly generous mentorship over the years and her exacting standard for clarity of thought and expression (every sentence!) are gifts I seek to pass along in all my teaching and writing.

Mary Gordon, Nancy Henry, Jonathan Grossman, Leona Toker, and the wonderful, so-necessary NAVSA Religion and Spiritualities Caucus, especially Mark Knight, Josh King, Cynthia Scheinberg, and Charles La Porte, have all enriched my understanding of George Eliot. For years, now, Jan-Melissa Schramm has been an esteemed and trusted fellow thinker on all matters Victorian, with George Eliot chief among them. Tim Larsen invited me to write this book with faith and enthusiasm, and his erudition and collegiality have made the process much less daunting than it would otherwise have been. Sheila Jelen got me writing when I was overwhelmed: "just write it" turned out to be surprisingly useful advice. I am grateful to my wonderful colleagues here in Israel: Yael Shapira, Evan Fallenberg, Michael Kramer, Bill Kolbrener, Marcela Sulak, Esther Schupak, Carra Glatt, and Daniel Feldman, and to our staff, in particular, our librarian, Smadar Wisper.

I am indebted to the Israel Science Foundation for a three-year grant, "Post-secular George Eliot," that supported the writing of this book, as well as my trips to the New York Public Library and the Morgan Library, where the staff so generously helped me review George Eliot's letters, manuscripts, and notebooks. The online George Eliot Archive, under the direction of Beverley Rilett, has been an invaluable resource, and the 2019 George Eliot Bicentenary Conference, hosted at the University of Leicester, was an inspirational meeting with so many gifted scholars who renew the work of George Eliot.

Thanks to *GE-GHL Studies* and to *Partial Answers* for permission to reprint segments of text.

Many thanks to the expert readers for Oxford University Press, whose perceptive and learned suggestions improved this book, and to Tom Perridge, Jamie Mortimer, Neil Morris, and all those at OUP who have seen it into print.

I am endlessly grateful to my family and friends.

List of Abbreviations

AB	George Eliot, *Adam Bede,* ed. Stephen Gill, London: Penguin Classics, 1980
DD	George Eliot, *Daniel Deronda*, ed. Barbara Hardy, New York and London: Penguin Classics, 1986
Essays	George Eliot, *Selected Essays, Poems and Other Writings*, ed. A. S. Byatt and Nicholas Warren, New York and London: Penguin Classics, 1990
Essence	Ludwig Feuerbach, *The Essence of Christianity*, trans. George Eliot, Amherst: Prometheus Books, 1989
Ethics	*Spinoza's Ethics,* trans. George Eliot, ed. Clare Carlisle, Princeton: Princeton University Press, 2020
FH	George Eliot, *Felix Holt,* ed. Peter Coveney, New York and London: Penguin Classics, 1972
GE	George Eliot
GEL	*The George Eliot Letters*, ed. Gordon S. Haight, 9 vols., New Haven: Yale University Press, 1954–78
Imp	George Eliot, *Impressions of Theophrastus Such*, ed. Nancy Henry, Iowa City: University of Iowa Press, 1994
Journals	Journals of George Eliot, ed. Margaret Harris and Judith Johnston, Cambridge: Cambridge University Press, 1998
MM	George Eliot, *Middlemarch*, New York: Bantam Classics, 1985
MOF	George Eliot, *The Mill on the Floss*, ed. A. S. Byatt, New York and London: Penguin Classics, 1985
Poems	George Eliot, *Collected Poems,* ed. Lucien Jenkins, London: Skoob Books, 1989
R	George Eliot, *Romola*, ed. Andrew Sanders, New York and London: Penguin Classics, 1980
Scenes	George Eliot, *Scenes of Clerical Life,* ed. David Lodge. London and New York: Penguin Classics, 1985
SM	George Eliot, *Silas Marner.* Bantam Classics. New York: Bantam Books, 1981
TTC	Benedict de Spinoza, *A Theologico-Political Treatise*, trans. R. H. M. Elwes, New York: Dover, 1951

1
"Longing to See and Know Many Things," 1819–1840

Born on November 22, 1819, Mary Anne Evans was a child of Middle England; in 1819, a child of the Midlands was necessarily a child of her parish. A week after her birth to Robert and Christiana Pearson Evans, their third child and Robert's fifth, she was baptized at Chilvers Coton parish church, at a historical moment in which it would have been reasonable to expect that she might be married, like her sister, and buried, like her father and brother, in the parish of her birth. Mary Anne was baptized in the Church of England by the resident vicar of Chilvers Coton, Bernard Gilpin Ebdell, who came from a Warwickshire clerical family, educated at Rugby and then at Oxford. Ebdell served nearly forty years and married off his daughter to one of the two leading families of Chilvers Coton, the Harpers, reflecting the stability and the tight nature of parish at the time of Mary Anne's childhood.

In 1819, the local still circumscribed the reaches of the knowable world for much of Middle England. When we grasp this fully, we can understand better the extraordinary ways in which a girl born into a life that might have remained parochial and provincial made it that life's aim to expand whatever was narrow into something wider, whatever was partial into something closer to whole, whatever seemed hermetically sealed and self-sufficient into part of a great web of human, historical, and natural relations. We might begin to understand, too, how spiritual loneliness could come to characterize the earliest phases of that lifelong effort. As we will see, the writer George Eliot would regularly describe the spiritual loneliness that could emerge for anyone seeking to be a "whole soul," in a world of limited people, limited

George Eliot: Whole Soul. Ilana M. Blumberg, Oxford University Press. © Ilana M. Blumberg 2024.
DOI: 10.1093/oso/9780192845092.003.0001

knowledge and experience, especially when accompanied by the intuition of a much wider world beyond (GEL 1:120).

When we think about where Mary Anne Evans was "from," we must imagine a world in which local maps—which were geographies but also records of human orientation—often ended at the parish boundaries.[1] The church parish was the basic ground of identity in the early and middle decades of the nineteenth century. This was especially true in the rural England of the Evans family, and it was true, as K. D. M. Snell has argued, across class, from landowners to the local poor. Each person had a "settlement," a parish identity that clarified to whom they "belonged": who would be required to take them in if poverty overtook them in the form of illness, disability, bankruptcy, fire, or any other catastrophe.[2] They paid their tithes or church rates within the parish as well. Local figures of standing, such as Mary Anne's male relatives from the Pearson side, served as churchwardens and parish constables.[3] Belonging to a local community and identifying religiously were difficult to separate.[4]

In the region of the Midlands, and especially in a "closed" parish like Chilvers Coton and the adjoining Arbury, where land ownership was concentrated in the hands of only two families—the Newdigates, for whom Robert Evans worked, and the Harpers (the clerical family succeeding Rev. Ebdell)—the Anglican Church tended to dominate over any form of Dissent.[5] Robert Evans managed the Newdigate Arbury estate, having followed his employer, Francis Parker-Newdigate, to this inherited estate from Kirk Hallam in Derbyshire. Unsurprisingly, the Evans family affiliated with the Church of England, in an identification that was common between land-based employees and their employers.[6] Relations between the two families were expressed in a context whose social and religious forms were inseparable. Robert Evans's first wife had been memorialized by the Newdigates, her longtime employers, in an unusual expression of cross-class connection, within Astley Church, reflecting the ways in which family and local history became materially inscribed in places of worship.

The move a few months after Mary Anne's birth to Griff House, attached to 240 acres of farmland, settled the family for twenty years, and provided Mary Anne with a powerful attachment to a particular landscape and the agricultural calendar, both of which would shape her fictions. As Robert Evans established himself as a rising professional in his capacity as the Newdigates' extraordinarily able land agent, he likewise established himself fully and firmly as a local force, sought after to manage and modernize other estates, as well as to keep books and to survey on behalf of the parish institutions of church, workhouse, and hospital.[7] When, twenty years later, he would move as a widower to Coventry, it was natural that his new parish church would immediately offer him a role in its leadership.[8] In Mary Anne Evans's youth, the orders of family, the broader social hierarchy, and the authority of the church all coalesced within the parish.

Yet the intensely local flavor of Midlands parish life did not determine the full range of Mary Anne's experiences, perhaps thanks to her father's concerted efforts to extend his children's educations and, also, to maintain his family ties outside the parish. For many English children before the 1880 educational reform, Sunday schools were the sole sources of learning, yet Mary Anne and her siblings were all educated well beyond that. Mary Anne's education began ordinarily enough for a country girl, though she left home earlier than most, perhaps because her mother had suffered the loss of twins a year and a half after Mary Anne was born. From then on until Christiana's own death in 1836, Mary Anne's mother seemed not to relish having her other children near at hand. From the young age of three, Mary Anne spent her days at a local dame school with her brother, Isaac, until he was moved to a school in Coventry; at age five, then, Mary Anne accompanied her sister, Chrissey, to Miss Lathom's school, boarding in Nuneaton.[9]

As letters written in her teens attest, Mary Anne's early exposure to denominational difference in the context of close personal and familial relations helped shape a capacious religious sensibility intensely focused on meeting the pressing and particular needs of individual human beings. As the Evans children got older, the circumstances of their education exposed them to distinct and varied religious affiliations that fostered in them differing sensibilities. At the age of nine, Mary Anne encountered at Mrs. Wallington's school in Nuneaton her first real mentor, the Irish-born head governess Maria Lewis, who would become her chief spiritual interlocutor and friend for ten years. While Maria Lewis was a passionate evangelical within the Church of England, prompting Mary Anne to a decade of avid evangelical belief, Mary Anne's brother, Isaac, was sent to a tutor in Birmingham, where he absorbed a version of the High Church attitudes that would later run contrary to Mary Anne's far more ascetic religious convictions (GEL 1: 25, n. 6). From 1832 to 1835, Mary Anne lived among Dissenters from the Anglican Church, as she studied and boarded at a highly selective school in Coventry, run by Mary and Rebecca Franklin, daughters of the Baptist minister Francis Franklin who preached at Cow Lane Particular Baptist Chapel. In Coventry, she led her fellow pupils in prayer meetings at school.[10]

Meanwhile, throughout Mary Ann's adolescence (during which she dropped the "e" from her name), Robert Evans maintained close ties with the extended family he had left behind in Derbyshire, an area especially hospitable to Dissent. This family included his devout brother, Samuel Evans, and his wife, Elizabeth, Arminian Methodist preachers in Wirksworth. As George Eliot would later depict, in the first two decades of Mary Ann's life, if one were an Anglican, a genuine openness to Dissent was not readily to be expected. In addition to religious differences, the Anglican Church stood as the undisputed home of the educated and the landed, so that even those Anglicans who were not members of this class could feel assured in looking down on Dissenters socially. Yet these distinctions did not dissuade Mary Ann, upon whom the Derbyshire Evanses, like Maria Lewis and the Franklin sisters, exerted a profound influence. Mary Ann described herself as yearning to imitate the self-denying exertions of her aunt "in *spirit* at least, if not in the particular practices by which that spirit discovers itself" (GEL 1: 39). Traveling in June 1840 with her father to visit this branch of the family allowed for some Christian sightseeing of the gardens and "architectural beauties both external and internal" of Lichfield Cathedral in Staffordshire, whose stained glass had been replaced in 1819 as part of a larger Victorian restoration that would extend into the later century (GEL 1: 55). They stopped as well at Derbyshire's Ashbourne Church, the "finest mere parish church in the kingdom," which likewise had been restored between 1837 and 1840 (GEL 1: 55). For the young Mary Ann Evans, then, religious life in the Midlands pushed beyond a small parish's limits and featured a good amount of religious variety, variety that would have been less likely both in manufacturing towns, where Dissent tended to dominate, and in urban areas like London, where

"*Longing to See and Know Many Things,*" *1819–1840*

the dominance and breadth of the Church of England might have made it less likely for an adherent to be exposed to other denominations at the time.

In 1835, Mary Ann returned home from school in Coventry to assist in the final phase of her mother's cancer and, after her death, stayed on as her father's housekeeper. While her father hired a tutor to teach her Italian and, later, German, the end of Mary Ann's formal education occasioned a shift to a self-directed reading marathon in which she read extraordinarily widely, seeking most of her books through a local bookseller where her father had opened an account for her. In addition, Maria Lewis lent and procured her books, and Mrs. Newdegate, mother of Charles, granted Mary Ann access to the Arbury library (GEL 1:40–1). While questions of whether fiction was appropriate reading for an evangelical Christian dogged Mary Ann, she was quick to read and also to recommend works from across the denominational spectrum to Maria Lewis and her schoolfriend Martha Jackson.

Mary Ann's letters attest to the remarkable success of a girl in the rural midlands keeping up with emerging Christian publishing. The literary historian Elisabeth Jay suggests she may have taken many of her reading suggestions from the reviews and advertisements of the evangelical publication *The Christian Observer*, and claims that Mary Ann rarely let as much as a year go by before getting her hands on what she saw noted.[11] All in all, there is a strong sense of contemporaneity. Reading was no escape from the world but a way of engaging it and engaging with her chief correspondents. To Maria Lewis, she recommended a new publication, "lately published, only five numbers out," noting that "[i]f you haven't seen it," I will "send you an abstract of his argument"; to Martha Jackson, she listed her impressions, "As you are so spirited in determining to see every book that is mentioned to you" (GEL 1: 38).

The letters from this period double as a reading journal in which Mary Ann listed books she had read, wished to read, was in the midst of reading, and her reflections on them, often noting the inspirational force of poetry or biography. Attentive to her own practices as a reader, she distinguishes among her commitment to different texts: she has "skimmed" a book, "studied it after the peripatetic system" (GEL 1: 36), "[read] eclectically" (GEL 1: 72), "read it attentively" or "cursorily read" (GEL 1: 45), even "devour[ed]" some works (GEL 1: 38). While she typically noted the denomination of the author, it is clear that Mary Ann simply sought to read as widely as possible and certainly not to miss any influential or major text. She repeatedly recommends the High Church poet John Keble's hymns in *The Christian Year* (GEL 1: 46, 48) even as she was profoundly moved by the five-volume life of the evangelical Anglican William Wilberforce (GEL 1: 12); refers with great interest to the writing of the Dissenting missionary John Williams, and with less enthusiasm for the Congregationalist John Hoppus's essay on schism (GEL 1: 25), comparing the latter with the Anglican Joseph Milner's *History of the Church of Christ* (GEL 1: 25); labors at the Tracts for the Times of the Oxford Movement writers (GEL 1: 46); and comments on the American Presbyterian Charles Grandison Finney's *Lectures on Revival* (GEL 1: 63).

Mary Ann expressed in her letters a distaste for "*morning calling* and *evening party* controversialists" and the "foot-balling of religious parties," who were preoccupied with disputes about which she could often not make up her mind, in spite of a deep understanding of the terms of debate (GEL 1:45). "I think no one feels more difficulty in coming to a decision on controverted matters than myself.... however congruous a theory may be with my notions, I cannot find that comfortable repose that others appear to possess after having made their election of a class of sentiments," she wrote in May 1839, on the matter of the visible church as defined by the Oxford Movement tract writers, chief among them John Henry Newman (GEL 1:25). They argued that it was the duty of all Christians to recognize the superior authority of the Church of England as the single ecclesiastical body having emerged in apostolical succession, and they extended fellowship toward Roman Catholics, which Mary Ann saw as an indicator of heresy (GEL 1: 26). It is not surprising that this contemporary question was one on which Mary Ann "veer[ed] to all points of the compass," since it was fundamentally a question of exclusive authority and the margins of inclusion (GEL 1: 25).

Mary Ann Evans's evangelical period is typically raced through in literary accounts of her life, in the rush to get to her mature intellect, her mature art, her mature friendships and partnership. Her available letters from this period, mostly to Maria Lewis, are often dismissed as priggish, little expressive of her originality, sense of humor, or sharp critical intellect, shot through as they are with biblical reference and habitual self-deprecation. But the intensity of her belief in her teen years asks for a fuller appreciation of context and content, particularly as she later described the way her "mind works with the most freedom and the keenest sense of poetry in my remotest past" (GEL 3: 128–9). Maria Lewis appears to have been the first adult to engage Mary Ann seriously in matters that lifted her out of the small world in which she grew. In writing to her, as well as to her Aunt and Uncle Evans, Mary Ann took on a regular writing practice alongside the more typical daily evangelical reading practice. Like the cleric that her first readers imagined "George Eliot" to be, Mary Ann Evans became a writer as an evangelical believer, preoccupied by narrating a life of active faith, with its doubts, vicissitudes, requests for support and sympathy, and attempts at consoling and comforting others. Let us absorb fully the significant fact that the novelist George Eliot emerged from a young woman whose earliest associations and experiences with *writing* were bound up with narrating a life of faith.

Active faith introduced to Mary Ann Evans a set of powerful forces: first, a tradition with immense intellectual and spiritual history, as well as a specifically literary inheritance via the Scriptures and Book of Common Prayer; second, a tradition still actively developing, with a voluminous scale of publication, in subfields and genres old and new, with the implicit possibility of her own participation; third, the idea of a body of believers united in spite of their differences by common language, values, and beliefs; and finally, a sense of the sacred in the divine and human realms.

For a girl of middling family in rural England, evangelicalism was probably the only force that could have conferred upon her a sense that her life bore monumental significance in spite of her "lowly and obscure station," as she described it on the cusp of her nineteenth birthday (GEL 1:12). Expectations for that life's work were high, even unattainable, and, also, not a matter of personal choice. In other words, evangelicalism was certainly the source for the deep, ingrained sense of unshirkable duty that George Eliot would address over and over in her novels (not in simplistic terms—she was often troubled by its seemingly relentless claims, or worried about the right response to conflicting duties). Feeling this sense of duty, of constant demand, one could not escape the sense of things *mattering*, the very opposite of nihilism.[12] Though Calvinism tended to emphasize God's action in salvation rather than the believer's quest for sanctification, Mary Ann does not focus in her letters on the doctrines of grace to the exclusion of a life of holiness and good works. She understood charity as a form of duty: in March 1840, she was busy arranging a Clothing Club (GEL 1:41), and in October 1841, saving items from a Leamington bazaar for an upcoming one "for the erection of Schools in our parish" (GEL 1:111). Later, upon her move to Coventry, the Misses Franklin would describe her as always ready to initiate such projects.[13]

Evangelicalism was also the primary source for a sense of self. Duty offered its subject an external standard by which to see and measure herself, even if she often—or always and necessarily—fell short. That external standard paradoxically fostered an interiority, an abstracted vision of a self who was worthy of attention. Rather than being a self who simply felt, acted, reacted, spoke, and thought, she was now a self who watched, evaluated, and often narrated herself doing those things. Such a self-division unsurprisingly revealed and contributed to a self in conflict. A gap opened up between personal desire identified and its realization; that gap was regularly thought of as temptation. The very self born of scrutiny needed to "die" to this world. As Thomas à Kempis wrote in *The Imitation of Christ*, a book that was precious to Mary Ann/Marian over the course of her life, "The man that is not yet perfectly dead to himself, is quickly tempted and overcome in small and trifling things"; "If we were perfectly dead unto ourselves...then should we be able to taste divine things."[14] Here are habits of restraint and self-division, as well as a consciousness structured by constant, extreme hierarchizing. What is not divine is by necessity small and trifling.

The evangelical focus on self-scrutiny posed for Mary Ann Evans not only the lifelong concern with temptation and wrongdoing even on the smallest scale but also the relentless problems of egoism and ambition of any kind. These problems would later serve as a motivating paradox for George Eliot's novels as they worked to imagine reality as seen from the perspective of the other's "equivalent centre of self, whence the lights and shadows must always fall with a certain difference" (*MM* 193). Appropriate selfhood for Mary Ann, writing in 1839, hinged on perspective. She notes at length the paradox of individual insignificance, on one hand, and, on the other hand, a Providence that does not overlook any sinner: even when "realizing our situation as one of a multitude that no man can number," still, "by taking an enlarged view of material and immaterial existence," human beings must recognize "that this does not hinder even the hairs of our head from being numbered" (GEL 1:32). At the same time, she worries that her own soul "seems for weeks together completely benumbed" and that her "lack of humility and Christian simplicity," as she wrote to her Aunt Evans in 1839, "makes me willing to obtain credit for greater knowledge and deeper feeling than I really possess" (GEL 1: 19).

Evangelicalism highlighted human imperfection and sin, and insisted on the human inability to save oneself or another; salvation was exclusively a divine prerogative effected through Christ's atonement on behalf of a sinful humanity. Yet Mary Ann's letters are not weighed down as they might easily have been by regular discussion of the inescapability of sin, nor by a focus on Christ's sacrifice; Satan gets very few mentions—one in reference to the learned appeal of the Tractarians as they pursue heretical ideas, and a second in quoting Milton (GEL 1: 26, 43). From the available elements, her imagination was drawn to the division between earthly and eternal aims, and by the limits to human power (perhaps as the inverse of ambition and egoism). The human will could never achieve salvation from sin, thus the appropriate response was submission; as Mary Ann described it to Maria Lewis in October 1839, "looking to Jesus" (Heb. 12:2) was the "all-powerful lever or rather the magnet that can alone lift our souls heavenward or quicken our steps in the paths of righteousness"; without such submission, she could imagine no peace (GEL 1: 32). Full submission to God's power, mercy, and grace was understood to require setting aside all worldly ephemera for the infinite, eternal, and holy.

For the young Mary Ann Evans, those distractions included music, art, and literature, when she was not devoted to religious purposes. Literature that constituted a sort of basic knowledge, "matter of constant reference," was acceptable; this list included Shakespeare, *Don Quixote*, *Robinson Crusoe*, Walter Scott, and others (GEL 1:21). But beyond such staples, Mary Ann worried that novels and romances were capable of malign influence on all "imitative beings," whether children or adults, influence that would end in action (GEL 1: 23). In an ironic twist for a woman whose monumental literary career was just beginning, Mary Ann's first publication (in *The Christian Observer*) was a poem whose refrain announced "Farewell" to "this bright, lovely world." The farewell extended from sun, moon, and stars to "Books that have been to me as chests of gold / Which, miser-like, I secretly have told / And for them love, health, friendship, peace have sold." The poem's speaker holds fast only to the single "Blest volume! Whose clear truth-writ page, once known / Fades not before heaven's sunshine or hell's moan" (GEL 1: 28).[15]

Having grown up with the Protestant emphasis on scriptural reading, it was not surprising that she argued in a letter that "those who ever read to any purpose at all, we cannot I say help being modified by the ideas that pass through our minds. We hardly wish to lay claim to such elasticity as retains no impress" (GEL 1: 23). Indeed, that "Blest volume" was a central means of self-expression for Mary Ann, whose letters are woven from scriptural verses, reworkings and meditations on scriptural figures, chapters of Psalms, and hymns.[16] Mary Ann could best express her own state of mind and soul by using the words of Scripture, by reading herself into and through a textual tradition.[17]

Self-understanding could also be a historical matter, ever more so as Mary Ann grew into a full-fledged intellectual and then novelist. Her earliest publication aim was to complete a "chronological view of Ecclesiastical history" (GEL 1:38), with its profits to go to the restoration of Attleborough Church by subscription and toward another unspecified private project. Over a few months in 1840, Mary Ann surveyed the ground, writing to Martha Jackson that she had "seen charts of profane history innumerable, or rather I should say secular history, but never one of Church history" (GEL 1: 38). What stands out in the letters is Mary Ann's intent for such a work not to answer her own private needs or desires, but to fill a genuine gap. She is aware of the different terminologies—profane versus secular—that define the tenor and assumptions of approach. She expresses concern not to have been "forestalled" by other works, and when she does encounter a small chart, she is relieved that it "trenches not on my ground" (GEL 1: 38, 48).

In a letter to Maria Lewis in March 1840, Mary Ann described what she envisioned as the work of approximately six months: a "series of perpendicular columns" containing the dates and descriptions of the Roman emperors, the bishops, "remarkable men and events in the several churches," "political and religious state of the Jews" and the relation of "heathenism and Judaism toward Christianity," the "chronology of the Apostolical and Patristical writings, schisms and heresies," General Councils, "eras of corruption," and possibly an "application of the Apocalyptic prophecies" (GEL 1: 44). She envisioned a "break in the chart" once Christianity was established as the "religion of the Empire" (GEL 1: 44). While on March 13 she had considered extending it to the Reformation, by two weeks later, for unknown reasons, she had revised the plan to end the chart in 606 with the acknowledgment of the supremacy of the Pope by the Eastern Roman Emperor, after which, she concludes dramatically and dogmatically, "Mahommedanism became a besom of destruction in the hand of the Lord, and completely altered the aspect of Ecclesiastical History" (GEL 1: 45).

For a woman who would become a translator of philosophy, an argumentative critic and essayist, then a prolific novelist and poet, and whose first publication was a pious poem written in the outpouring of first person, an ecclesiastical chart might seem a surprisingly dry and non-narrative endeavor. Likewise, for a novelist who would famously describe all relations as a "web," and who delighted in narrating horizontally, a chart with rectangular columns seems singularly unamenable. Perhaps the chart answered best as an act of practical Christian piety. The project, it is important to note, failed, and when it failed, Mary Ann described no sorrow. Indeed, she did not dwell on the failure beyond the moment she saw the work that had superseded hers. She felt justified in having correctly identified a "desideratum," but relieved that it was "executed much better than if left to my slow fingers and slower head"; while the phrasing might arguably be read as performative self-effacement, it seems equally likely to have been genuine (GEL 1:51). The chart that forestalled her project was published in 1840 by the prominent religious publishers Seeley and Burnside. Mary Ann's appreciative note on its content was that it answered "the purpose of presenting epochs as nuclei round which less important events instinctively cluster" (GEL 1:64). Her attempt to chart events in rectangular columns of official chronicle had already been replaced by an appreciation for evaluative sense-making.

The idea of the chart had temporarily provided Mary Ann with a path of authorship that disciplined and directed her mind, without unduly indulging her ego. In designating its proceeds in advance to Christian causes, Mary Ann served Christ. But perhaps even more, she had chosen a project that could discipline a mind that seemed at times nothing but

> an assemblage of disjointed specimens of history, ancient and modern, scraps of poetry picked up from Shakespeare, Cowper, Wordsworth and Milton, newspaper topics, morsels of Addison and Bacon, Latin verbs, geometry entomology and chemistry, reviews and metaphysics, all arrested and petrified and smothered by the fast thickening every day accession of actual events, relative anxieties, and household cares and vexations. (GEL 1:29)

The rhythmic, syntactically pleasing accretion of this single sentence testifies to the richness but also the unruliness of Mary Ann's learning (and to her metaphoric bent toward the scientific and geological). Whenever she mentioned the chart in her correspondence, she spoke not in terms of writing nor of "authorship" (as she described her "Farewell" poem), but of "completing" the chart, bringing it from the condition of "airy vision" to solidity (GEL 1: 45, 51). Wits so "irretrievably scattered," and a mind "never of the most highly organized genus...more than usually chaotic," that would require nothing short of a lens "equal to...Herschel's fabled telescope" to "collect them in a focus": these conditions and predilections were not helpful to the Christian (GEL 1: 29). As Mary Ann wrote to Martha Jackson, "Though God is best served by diligence in occupations that His providence points out or permits, still the first of His requirements...is the giving up of the heart to him, not at one particular epoch, but daily, hourly, as a living sacrifice and oblation. I am conscious of having straitened myself by the adoption of a too varied and laborious set of studies, having so many social duties" (GEL 1: 48).

The problem of boundaries—whether to allow for a range of learning that would challenge the limits of human vision and traverse all of natural history—was Mary Ann's palpable challenge as a young believer. Learning and thus living without God-given boundaries posed the risks of greed and egoism. Learning was as great a risk as any other source of temptation, as Thomas à Kempis and countless evangelical preachers insisted: "Cease from an inordinate desire of knowing, for therein is much distraction and deceit"; "There may be many things, which to know doth little or nothing profit the soul."[18] When, in March 1839, Mary Ann had tried to delineate reading acceptable for the Christian, she had made one exception: the books of "persons of perceptions so quick, memories so eclectic and retentive, and minds so comprehensive, that nothing less than omnivorous reading...can satisfy their intellectual maw, for (if I may parody the words of Scripture without profaneness), they will gather to themselves all facts and heap unto themselves all ideas. For such persons we cannot legislate" (GEL 1: 21). Notable here is that Mary Ann had set out to describe the books allowable to Christian readers. Yet she found herself imagining what might be permissible reading for the *authors* of those books. It was as much for those authors as readers, as about those authors as writers, that she would not legislate.

She, too, was such an author, a "mind so comprehensive." Her own "omnivorous reading," her own gathering to herself of all facts and ideas, were powerful but dangerous.

Indeed, the verses Mary Ann was parodying, Habakkuk 2:5, read in prayer the third Monday after Epiphany, were dark ones, describing those who were "arrogant and never at rest. Because he is greedy as the grave and like death is never satisfied, he gathers to himself all the nations and takes captive all the peoples." Authorship required the kind of reading, the kind of arrogance and restless greed, that challenged faith: "But the just shall live by his faith," the prophecy in Habakkuk went on, as Mary Ann Evans surely knew. The questions of legislation, of authority, of divine and human perspective, within a life of faith would accompany Mary Ann Evans into her adulthood.

Notes

1. K. D. M. Snell, *Parish and Belonging: Community, Identity and Welfare in England and Wales, 1700–1950* (Cambridge: Cambridge University Press, 2006), p. 36. The personal descriptor "Of this parish" marked both marriage registers and burial monuments and persisted, reflecting strong affiliation at the local level, throughout the century, until civil and ecclesiastical forms of authority began to separate (pp. 14–15, 17).

2. Snell, *Parish*, p. 103. The exception were certain national immigrants who did not have settlements.
3. Kathryn Hughes, *George Eliot: The Last Victorian* (London: Fourth Estate, 2000), p. 16. The basic facts of George Eliot's life are well established and therefore I will cite biographical texts only for lesser-known details or interpretive commentary. I refer readers to the following major biographies: Rosemary Ashton, *George Eliot: A Life* (New York: Viking, 1997); Gordon S. Haight, *George Eliot: A Biography* (New York: Oxford University Press, 1968); Hardy, *George Eliot*; Nancy Henry, *The Life of George Eliot: A Critical Biography* (Malden, MA: Wiley-Blackwell, 2012); Frederick Karl, *George Eliot: Voice of a Century: A Biography* (New York: W.W. Norton, 1995); Ruby Redinger, *George Eliot: The Emergent Self* (New York: Knopf, 1975).
4. Snell, *Parish*, p. 15.
5. K. D. M. Snell and Paul S. Ell, *Rival Jerusalems: The Geography of Victorian Religion* (Cambridge: Cambridge University Press, 2000), p. 304. Anglican clergymen also evinced strong Tory voting preferences, in contrast to the Whig/Liberal preferences of Catholic, Independent, Baptist, Unitarian, Presbyterian, and (after 1832) Methodist ministers (p. 74).
6. Snell and Ell, *Rival Jerusalems*, p. 81.
7. Hughes, *George Eliot*, p. 19.
8. Managing the many names of George Eliot is a challenge for any critic. I have tried to use "Eliot" or "George Eliot" when referring to the author of the works published under that name (to be distinguished whenever possible from the narrator of those works). She was baptized as Mary Anne and dropped the "e" around 1837 when her sister married and she took on the title of "Miss Evans." I use Mary Anne/Ann/Marian when referring to the historical subject, even when I describe her work as editor and journalist, since she did not carry out either role under any professional name. I have chosen to use her first name rather than her last because of the challenges involved there as well: she was Evans until she began to live with G. H. Lewes, at which point she signed herself "Marian Evans Lewes," though this was not her legal name until a brief window following Lewes's death when she was settling her finances. Once she married John Cross, she signed herself "M. A. Cross." I must confess that I think of her as MAE, MEL, and GE, but none of those seemed feasible for a biography.
9. Much of the common knowledge about the childhood comes from John Walter Cross, *George Eliot's Life as Related in Her Letters and Journals* (Boston and New York: Jefferson Press, n.d., orig. pub. 1888).
10. Cross, *George Eliot's Life*, Vol. 1, p. 20.
11. Elisabeth Jay, *Religion of the Heart: Anglican Evangelicalism and the Nineteenth-Century Novel* (Oxford: Oxford University Press, 1979, p. 227).
12. Here, I contest Christopher Herbert's claim in his study *Evangelical Gothic: the English Novel and the Religious War on Virtue from Wesley to Dracula* (Charlottesville: University of Virginia Press, 2019), that moral nihilism was not only compatible with evangelicalism but necessary to much of its orthodoxy.

13. Cross, *George Eliot's Life*, Vol 1, p. 20.
14. Thomas à Kempis. *The Imitation of Christ* (London and Glasgow: Blackie & Son Limited, n.d.), pp. 11, 17.
15. See Miriam Elizabeth Burstein's "Hybridous Monsters: Constructing 'Religion' and the 'the Novel' in the Early Nineteenth Century," in Joshua King and Winter Jade Werner, eds. *Constructing Nineteenth-Century Religion* (Columbus: Ohio State University Press, 2019), pp. 171–89, for helpful context. Burstein describes the moral and religious dangers that were associated with the spread of commodified fiction in the first half of the century, especially the range of religious fictions that sought, often unsuccessfully, to combine pleasure and instruction. This history of the controversies surrounding the reading and marketing of religious novels is also instructive when we encounter Eliot's reviews and her insistence on realism.
16. See Christine L. Kreuger's important study *The Reader's Repentance: Women Preachers, Women Writers, and Nineteenth-Century Social Discourse* (Chicago and London: University of Chicago Press, 1992), describing the eighteenth-century female preachers who assumed a feminist authority, albeit a conflicted one, and generated a tradition of public voice for exceptional women writers such as George Eliot. Admirably, Kreuger does not shy away from the complications—the pursuit of feminist autonomy and the complicity with patriarchy—lived by religious women preachers and writers, noting the particular predicament of Eliot, who gave up evangelical dogmatism in spite of her "desire for the power invested in its language" (p. 243).
17. Mark Knight, *Good Words: Evangelicalism and the Victorian Novel*, (Columbus: Ohio State University Press, 2019), excludes Eliot from his study of evangelicalism's impact on the novel, arguing that, on Eliot's reading, "evangelicalism can be explained most fully through a secular language that she helps to develop," and he astutely notes that critics bow to her analysis rather than analyze it (p. 20). I attempt here not to take her analyses of religion at face value, as the truth claims of a philosopher, but to read them as traces of a lifelong engagement with tradition and evolving forms of knowledge.
18. à Kempis, *Imitation*, p. 4.

2
"New Treasures," 1840–1842

In March 1840, in the midst of a letter detailing her ecclesiastical chart, Mary Ann related to Maria Lewis that Henry Richard Harper of Chilvers Coton (the brother of Lewis's employer) had lent her a Tractarian novel, *Portrait of an English Churchman* (1838), written by the prolific Revd W. Gresley. Mr. Henry Harper "begg[ed] me to read it, as he thought it was calculated to make me a proselyte to the opinions it advocates" (GEL 1:45). After having "read it attentively," Mary Ann reports feeling "pleased" with its "spirit of piety," yet resisting it nonetheless, on the grounds that "there is unfairness in arbitrarily selecting a train of circumstances, and a set of characters as a development of a class of opinions" (GEL 1:45). How equally easy, she writes, would it be to "make atheism appear wonderfully calculated to promote social happiness" (GEL 1:45).

Whereas seven or eight years earlier Mary Ann had found herself subject to a low-grade crisis of reading, occasioned by a novel that celebrated atheism in the person of a moral hero (Bulwer Lytton's *Devereux*), by this point in her life she stood her ground while reading. She had become too intelligent and critical a reader to fall under the sort of "powerful influence" she imagined a book such as Gresley's could exert on the "minds of small readers and shallow thinkers" (GEL 1:45). Far from becoming a proselyte to the opinions she read, she was increasingly capable of forming her own conclusions, even in direct opposition to the intentions of certain authors, whether clerical novelists or theologians. Barely a paragraph later in her letter, she notes ironically that "Certain divines enjoin us to consult ecclesiastical records for the settling of our faith, a result the very opposite to what they appear likely to produce, in my humble and narrow appreciation" (GEL 1:46).

While it would be nearly two years before Mary Ann made the significant move not to accompany her father to church, her letters suggest that she had entered a phase of her life that we might identify as "critical." In March 1841, she and her father left her beloved home at Griff to her brother, Isaac, and his new wife. Writing to Martha Jackson that the removal was "like dying to one stage of existence," Mary Ann and her father settled at Foleshill, which was under a mile from Coventry (GEL 1:86). Although the move was calculated to enhance Mary Ann's marital prospects, its chief effect was to introduce her to the friendship of the freethinking Bray and Hennell families that centered in nearby Rosehill. They would supplant Maria Lewis and the near and distant Evans family as her most intimate friends and intellectual partners in what was definitively a new "stage of existence." This stage was characterized by her personal rejection of Christian dogma and a series of intensive projects translating texts that read Scripture critically and resisted orthodox efforts that sought to reconcile or substantiate the accounts of the Gospels in order to safeguard the binding, sacred nature of revelation. From David Friedrich Strauss's *The Life of Jesus* (1835) to Ludwig Feuerbach's *Essence of Christianity* (1841) to Benedict de Spinoza's *Ethics* (1677) (though the last translation, completed in 1856, did not see publication in her time), the texts Mary Ann would translate ushered in a new "stage of existence" for English intellectuals, as they collectively encountered German higher criticism and contemplated an ethical modernity that did not rely upon supernatural dimensions of a divine revelation, nor promise salvation through Jesus Christ's death, nor preach the hierarchy of an eternal realm truer than this world.

In this third decade of her life, Mary Ann was still fundamentally a reader, yet now she was expanding the tendency visible in her letter writing to respond to so much of what she read in written form for an audience beyond one or two intimates. In a word, translation, for Mary Ann Evans, seems to have been associated with teaching, first herself and then others. In September 1841 she wrote to Maria Lewis, who was, of course, a teacher, a very long reflection on a kind of study that would issue in writing the truths of Scripture, "in other words":

> I thought the other day that a mode of studying Scripture very beneficial to adults might be made equally so to your pupils. It is that of

taking the parables or other portions of the New Testament for analyzation—writing in words other than those of Scripture the general truths contained or implied in the passage. . . . The frequent and indeed constant use of this plan would I am convinced give a clearness and comprehensiveness to our knowledge of Scripture truths that I have not found common, and the lack of which I am earnestly desirous to supply in myself. (GEL 1: 106)

By way of example, she takes the "familiar but impressive" parable of the sower, from Matthew 13, and lists seven "heads for reflection," noting that there are "perhaps many more" to be gleaned. Fascinatingly, this parable is followed by the disciples coming to Jesus and asking why it is that he preaches to the people in parables. He answers, "Because the knowledge of the secrets of the kingdom of heaven has been given to you, but not to them. / Whoever has will be given more, and they will have an abundance. Whoever does not have, even what they have will be taken from them. This is why I speak to them in parables: / Though seeing, they do not see; though hearing, they do not hear or understand. / In them is fulfilled the prophecy of Isaiah" (Matt. 13:11–14).

From Jesus's explanation not only of the parable of the sower but of the parable of speaking in parables to those who do not have, see, or hear, who themselves are unknowingly fulfilling a prophetic teaching, Mary Ann extended the teaching work of Jesus to herself. Now she steps in as explainer of parable, drawing seven general truths, three of which are explicitly concerned with how to receive the "preached word" (GEL 1: 106). The fifth truth she recorded as follows: "The saving reception of the word is invariably marked by strong effort on the part of the recipient to 'hold fast' what he has heard. 'Having heard the word, *keep it*'" (GEL 1: 106). For Mary Ann, the way to keep the word was to put it into her own words, and then to teach it, in the sort of paradox beloved of the New Testament, in which giving, losing, and receiving coalesce in spiritual plenty. Near the end of the chapter in Matthew, when Jesus confirms that the disciples have understood the parable of the net, he says to them, "Therefore every teacher of the law who has become a disciple in the kingdom of heaven is like the owner of a house who brings out of his storeroom new treasures as well as old," a simile that Mary Ann used repeatedly in her letters when seeking to console her correspondents with religious truths cast in different modes of expression (Matt. 13:52).

Mary Ann's impulse to analyze and to recast ideas in her own words appears to have begun as a work of faith, expressing her desire for clarity and comprehensiveness in her own knowledge of scriptural truths. Perhaps it was an effort to shore up her faith. Yet it also testified to confidence: a sense that she was one to whom it had been given in abundance to hear, to see, to understand, and to teach. In reading her letters, it is remarkable to recognize that her renunciation of the orthodox dogma was not preceded by any discussion with her chief interlocutors. Whatever internal process she underwent, there is no sign of it in her letters, other than comments such as the following to her uncle Samuel Evans, "I am often, very often stumbling," or noting that a passage in Joel comforts her "when conscious of the desolating effects of back-sliding on my heart," both precisely the sorts of comment that could have testified equally to *living* in great faith as to *losing* such faith (GEL 1: 114).[1] The only clue is the well-known extract from a letter to Maria Lewis on November 13, 1841, in which Mary Ann asks, "Think—is there any *conceivable* alteration in me that would prevent your coming to me at Christmas?" at the end of a letter which begins, "My whole soul has been engrossed in the most interesting of all enquiries for the last few days, and to what result my thoughts may lead I know not—possibly to one that will startle you, but my only desire is to know the truth, my only fear to cling to error" (GEL 1: 120–1). No scriptural verse succeeded this statement.

On January 2, 1842, Robert Evans recorded his own attendance at Trinity Church, along with Maria Lewis who was visiting. He notes, "Mary Ann did not go" (GEL 1: 124). Again, on January 16, "Mary Ann did not go to church" (GEL 1: 124). Weeks later, in February, when she wrote to her father a full explanation of her position, she described church attendance as "worship which I wholly disapprove" (GEL 1: 129). As remarkable as her silence in the letters leading up to this shift is the ideological clarity Mary Ann mustered. She knew, seemingly, precisely what she did and did not believe, as if it had come out of the fire fully formed. On January 28, she scribbled "hastily" the following to Mrs. Elizabeth Pears, the Evans's closest neighbor and the sister of Charles Bray, who had introduced Mary Ann into her brother's family's society:

> though I cannot rank among my principles of action a fear of vengeance eternal, gratitude for predestined salvation, or a revelation of future glories as a reward, I fully participate in the belief that the only heaven here or hereafter is to be found in conformity with the will of the Supreme; a continual aiming at the attainment of that perfect ideal, the true Logos that dwells in the bosom of the one Father. (GEL 1: 125–6)

Ten months later, her good friend Mary Sibree, daughter of an Independent minister in Coventry, described Mary Ann as declaring that "Calvinism is Christianity, and this granted,...it is a religion based on pure selfishness" (GEL 1: 151, n. 2, as quoted in Cross.[2])

What prompted such a turn from the intense evangelical affiliation of more than a decade, not to say the familial Anglican identity of her entire life? We can trace her immersion in geology and astronomy, both radical and weakly conciliatory; the tomes of church history; the tracts and pamphlets and novels and sermons on the contemporary church controversies that dogged her times and whose sectarianism repelled her. We can note her admiration for a writer such as Thomas Carlyle, "not orthodox," yet whose "soul is a shrine of the brightest and purest philanthropy, kindled by the live coal of gratitude and devotion to the Author of all things," and her great love of William Wordsworth's romantic embrace of the natural world (GEL 1: 123). Her letters declare that sectarianism was greatly dissuasive to her. And retrospectively, in 1844, she offers a hint that some of the unhappiness of her childhood may have stemmed from bad doctrine, mixed, perhaps, with the historical reality of infant illness and death, then adult mourning, such as she had witnessed at the death of sibling twins when she was herself but three years old: "to the child [childhood] is full of deep sorrows, the meaning of which is unknown. Witness colic and whooping-cough and dread of ghosts, to say nothing of hell and Satan, and an offended Deity in the sky who was angry when I wanted too much plum cake. Then the sorrows of older persons which children see but cannot understand are worse than all" (GEL 1:173).

Most immediately, we can identify her reading of Charles Hennell's *Inquiry Concerning the Origin of Christianity* (1838) in 1841, before she had met the Hennells and the Brays. The text offered a historical analysis of "the four Gospels, proceeding on the admission that they may contain a mixture of *truth and error*," in terms that Mary Ann echoed exactly in her letters to Maria Lewis, to Elizabeth Pears, and to her father.[3] Hennell's work had been taken up at the request of his sister, Cara (Caroline) Hennell Bray, soon after her marriage to Charles Bray clarified how fully his views challenged even the liberal Unitarian beliefs upon which she and her siblings had been raised (GEL 1: lvi). While Mary Ann would invest years in Strauss's analysis, it still seems meaningful that she first encountered this sort of inquiry written not by the distant German and published in 1835 (she records only in February 1840 that she hopes to begin lessons in German the next month [GEL 1: 38]), but by an Englishman closely linked to her own trustworthy neighbor. Right on her own doorstep, so to speak, were good people who had made meaningful, imaginable lives outside the frameworks she had known. "Heretics" had first names and families. They might be encountered off the page, where they need not look so "pestering" in "their wide uniformity and their narrow differences," as she had written to Maria Lewis on March 30, 1840 (GEL 1: 46).

In fact, as heretics went, Hennell would always be preferable to Strauss for Mary Ann. When, in September 1847, after she had already completed the translation of Strauss, Mary Ann reread Hennell, she found herself newly impressed with a "delight and admiration" she might not have been able to allow herself on its first reading (GEL 1: 237). The work, which "furnishe[d] the utmost that can be done towards obtaining a *real* view of the life and character of Jesus by rejecting as little as possible from the Gospels," was written with strong reason, high style, and wit, and an "animus so candid and even generous" (GEL 1:237). Likely it was this animus and wit that distinguished it from Strauss, whose endless dissections made her certain that "I do not know *one* person who is likely to read the book through" (GEL 1: 218). By contrast, Mary Ann had a clear image of the benefit to Hennell's readers: "No one fit to read it at all could read it without being intellectually and morally stronger" (GEL 1: 237). Translating Strauss, a two-and-a-half-year project she took over from Charles Hennell's wife, Rufa Brabant, who had completed only a part of the first of three volumes, Mary Ann regularly felt depleted and "Strauss-sick" from the "soul-stupefying labour" (GEL 1: 206, 185). She drew inspiration only from a Christ figure and engraving she kept before her on her table and, less noted, from the regular consultation regarding the work with Sara Hennell, Cara's sister, who quickly became Mary Ann's closest correspondent.

In the kind of personal reading of authors (as distinct from books) she had done for years, noting whenever she determined a strong likeness between her own sensibility and that of what she read, Mary Ann here imagined being the writer of a book such as Hennell's:

> I am sure if I had written such a book I should be invulnerable to all the arrows of all spiteful gods and goddesses. I should say, "None of these things move me neither count I my life dear unto myself," seeing that I have delivered such a message of God to men. (GEL 1: 237)

Splicing "heathen" mythology with Scripture, while amending the verse in Acts 20:24 (which ends, "so that I might finish my course with joy, and the ministry, which I have received of the Lord Jesus, to testify the gospel of the grace of God"), Mary Ann satirically imagined objectors to Hennell's critical inquiry as the mythical gods and goddesses subject to unrefined human spite. Meanwhile, Mary Ann recouped Hennell's own work, which argued for the mythical nature of elements of Gospel, as the Gospel itself: the message of God to men. Religious sanction for free inquiry could be given no clearer expression than hers here.

By 1847, Mary Ann risked nothing in expressing semi-privately such confidence in a book that she—not at all incidentally—had *not* written and never would write. (Strauss, too, came out without her name.) But, in January 1842, Mary Ann risked everything in suddenly refusing to attend church, thereby visibly separating herself from Maria Lewis and her father, whom she could not distance ironically and narratively as "spiteful gods and goddesses" but had to acknowledge, as her nearest friend and the single living parent who provided her with home, protection, and identity. Mary Ann's decisive public act prompted her father to threaten her with leaving Foleshill altogether. Over the course of a few months in which the family reeled from the daughter's act and the father's response, Mary Ann went to stay with her brother at Griff. Recognizing that she could make no home as a hanger-on, she considered the drastic step of taking her own lodgings in Leamington, all the while corresponding with her new "family," the Rosehill friends, who sought to counsel and assist her in patching things up with her father, as did Rebecca Franklin and the Pears neighbors.

It is hard not to think that Mary Ann was looking for a "Holy War" (GEL 1: 133). Refusing to go to church—did she decline or refuse? What did she say? How did she say it? To whom and in whose listening presence?—could not have been more dramatic and confrontational in its nature. Over the course of her life, it would be her tendency to come to decisions privately and silently, and then enact them in full, thus surprising, if not downright shocking and insulting, those who thought they were her intimates. The defection from church was the first of such acts: traveling abroad with the married George Henry Lewes was the second; becoming a fiction writer under an assumed name, the third; and marrying John Cross after Lewes's death, the fourth. The path toward these decisions can only be sketched retrospectively and conjecturally, yet the four events together may help us cast light on the first. Each posed a great risk—or, at least, a great challenge—to her own public reputation, with implications for the reputations of others, whether family or friends; each was certain to occasion her friends' and family's remonstration or the advice to compromise or cancel her plans. At the same time, each decision was tied up with the most internal set of needs, desires, convictions, hopes, such as could not have been narrated in full to others and likely not even to herself. Certainly, it would have been immensely difficult, both emotionally and intellectually, to narrate motivation and intention, and to account for risk, *before* the acts were carried out; these stories required retrospect for full intelligibility.

Later, when Mary Ann became a novelist who delighted in narratorial omniscience and instructive commentary, she could record the incremental steps, the small, seemingly inconsequential actions and habits of thought, that led to predictability and intelligibility of human character, for the reader if not for characters enmeshed in the forward-moving, ground-level plot. Yet documented and signposted paths into character were the province of the novelist who knew where she was headed with the story. In real life, Mary Ann seemed to trust nothing but public, decisive, controversial, and unexpected action to get the job of living her life done. These swerves testified to subterranean developments that had a rhythm and a force of their own; once these had come to a head, Mary Ann had immediately to adjust the externals to the internals. Those around her were left to catch up on their own time.[4]

Indeed, after her public apostasy, some friends tried to persuade Mary Ann back to the fold. In hopes of reconverting her, Mary and John Sibree's mother introduced her to the professor of theology Francis Watts, who had founded a college in 1838 to train Independent ministers and was well read in higher German thought (in one of few comic interludes in this period, he immediately reported back to the Sibrees that "*She* has gone into the question" [GEL 1: 135, n. 7, as quoted in Cross]). In her brilliant study of the letters of Mary Ann Evans, Rosemarie Bodenheimer has noted that to read Mary Ann's apostasy in purely psychological terms denies its intense intellectual dimension.[5] Yet the letters tend to explore less deeply than we might have expected the theological content of Mary Ann's doubts, leaving still mysterious what forced a rupture of such moment. Did particular beliefs pose for her an ethical or spiritual crisis?[6] Had historical argumentation and scientific advance simply won the day? Her silence attests to the mystery of human change and rupture, the insufficiency of narratives of direct cause and effect, that she would later redress so ambitiously and creatively in her novels.

The correspondence with Watts is the rare one in the midst of the domestic drama to pick up the theological debate. In what appears to have been the extension of a personal conversation, Mary Ann rejected the resolution proposed by the major Anglican theologian Bishop Joseph Butler in his *The Analogy of Religion* (1736), a "revered classic defense" of the Christian faith for Victorians.[7] It is not easy to reconstruct precisely what constituted the source of her doubt, since she argues procedurally and without reference to a particular passage.[8] The *Analogy* begins by arguing, via analogy to natural law, for the probability and "credibility of a future life"; given that this is a necessity for any religious belief, Butler suggests that once its likelihood has been satisfactorily established, by extension further doctrines of religion should also be given serious consideration.[9] Quite possibly the entire basis for Butler's theology did not satisfy Mary Ann, but her letter suggests that she was specifically troubled by his analysis of Divine Government and its implications for the problem of free will. Butler suggested that vicarious punishments might be "fit, and absolutely necessary" to the "moral scheme"; further, human beings were not in a position to judge based on their inability to grasp the entire scheme. Just as in natural relations, Butler writes, "we see in what variety of ways one person's sufferings contribute to the relief of another," so in the divine scheme, "for aught we know" (a phrasing that repeats eleven times in the *Analogy*), the same principle may be operative.[10]

Yet for Mary Ann, this solution—the extrapolation from natural law to the spiritual balance of "the eternal woe of a limited number to the eternal bliss of a larger multitude"—suffered from inadequate evidence (GEL 1: 135). Further, she could not accept it on the basis that no other system dealt better with such problems, as Watts had apparently suggested via Butler. While she did not expand upon what she called the "vexed question of free-will," she referred to it as an "immense" difficulty, "so contradictory to a priori conceptions" (GEL 1: 135). Since she was exiting from a Calvinist theology whose doctrine of predestination posed such difficulties for the meaningful effects of free will, it is hardly surprising that Mary Ann would have rejected any alternative that so compromised it. Yet the strongest legacy Christianity left her was the recognition of the undeniable reality of human suffering. This recognition left her to contend over the course of her career with the issues of vicarious suffering and uneven suffering—the former, the basis of atonement theology, and the latter, a painful difficulty for any who rejected the theology of an afterlife.

Mary Ann concluded by aligning herself with Samuel Coleridge's broad analysis that "the notion of Revelation abandoned, there is ever a tendency toward Pantheism, and the personality of the Deity is not to be maintained quite satisfactorily apart from Christianity" (GEL 1: 136). Yet all of her objections and claims are presented to Watts with scrupulous respect and gratitude: "I am aware of my inadequacy, with the inexperience and ignorance of twenty-two years, to judge on a subject so difficult" (GEL 1: 136). Even more, she writes to him about her sense of loss and uncertainty, with no comprehensive new theory yet ready to replace the old: "It is no small sacrifice to part with the assurance that life and immortality have been brought to light, and to be reduced to the condition of the great spirits of old who looked yearningly to the horizon of their earthly career, wondering what lay beyond" (GEL 1: 136). The term "sacrifice" here with regard to giving up her faith prompts us to recognize that she saw her path as one consecrated by her commitment to truth in spite of comfort; possibly, this language was adopted in instinctive defense, to recast definitively what might be seen by many, including her family, as selfishness.

The issue of immortality would remain one of the most painful renunciations for Mary Ann long beyond her apostasy, first prompting her to envision a study of the subject itself (which she did not execute) and eventually requiring the humanist glorification of history and memory that she described in 1867 as "the choir invisible / of those immortal dead who live again / In minds made better by their presence" (*Poems* 49). Even at this early point, though, she insisted to Watts that she could not believe that only the belief in immortality would succeed in producing "elevated and heroic virtue and the sublimest resignation" (GEL 1: 136). Here, she began the intellectual labor of dividing morality from religion.

The earnest nine-month dialogue between Mary Ann and Watts is a wonderfully instructive instance of Victorian religious culture. In their correspondence, we encounter a mutually appreciative conversation between two intellects who have read many of the same works and found passionate interest in the same theological and cultural developments, but ultimately reached two utterly different endpoints with regard to faith. Their letters record the loan of numerous books from Watts to Mary Ann, and even address the possibility of his advising as a "foster-father to the work" of Mary Ann's translation of the major Swiss theologian Alexandre Rodolphe Vinet, who had led a liberal Protestant break from the state church (the translation did not come to pass) (GEL 1: 136; 142). Yet the very texts that upheld Watts in his faith did not sway Mary Ann Evans in the same way.[11]

Given that the intellectual tussle of the times was not inevitably weighted toward the loss of faith, Mary Ann's decision cannot simply be read as an account of "progress." Her letters to Watts do give us more to work with, however. In August 1842, Mary Ann offered a "confession" to Watts that seems genuinely revelatory in the story of her movement away from evangelicalism and church affiliation more generally. Its content, anomalous in her correspondence, cries out for notice:

> I confess to you that I feel it an inexpressible relief to be freed from the apprehension of what Finney well describes, that at each moment I tread on chords that will vibrate for weal or woe to all eternity. I could shed tears of joy to believe that in this lovely world I may lie on the grass and ruminate on possibilities without dreading lest my conclusions should be everlastingly fatal.   (GEL 1: 143–4)

A sentence later she begs, "Pray pardon my freedom," but the freedom is precisely the point (GEL 1: 144). Two months later, she expresses her conviction that, to advance mankind, "We cannot fight and struggle enough for freedom of enquiry," yet this grand program for freedom is far less moving than her "confession" above (a "full confession," she asserts *in situ*, is "far better than *pro*fession" [GEL 1: 163]). Mary Ann's freedom—from apprehension, from dread, from eternity, from the everlasting, from fatality, from conclusions—allows her, so simply, the relief of lying bodily on the grass and ruminating on possibilities without implications or consequence. Without responsibility, without the future—to all eternity, everlastingly—weighing upon "each moment." This is a profound alteration in consciousness. One feels its inexpressibility.[12]

From the distance of about nine months from her public apostasy, but perhaps "a year or two" from the beginning of her shift, Mary Ann would write at much greater length to Sara Hennell the famous account that begins "When the soul is just liberated from the wretched giant's bed of dogmas on which it has been racked and stretched ever since it began to think, there is a feeling of exultation and strong hope" (GEL 1: 162). Yet here she tempered the exultation of moving from the rack of the giant's bed to lying on the grass, describing a succeeding period of "reflection and the experience of our own miserable weakness," an evangelical-sounding amendment if ever there was one. She ended with her pronouncement that "speculative truth begins to appear but a shadow of individual minds... and we turn to the *truth of feeling* as the only universal bond of union" (GEL 1: 162). The letter is an extremely important one, full of hard-earned wisdom about the mistake of zealous proselytizing and a recognition of the difference between the possible "harmony," though not "union," "with those who are often richer in the fruits of faith though not in reasons, than ourselves" (GEL 1: 162). The letter concludes with a reference to Romans 14–15, in which St. Paul directs Christians, distinguishing between the strong and the weak, to refrain from passing judgment on others and to act in ways that lead towards peace (Rom. 14:13,19). Then Mary Ann laments, "But I have not said half what I meant to say. There are so many aspects in which the subject might be presented that it is useless to attempt to exhaust it" (GEL 1: 163).

Mary Ann's reflection on her own experience among "persons whose views on religious matters undergo a change early in life" is never picked up again in direct fashion, only in significantly transposed form; even in this letter she generalizes, abstracts, and evades her own intimate experience (GEL 1: 162). What we know is that the shift offered her "inexpressible relief," so inexpressible that she could never return to that precise moment again, not in her letters nor in her novels. We know as well that her own shift was played out primarily against her father, on one hand, to the spectatorship of her new circle of intimates, on the other; with her brother, who would later occupy a central role in assenting to and withholding assent from her unions, acting this time as a reconciling force. The drama was a painful one that ended in May with Mary Ann's return to church, now determined that her independence of mind could be sustained internally and that her revolution could not take human relations as its cost. Her compromise followed the logic of the less rigid mind yielding to the needs and expectations of the more rigid (a transmutation of Paul's distinction between the stronger and the weaker), in a pattern that would surface repeatedly in her fiction.[13]

By May, it was clear that such a return was the only way to salvage her ties with her father. Months earlier in February, Mary Ann had taken the step of writing to her father from within the same household, after conversation had apparently failed. Mary Ann's long letter clarifies matters of opinion and feeling. She stated that she was not "inclined visibly to unite myself with any Christian community" (GEL 1: 128). At stake was the divine inspiration of both Old and New Testament:

> I regard these writings as histories consisting of mingled truth and fiction, and while I admire and cherish much of what I believe to have been the moral teaching of Jesus himself, I consider the system of doctrines built upon the facts of his life and drawn as to its materials from Jewish notions to be most dishonourable to God and most pernicious in its influence on individual and social happiness. In thus viewing this important subject I am in unison with some of the finest minds in Christendom in past ages, and with the majority of such in the present. (GEL 1: 128)

It is worth noting that Mary Ann's assessment of the divine inspiration of Scripture would not have made it impossible for her to remain within the liberal Broad Church movement of the time, which sought to embrace critical reading methods without directly contravening the Thirty-nine Articles of Religion of the Anglican Church. Yet Mary Ann rejected Christian doctrine here in toto and argued, with none of the humility that characterized her exchange with the highly educated Rev. Watts, that Christian doctrine did not glorify God but instead harmed individuals and society (in part because of what she then perceived as its "low" Jewish origins, a view she later revised, as we will see [GEL 1: 247]). God's existence, we might note, is here affirmed; Mary Ann ends the letter by affirming that she loves her father and that, in parallel, she seeks to "obey the laws of my Creator and to follow duty wherever it may lead me" (GEL 1: 130). Yet worshipping under these circumstances would be a singular act of hypocrisy "for the sake of [her] supposed interests," and while she would undergo any other pain to satisfy her father's desire, she cannot undergo this one (GEL 1: 129).

The notable feature of Mary Ann's letter—which went unanswered by her father, at least in the form of a return letter—is hardly doctrinal. What stands out is the extent to which Mary Ann and her father had come to live in utterly different universes. Mary Ann was on her way to being one of the best-read minds in England (think: "*She* has gone into the question!"). Soon she would become a full-fledged member, then a leader, of the nation's intellectual avant-garde, at a time when, as a woman, she could not attend its universities nor enter most libraries. Yet the father of this woman had recorded her apostasy in a journal entry of five words: "Mary Ann did not come." How could Mary Ann have expected that the views of the "finest minds in Christendom," past or present, would prove relevant for her father's faith and piety, his unified identity in family, parish, and nation, his professional ambition and achievement? On one hand, Mary Ann honored her father by turning to him in the language native to her mind, a language he had made it possible for her to learn. On the other hand, in asserting her independent assessment of doctrine in a long, articulate, emotionally and structurally complicated letter, Mary Ann announced her intellectual superiority over her limitedly read, solidly Midlands, Tory, Anglican father who could not follow her where she now traveled.

Mary Ann bridged the chasm between them by deciding, with her brother's support, to separate private conviction from filial duty and familial participation. The highest duty was to her father. For the man and the value, she would sacrifice the consonance between inner and outer lives (she would sacrifice, too, the tempting, public role of martyr). The "mingl[ing]" of "truth and fiction" that characterized the history of Jesus would come to describe Mary Ann's identity, as well. It was a better divide than "truth and error."

Notes

1. For this important argument, see Timothy Larsen, *Crisis of Doubt: Honest Faith in Nineteenth-Century England* (Oxford: Oxford University Press, 2006): "The Victorians...frequently discussed and wrote about the crisis of faith. Many of them did this because they prized faith so much and therefore feared and cared about its loss" (p. 10). Larsen argues that literary scholars, in particular, have miscast the loss-of-faith narrative as the central and representative Victorian experience, not recognizing the powerfully religious context of the time nor the exceptionality of the novels and novelists that foregrounded it.
2. John Walter Cross, *George Eliot's Life as Related in Her Letters and Journals* (Boston and New York: Jefferson Press, n.d., orig. pub. 1888).
3. Charles Hennell, *Inquiry Concerning the Origin of Christianity* (London: Smallfield, 1838), p. iv, HathiTrust, https://catalog.hathitrust.org/Record/005767369, emphasis mine. See Mary Ann Evans's letter of January 28, 1842, to Elizabeth Pears: "Nor will I quarrel with the million who, I am persuaded, are with me in intention though our dialect differ. Of course I must desire the ultimate downfall of error: for no error is innocuous, but this assuredly will occur without my proselyting aid, and the best proof of a real love of the truth, –that freshest stamp of divinity, –is a calm confidence in its intrinsic power to secure its own highest destiny, – that of universal empire" (GEL 1:125).
4. Rosemarie Bodenheimer, *The Real Life of Mary Ann Evans: Her Letters and Fiction* (Ithaca: Cornell University Press, 1994), suggests that the choice was perhaps a New Year's resolution "to publicize the conviction that had been developing in the deep privacy of her mind for some time. Its abruptness—if we can assume that the refusal was her first outward sign—signals the depth of the gap between her inner life and her family life" (p. 61).
5. Bodenheimer, *Real Life*, p. 66.
6. See Dominic Erdozain, *The Soul of Doubt: The Religious Roots of Unbelief from Luther to Marx* (Oxford: Oxford University Press, 2016), p. 5, for his compelling argument that "assaults on religious orthodoxy...are typically prompted by moral or spiritual anxieties....A visceral sense of right and

wrong, rather than a scientific or historical suspicion of supernatural truth claims, has served as the primary solvent of orthodoxy in the West." Bodenheimer, *Real Life*, also notes that "her rejection of Christian religious doctrine was undertaken in a militantly religious spirit, as a quest for truths worthy of God" (p. 64).
7. Timothy Larsen, *John Stuart Mill: A Secular Life* (Oxford: Oxford University Press, 2018), p. 209. In 1859, Sara Hennell's *Essay on the Sceptical Tendency of Butler's Analogy* was published by Chapman.
8. Haight suggests that GE's allusion is to a passage in Butler's chapter 7, but I venture that she was objecting to the passages in chapter 5 on vicarious punishment (GEL 1: 135, n. 9).
9. Joseph Butler, *Analogy of Religion to the Course and Constitution of Nature* (Philadelphia: J.B. Lippincott, 1873), p. 218; Project Gutenberg, https://www.gutenberg.org/ebooks/53346.
10. Butler, *Analogy*, p. 458.
11. It was also the case that Mary Ann's half-sister Fanny Houghton had read both Strauss and Hennell, "by stealth," as Cara Bray put it in a letter to her sister, Sara, and "always had regarded the miraculous part of Christianity as purely mythical," but "the good lady has no idea of making herself singular and obnoxious by an avowal of her opinions, and thinks M.A. very foolish not to keep her notions snugly to herself" (GEL 1:157).
12. Erdozain, *Soul*, p. 196, gives us a helpful framework, noting that the word "freedom" had been a hallmark of conversion narratives in the era of Wesley, when evangelicalism had "flourished as a joyous antidote to a religion of law and terror"; he sees the "hardening" of the movement in the middle decades of the century as having prompted precisely the kind of reaction we see in Mary Ann's account.
13. Bodenheimer, *Real Life*, p. 83. Bodenheimer's account of the Holy War is full of invaluable insights, especially the argument that we witness here the invention of a motif in which Eliot's scenes of mental liberation are followed by the heroine's "chastened [moral] return" (p. 84).

3
"Giving Full Faith to Every Symbol," 1843–1849

Mary Ann would go to church. She would go on living with her father. This much was decided. She would continue to serve as the mistress of the house, as she had since her mother's death, involved in all its most practical responsibilities. She would maintain her friendship with Maria Lewis and Rebecca Franklin, keep up strong ties with her brother, Isaac, at Griff; her sister, Chrissey, and her growing family; her half-sister, Fanny. At the same time, Mary Ann's ties to Rosehill, to the Brays and Hennells, would allow her the intellectual and spiritual life that sustained her through her father's death in 1849 and positioned her for an independent move to London in 1851.

In her mid-twenties, the question of Mary Ann's future was an open question. Isaac Evans wanted Mary Ann to pursue marriage prospects as far as possible from the "radical" Rosehill circle. Isaac's anxiety concerned their politics and religion, and would only have intensified had he known that Charles and Cara Bray had agreed upon an open marriage, in which Charles had lovers and children outside of wedlock, one of which he and Cara adopted, and Cara herself had an intense relationship with a man who came and went from Rosehill.[1]

Through Fanny's family, Mary Ann was introduced in April 1845 to a young picture restorer who enthusiastically hoped for an engagement. Unlike the major attachments of her life which Mary Ann would make without any advice or consultation, this one was made in full view of Fanny's family and discussed with the Brays, and it was botched. The suitor's overtures were first accepted joyfully, then rejected in confusion and worry "that she could never love or respect him *enough* to marry him and that it would involve *too great a sacrifice* of her mind and pursuits," as Cara Bray put it to her sister Sara in a letter (GEL 1: 184 my emphases). Mary Ann herself confirmed the sense of mistake in her own account to Sara: "If the circumstances could be repaired with the added condition of my experience I should act very differently" (GEL 1: 185–6). Cara summed it up, "poor girl, everything seems against the grain with her" (GEL 1 :186). Mary Ann's language of "enough" and the question of the worthiness of sacrifice in this case reflect a tension between her ideal of a marriage as weighed against its probable personal costs. Yet there is no way to know what, at this transitional stage, she envisioned her future pursuits to be.

The translation of the *Leben Jesu* and the sustaining force of her all-important relationship with Sara ("I have no loves but those that you can share with me") provided the framework for her days, which were punctuated by musical nights at the Brays, intermittent speakers at the Mechanics' Institute of Coventry, meeting Harriet Martineau and family, occasional visits from the Pears neighbors, Rebecca Franklin, and Maria Lewis (GEL 1: 186). From the demanding work of the Strauss translation, Mary Ann suffered headaches and low moods. The translation was all-consuming, from the daily work at 1,500 pages, to the totalizing vision of Strauss's project, to Mary Ann's worry as to whether all her effort would pay off in a finished and published product. While there was to be no serious financial gain from the project (in the end, she received the very low sum of twenty pounds; it would have been about as lucrative to serve for one year as a governess), she worried about the backing for the publication, which had been assured in 1844 but needed renegotiation later, in July 1845. In the end the greatest reward of the work was probably nothing that Mary Ann could have foreseen: John Chapman's publication of the translation would lead into the next significant phase of her writerly life, working as editor after his acquisition of *The Westminster Review* in 1851.

Mary Ann's translation of Strauss was not the first in English. The first had been translated from a French version, rather than the German, and circulated primarily in working-class, overtly infidel, circles.[2] Mary Ann's work was painstaking and seems always to have been intended for educated readers, probably with scholarly interests. She translated not only the German but also all the quotations within the text, from Greek, Latin, and Hebrew, seeking assistance and confirmation when she needed it from Charles Hennell and Rufa Brabant's father, Dr. R. H. Brabant, who himself had initiated the translation of his friend Strauss. Mary Ann insisted on correcting and revising her own proofs on the heels of all her consultations and took interest in all the details of publication, as she would when it came later to her novels. Constant communication with Sara Hennell as to the rendering of terms and the consistency of approach made Sara a partner to the labor.

Yet the entire project, which should have seemed a significant, if highly challenging, undertaking, seems never to have seized hold of Mary Ann's imagination; this in spite of the extraordinary commitment it required and the genuinely unprecedented contribution it made to the English educated classes, few of whom could contend with German texts. In May 1845, Mary Ann described to Sara Hennell her frustration and impatience at the renegotiation of the publication, noting that her "only real satisfaction just now is some hope that I am not sowing the wind. It is very laughable that I should be irritated about a thing in itself so trifling as a translation, but it is this very triviality of the thing that makes delays provoking. The difficulties that attend a really grand undertaking are to be borne, but things should run smoothly and fast when they are not important *enough* to demand the *sacrifice* of one's whole soul" (GEL 1: 191, emphases mine). In her ready-to-hand terms, Mary Ann again tested value by weighing how much and what sort of sacrifice it justified. At this stage translation seemed to her trivial, even if the text in question was major. Yet Mary Ann would go on to translate Spinoza and Feuerbach, too, even as she began to write her own reviews and essays, first for the small-scale *Coventry Herald*, owned by Charles Bray, and then for *The Westminster Review*, the progressive journal seeking a return to its most successful era under John Stuart Mill's editorship. With Chapman, Mary Ann would edit the decade's most vibrant intellectual platform, publishing writers including Herbert Spencer, Thomas Huxley, Harriet Martineau, and Robert Chambers on matters of scientific, economic, theological, and literary thought. But all that was in the future.

Like the work of putting scriptural lessons into her own words for the sake of self-discipline, mastery, internalization, and intelligibility for those less able than herself, Mary Ann moved into translating some of the great statements of a new sort of faith before turning to editing, original journalism, and fiction. To have any sense of community on the cusp of a new time, shared texts needed to be identified and made available; they needed to be tested in different environments to see how they were variously received and what meaning they contributed. Only then could they join an evolving tradition capable of nurturing a culture into its future. It is no exaggeration to say that Mary Ann Evans played a central role in that constructive process in mid-nineteenth-century England.

As philosopher Charles Taylor has written about the period, "in face of the opposition between orthodoxy and unbelief, many, and among them the best and most sensitive minds, were cross-pressured, looking for a third way."[3] Strauss and, like him, the Unitarian Charles Hennell (whose work Strauss liked so much he sought its translation into German) were indeed looking for a third way. They represented a kind of freethinking that was respectful and at times surprisingly reverent about the Scriptures it analyzed. While popular conceptions of Strauss (often suffering from hearsay or limited knowledge) held his text to be a purposeful damaging of religious belief, the introduction to his text could not have been more clear: "The supernatural birth of Christ, his miracles, his resurrection and ascension, remain eternal facts, whatever doubts may be cast of their reality as historical facts. . . . no injury is threatened to the Christian faith."[4] Distinguishing the eternal from the historical was protective, on Strauss's view, not destructive. In seeking to retain the essential, Strauss was, as Timothy Larsen has argued, "*less* radical than alternative skeptical voices; his approach was *more* palatable for those with lingering pious convictions or sensibilities."[5]

Strauss's approach immersed itself in an interpretive tradition that emerged within the church as early as Origen and proposed a new sort of reading in order to bring the understanding of Scriptures into accordance with modernity, rather than allowing it to wither as a clearly archaic and obsolete relic. For Strauss, the question of the precise boundary line between the historical and the unhistorical, "the most difficult question in the whole province of criticism," was ultimately only the starting point.[6] The unhistorical dimensions of the Gospels were not untrue and thus not "error," by the church's terms. They occupied a different category altogether: myth.

Certainly, Strauss distinguished himself from English theologians on this point, but it is worth noting that his method also distinguished him from many English *freethinkers*. His path was to refute not only the supernaturalist reading of Scripture that claimed the historicity of miracles and inspiration but also to refute avowedly scientific explanation, in a break from many English rationalists. Britons were yet absorbed with the questions of historicity—how best to reconcile the Gospels so that they could still be considered the infallible and true word of God? How to explain a miracle so that it could be rationally conceivable? Meanwhile, Strauss, in his Continental context, post Spinoza, post Friedrich Schleiermacher (Strauss's own teacher), was in conversation with a hermeneutic tradition that had wrestled for centuries with challenges to Scripture's authority and with the consequences for the doctrine of Scripture's infallibility, a doctrine whose assent was judged necessary to salvation.

For his part, Strauss argued that the writings of Scripture reflected a civilization less mentally developed; in the ancient Eastern world, he wrote, causes and effects could not be traced through scientific method and "the religious tendency was so preponderating" that "[a]t every link there was a disposition to spring into the Infinite, and to see God as the immediate cause of every change in nature or the human mind. In this mental condition the biblical history was written."[7] Such a history was a sacred one: "a history of events in which the divine enters, without intermediation, into the human."[8] Yet the processes of mental cultivation allowed later human beings to see history differently: to trace *natural* causes and effects. Thus the rationalists had broken from the supernaturalists in seeking to reconcile their more cultivated mental habits with Scripture by trying to prove either that the divine did not manifest itself in the manner related—thus the record was not historical—or, alternatively, that what was seen was not divine.

Strauss instead took the writers of the Gospels as readers themselves, disciples predisposed to see in the events of their time the fulfillment of Old Testament prophecies. The messianic era was supposed to be characterized by signs and wonders. Even before Jesus came on the scene, this promise came to be taken literally rather than figuratively. But with the belief that Jesus was the messiah, proven by his resurrection, then, retroactively, whatever Scripture had said about the messiah had to be true of Jesus. The writing of the Gospels was thus shaped by that need for fulfillment. Yet from the vantage point of the mid-nineteenth century, Strauss argued that the matters related in the Gospels had to be seen "in a light altogether different from that in which they were regarded by the authors themselves."[9] Distinguishing myth from allegory, Strauss maintained that allegory understood the higher influence on an account to be divine; whereas in the case of myth, the higher influence was the "spirit of a people or a community."[10] "Fiction," he summarized, "met with faith of a multitude is myth."[11]

With all this Mary Ann Evans agreed. In her important 1851 review of Robert William Mackay's *The Progress of the Intellect, as Exemplified in the Religious Development of the Greeks and the Hebrews*, she would set out consonant ideas at length, in her own words, though not under her own name:

> Our civilization, and, yet more, our religion, are an anomalous blending of lifeless barbarisms, which have descended to us like so many petrifactions from distant ages, with living ideas, the offspring of a true process of development. We are in bondage to terms and conceptions which, having had their root in conditions of thought no longer existing, have ceased to possess any vitality.... Now though the teaching of positive truth is the grand means of expelling error, the process will be very much quickened if the negative argument serve as its pioneer; if, by a survey of the past, it can be shown how each age and each race has had a faith and a symbolism suited to its needs and its stage of development, and that for succeeding ages to dream of retaining the spirit along with the forms of the past, is as futile as the embalming of the dead body in the hope that it may one day be resumed by the living soul.[12]

For Mary Ann, the "anomalous blending" of lifeless barbarisms with living ideas held English religion in bondage. The need, above all else, for "vitality," in terms and conceptions, meant abandoning the dream of a present inspired by a petrified faith and symbolism. An embalmed dead body will never be resumed by a living soul, she wrote, metaphorically, meanwhile, negating any supranaturalist resolution. Mary Ann ended her review essay with a suggestion to theological teachers to help their own cause by stepping back from dogma and allowing for the more "liberal views of biblical criticism"; these views would enable Christianity to "strike a firm root in man's moral nature, and to entwine itself with the growth of those new forms of social life to which we are tending" (*Essays* 281). Each religion needed to be in its own present, to answer the needs of its moment.

Mary Ann concluded by reversing and thus revivifying the terms and conceptions of religion and atheism:

> The spirit which doubts the ultimately beneficial tendency of inquiry, which thinks that morality and religion will not bear the broadest daylight our intellect can throw on them, ... is the worst form of atheism; while he who believes, whatever else he may deny, that the true and the good are synonymous, bears in his soul the essential element of religion. (*Essays* 281–2)

As Dominic Erdozain has argued about unbelief more generally, the reversal of terms that Mary Ann instituted here was a sort of free-thinking critique of the faith from within the faith.[13] Mary Ann's "holy war" was not ironic, but a battle for the essential elements of religion; those elements were not available via dogma but needed to be brought into being in what Mackay suggestively saw as an ongoing form of revelation: "divine revelation is not contained exclusively or pre-eminently in the facts and inspirations of any one age or nation, but is co-extensive with the history of human development, and is perpetually unfolding itself to our widened experience and investigation, as firmament upon firmament becomes visible to us in proportion to the power and range of our exploring instruments" (*Essays* 270–1). For both Mackay and Mary Ann Evans, science and inquiry—Herschel's telescope comes to mind—were not enemies of religion, nor even of revelation, but their very tools (note the scriptural "firmament upon firmament").

All the same, translating Strauss in his methodical journey through every moment of Jesus's life as rendered by the different Gospels did not inspire Mary Ann, in spite of the stakes of this holy war. Biographers and scholars tend regularly to note the dryness of Strauss, taking their cue from Mary Ann's own despair at his dissections of texts that she loved. Yet the despair may also have been a form of inchoate wondering in what language she would be able to speak originally. In an October 1855 review in *The Leader*, "Translations and Translators," she would recognize that translations of works "of reasoning or science can be adequately rendered only by means of what is at present exceptional faculty and exceptional knowledge" (*Essays* 340).

She would note that "a good translator" is "infinitely above the man who produces feeble original works" but insisted that he was still "infinitely below the man who produces good original works" (*Essays* 342). (Nine years earlier, Mary Ann had described attempting to convince a naïve former schoolfriend that a life of ceaseless, laborious translating from French and German in London, with the aim of financial independence, was far less pleasant than a life as a governess [GEL 1: 212].) In the mid-1840s, Mary Ann was a woman who had proven herself to be of exceptional faculty and knowledge, possessed of intellectual and personal courage. What else did she hold and what in the world would she produce?

Here, it might be useful to jump forward in chronology and consider how really, deeply unexpected it was for an intellect of her caliber—a self-trained scholar of church history, philosophy, and theology, a critical reader of the natural and social science emerging in her time, the learned translator of some of the most avant-garde thinking that crossed the Channel in her time, capable of working in French, Italian, Greek, Latin, German, and some Hebrew—to have chosen in the end... *fiction*.[14] Why not a major philosophical inquiry? The work she considered on the "Idea of a Future Life" (GEL 1: 240, n. 1)? A history to rival Michelet and Burckhardt, to counterpoint Macaulay? A national literary reckoning, from Milton and Shakespeare to Scott and Wordsworth? An account of the fine arts in relation to religion? Or poetry, the most highly esteemed genre of her time?

Further, who would have expected the *sort* of fiction she wrote? Not social problem novels, though she was highly alive and informed as to the ills of her time, not the loss-of-faith novels that moved her in her own reading, not novels driven by any programmatic moral, but instead page-turning novels of psychological complexity and dramatic interpersonal incident, set mostly in an English past so recent it could still be remembered. Novels that made a writer vulnerable by setting her own psyche in intense, if transposed, forms on the page. And novels that, while challenging and educative, were most certainly popular sensations, replete with murders, illegitimate children, adultery, mesmerism, lawsuits, bankruptcies, and blackmail. In other words, she wrote not only for the elite minds among which she numbered but for thousands of novel readers at mid-century.

The great unlikelihood of this development has been obscured by our knowledge that George Eliot did in fact emerge from Mary Ann Evans. But, if anything, the translations and review essays might easily have been preparation for or the early stages of a different career entirely. The translation period, which lasted about a decade, saw Mary Ann wrestle to find a sensibility and an idiom with which to analyze and dissect, but also to invent and explore new frameworks of meaning. Putting the Thorvaldsen statue of the risen Christ on her desk—at 20 inches tall, it was a miniature primarily by comparison with the major original—as well as an engraving of a painting by Paul Delaroche, was a push to move beyond the abstraction of text and system, to ideas made incarnate, ideas "wrought back," as she would later write in *Middlemarch*, "to the directness of sense, like the solidity of objects" (*MM* 193).[15] The objects in her study were not natural objects either, but human artifacts, and human artifacts with the potential for imitation and reproduction: widely shareable, capable of great, diffuse, and varying influence in whatever settings they found themselves. Capable, too, of comfort, solace, and pleasure. "Do you not feel how hard it is not [to] give *full faith* to every symbol?" she wrote to Sara Hennell in 1844 (GEL 1: 182).

When the translating of Strauss was complete in October 1845 (as she wrote in September about the proofs, "To see the first sheet is the next best thing to seeing the last" [GEL 1: 199]), Mary Ann celebrated by traveling abroad to Scotland, with the Brays, a trip that nearly did not take place because of her brother-in-law's bankruptcy but then was reinstated, only for Mary Ann to be called back almost immediately by brother and father. Her father had fallen and broken his leg. From here, his health was precarious and failing, especially in the months leading up to his death in May 1849, and Mary Ann was his primary companion and nurse. As she kept him company and traveled with him in England for his health, reading aloud to him when he wished and playing piano when she could, Mary Ann took on no new big projects, publishing limited reviews and short essays for the *Coventry Herald* anonymously. We have no record that her father knew that she was the translator of Strauss after its publication in June 1846, nor whether they discussed her future plans. Everything in those three years returned to the matter of his health.

From Foleshill in 1848 Mary Ann carried on a short, intense correspondence with John Sibree, whose family were the Evanses' near neighbors, among those who had sought years earlier to return Mary Ann to the fold. At that time, John, the son of an Independent minister in Coventry, had tutored Mary Ann in Greek while she gave lessons in German to his sister, Mary. In 1848, from his post at Spring Hill College in Birmingham, John made Mary Ann a sharer in the doubts which would ultimately cause him to renounce his religious calling. While his parents suspected Mary Ann's freethinking influence, his sister, Mary, denied it in her own account of the relationship.[16]

While biographers have not read this correspondence as evidence of a romance, John Sibree and Mary Ann were only four years apart in age and had a good deal in common. John was in the process of leaving a clerical life, with all the risks that entailed, and stood on the cusp of a major translation from German of Hegel's *Lectures on the Philosophy of History* (1849). He was also ready for marriage and, indeed, married soon after, in 1850. That Mary Ann was largely silent about the correspondence with the Brays and Hennells until after its end, when she spoke of the Sibrees unusually disparagingly, makes it more, rather than less, likely that the relationship meant a good deal to her.

Mary Ann's letters to Sibree, traversing a range of subjects, from the revolution in France to differences between the French and English working classes, to the fate of music and sculpture, to artistic power and originality, flash with intelligence and imagination, and a good deal of brashness, too.[17] While Mary Ann could position herself as an elder (perhaps self-protectively)—"I have gone through a trial of the same genus as yours, though rather differing in species"—and ironically (but perhaps pointedly) claim "feminine dependence and stupidity"— her letters to John more generally reflect both self-fashioning and abandon (GEL 1: 260, 253). A desire for intimacy, freedom, and mutual confession comes out, as she asks John to burn her letters (thereby endowing them with sacred and sacrificial value) and promises him her own extreme caution with respect to anything he might say of himself: "It is necessary to me, not simply to *be* but to *utter*, and I require utterance of my friends.... If the perfect union comes occasionally, as in music, it enhances the harmonies.... Is not the universe itself a perpetual utterance of the One Being? I want you to write me a Confession of Faith – not merely *what* you believe but why you believe it... utter, utter, utter" (GEL 1: 255). Had anyone ever asked that of her, in just such an affirmation?

Mary Ann urged him with the sort of advice she might have wished others could have given—or would still give—to her:

> Only persevere – be true, firm and loving – not too anxious about immediate usefulness to others—that can only be a result of justice to yourself.... Do we not commit ourselves to sleep, and so resign all care for ourselves every night? Lay ourselves gently on the bosom of nature or God? A beautiful reproach to the spirit of some religionists and ultra-good people. (GEL 1: 261)

Mary Ann was urging justice to the self: the setting aside of anxiety about busy duty and a gentle reliance on something greater than the self, for the sake of the self. In casting this kind of shift as the truest faith, the deepest utterance of the religious sensibility, Mary Ann was returning to the letter to Francis Watts in which she yearned for the rest that she associated with freedom. These letters to John Sibree thus read as Mary Ann testing—or writing into being—a relationship that might have held the power to ease some of her most difficult habits of mind, habits that reflected a profound sense of solitude. Yet the relationship did not develop into romance, perhaps in part because of his parents' anxiety over Mary Ann's influence. Mary Ann encouraged his independent travel to Germany, imagining him there with vicarious pleasure. The engraving of the Delaroche Christ that had accompanied her as solace through her Strauss translation she gave to John, though we do not know where or when.

The full year preceding Robert Evans's death, from the spring of 1848 through May 1849, was an exceedingly intense one for Mary Ann, in which she expressed the extremes of her intellectual and spiritual life in the most charged language she knew, that of the trials of religious faith. She read the novels of Scott aloud to her father, she watched him searchingly, and she took care to answer his every answerable need: "My heart bleeds for dear Father's pains, but it is blessed to be at hand to give the soothing word and act needed" (GEL 1: 270). Every word here bespeaks religious experience: bleeds, blessed, soothe, dear Father's pains, heart, hand, word, and act. Mary

Ann described her state to the Brays and the Hennells, writing to Sara:

> Alas for the fate of poor mortals which condemns them to wake up some fine morning and find all the poetry in which their world was bathed only the evening before utterly gone—the hard angular world of chairs and tables and looking-glasses staring at them in all its naked prose. It is so in all the stages of life—the poetry of girlhood goes—the poetry of love and marriage—the poetry of maternity—and at last the very poetry of duty forsakes us for a season...this is the state of prostration—the self-abnegation through which the soul must go, and to which perhaps it must again and again return, that its poetry or religion, which is the same thing, may be a real ever flowing river fresh from the windows of heaven and the fountains of the great deep—not an artificial basin with grotto work and gold fish. (GEL 1: 264)

All readers of the novels know this moment of "disenchantment," as the great Eliot scholar Barbara Hardy named it.[18] We recognize its recurrence in *The Mill on the Floss*, in *Silas Marner*, *Middlemarch*, and *Romola*. Intense depression, as the comprehensive loss of faith within the unyielding domestic space of chairs, tables, looking glasses: objects designed to meet basic need, offering harsh reflection rather than transformation. The sense of finding something that had been naturally present suddenly "utterly gone," the sense of all enthusiasm having "forsaken" her, was the deeply religious language of Mary Ann's depression.

To describe the work of the soul in this crisis, its need for rebirth into a new stage of life with its own poetry or religion, Mary Ann went back to the language of the Bible, to the story of the flood God brings upon the earth in a destruction of the first creation: "In the six hundredth year of Noah's life...the same day were all the *fountains of the great deep* broken up, and the *windows of heaven* were opened" (Gen. 7:11, emphasis mine). While the biblical account describes these fountains and windows opening to the destructive force of the floodwaters, Mary Ann describes them as necessary life forces. Heaven and the great deep serve as the sources for a "real ever flowing river" (no commas, just the cascade itself) that makes continuity, fluidity, eternity available once again to human experience.

Mary Ann waited out her periods of deep depression, believing that they would pass, in what she characterized as a sort of religious practice, a *rhythm* in which she could anticipate feeling forsaken, then needing to "possess [her own soul] in patience," until enthusiasm (itself a term with definitively religious associations for her, as for other Victorians) could return. As she wrote to Charles Bray, "The enthusiasm without which one cannot even pour out breakfast well (at least *I* cannot) has forsaken me.... I can never live long without it in some form of other. I possess my soul in patience for a time" (GEL 1: 265). Thought and love, she continued, worked against sadness: with thought as a formative power and love as a vitalizing one, "They are in themselves a more intense and extended participation of a divine Existence—as they grow the highest species of faith grows too" (GEL 1: 266).

This period, in which Mary Ann neared thirty, saw her involved in self-scrutiny reminiscent of her evangelical youth. To Sara Hennell she wrote, "I am entering on a new period of my life which makes me look back on the past as something incredibly poor and contemptible... I never felt my own insignificance and imperfection so completely" (GEL 1: 269). To Fanny Houghton she described holding a "court of conscience," in which she entered

> a protest against that superficial soul of mine which is perpetually contradicting and belying the true inner soul. I am in that mood which, *in another age of the world*, would have led me to put on sackcloth and pour ashes on my head, when I call to mind the sins of my tongue—my animadversions on the faults of others, as if I thought myself to be something when I am nothing. When shall I attain to the true spirit of love which Paul has taught for all the ages?... I only want to remove the shadow of my miserable words and deeds from before the divine image of truth and goodness, which I would have all beings worship. (GEL 1: 276, emphasis mine)

"In another age of the world": and yet, Mary Ann was intensely aware of where she found herself in human history, of what behaviors and beliefs had met human needs earlier in time and were no longer vital but merely vestigial at the midpoint of the nineteenth century. In the absence of prayer, mourning, and repentance, she turned to confession and the eternal facts of the Gospel. She set out the difference between falsity and truth, though not as a matter of opinions but as the divide between the surface and the inner soul.

"Giving Full Faith to Every Symbol," 1843–1849

As Mary Ann confronted her father's mortality, it was likely not mortality itself that overwhelmed her. Death, timely and untimely, had been a part of her life since her earliest childhood; it dots her letters without a sense of crisis. Her father had lived long and well and, as Mary Ann wrote to Fanny, "no evil threatens him...for *his sake* there is absolutely no regret" (GEL 1: 283). For Mary Ann, though, as for other Victorians who had set aside Christian doctrine, apostasy's greatest cost came as they confronted the blank that succeeded death. That Mary Ann had thought to write, of all subjects, on the idea of a future life was not incidental.

In this period, her letters repeatedly feature the term "utterance" (as in the important letter to John Sibree). "Utterance" was emerging as Mary Ann's contemporary/provisional response to death in a world no longer defined for her by Christian dogma: "I will talk and caress and look lovingly until death makes me as stony as the Gorgon-like heads of all the judicious people I know. What is anything worth until it is uttered? Is not the Universe one great utterance? Utterance there must be in word or deed to make life of any worth. Every true pentecost is a gift of utterance" (GEL 1: 279). For Mary Ann, utterance was life and the bringing forth of creation by spoken word, as Genesis and John described it. It was the most fundamental standard of value ("worth"). Utterance was the substitute for sacrifice, and it merged the human and the divine. "Utterance" could do all this for Mary Ann because when she spoke, she, too, was giving utterance to other words and gesturing to other Pentecosts: "And they were all filled with the Holy Ghost, and began to speak with other tongues, as the Spirit gave them utterance" (Acts 2:4).

Mary Ann seems at this time to have sought out and recognized utterances that felt to her inspired. Beyond the correspondence of her closest friends, the "utterances" she valued most were those of especially gifted writers, regardless of their lives or opinions: George Sand, Jean-Jacques Rousseau, and her contemporaries Francis Newman and J. A. Froude. Rousseau's genius, she wrote in a letter to Sara Hennell, "has sent that electric thrill through my intellectual and moral frame which has awakened me to new perceptions, which has made man and nature a fresh world of thought and feeling to me— and this not by teaching me any new belief" (GEL 1: 277). Turning to the metaphors of wind and fire, again from Acts 2, she went on: "It is simply that *the rushing wind* of his inspiration has so quickened my faculties that I have been able to shape more definitely for myself ideas which had previously dwelt as dim 'anhungen' in my soul—*the fire* of his genius has so fused together old thoughts and prejudices that I have been ready to make new combinations" (GEL 1: 277). George Sand, Mary Ann contended, wrote "as the spirit moved her and trusted to Providence for the catastrophe" of her plots; in a phrase probably never used for the writings of George Sand before or since, Mary Ann "bow[ed] before her in eternal gratitude to that 'great power of God' [Acts 8:10] manifested in her" (GEL 1: 277–8).

Closer to home, Mary Ann exalted J. A. Froude's controversial loss-of-faith novel, *The Nemesis of Faith* (1849), in a review in the *Coventry Herald*, as no ordinary reading experience but "companionship with a spirit, who is transfusing himself into our souls, and is vitalizing them by his superior energy" (*Essays* 265). Francis Newman's *The Soul; Her Sorrows and Her Aspirations* she called a Carlylean "yea" (GEL 1: 282). All these productions prompted Mary Ann to contrast the poverty of the individual soul—"Poor and shallow as one's own soul is"—with the blessedness "by which the greater ones can live in us" in their "greatness, beauty or bliss" (GEL 1: 280). She called this "a sort of transhumanation": "the living soul – the breath of God within us" (GEL 1: 280).

In the intensity of watching her father's life come to an end, Mary Ann reached beyond individual consciousness to something more like the species-consciousness she would encounter in the work of Ludwig Feuerbach. She kept after that prefix "trans," seeking a way to describe some movement *across* or between human beings, *across* time: *trans*human, a *trans*fused spirit, living *in us*.[19] This human greatness, beauty, or bliss was "the living soul," the breath of God. Mary Ann closed the letter to Sara Hennell on Rousseau and Sand with a return to her beloved *Imitation of Christ*, "I have at last the most delightful 'de imitation Christi' with quaint woodcuts. One breathes a cool air as of cloisters in the book—it makes one long to be a saint for a few months. Verily its piety has its foundations in the depths of the divine-human soul" (GEL 1: 278). The breath, the soul, the depths, the divine-human, and the impulse to be a saint, "for a few months": all these were the keywords of Mary Ann Evans as she nursed her father and fused her new combinations.

A little less than a decade earlier, in 1840, Mary Ann Evans had channeled Calvinist evangelical certainty, declaring that

> the Christian is greater than others in that he knows the object, the end of all his chastisements, the state to which he is tending, and while all mankind beside are either dizzy with intoxication, locked in the stupor of indifference, or shuddering at the spectre of despair, he alone walks calmly and wakefully, and with an eye freed from the film of pride, prejudice and discontent he sees all things in Nature and in Providence in those soul gladdening hues with which the great Fountain of Light has clothed them. (GEL 1:56)

Mary Ann no longer spoke or wrote of an elect (male) few—"he alone walks calmly"; there was no doctrine to declare "the Christian" greater than all "the rest of mankind," possessed of the Light. Mary Ann's pronouns had shifted in the near decade that had passed. It was often first-person plural now, a "we" or "us" that expanded beyond creed and sect, that was testing its limits and its authority.[20] To be calm, wakeful, able to see divine light was no longer her patrimony. When her father died and was buried on June 6, 1849, in Chilvers Coton, filial duty was done. Within a week Mary Ann, mournful but free, would be off to the Continent with the Brays, leaving the parish boundaries far behind.

Notes

1. Hughes, *George Eliot*, pp. 82–5. See pp. 82–122 for Hughes's account of Mary Ann's struggles with a series of men, some older and married, some as yet unmarried, in her intense desire for intimacy. Hughes also understands Mary Ann's names that described Sara as a wife or beloved spouse in terms of that intense desire (cf. GEL 1: 285). Cross, however, deleted those names in his account, suggesting their non-normativity.
2. See Timothy Larsen, "Biblical Criticism and the Crisis of Belief: D. F. Strauss's *Leben Jesu* in Britain," in *Contested Christianity: The Political and Social Contexts of Victorian Theology* (Waco, TX: Baylor University Press, 2004), pp. 43–58.
3. Charles Taylor, *A Secular Age* (Cambridge: Belknap Press, 2007), p. 302.
4. David Friedrich Strauss, *The Life of Jesus, Critically Examined* (London: Chapman, 1846), p. xi. HathiTrust, http://hdl.handle.net/2027/hvd.rslfjs.
5. Larsen, *Contested Christianity*, 58.
6. Strauss, *Life*, p. 92.

7. Strauss, *Life*, p. 74.
8. Strauss, *Life*, p. 2.
9. Strauss, *Life*, p. 43.
10. Strauss, *Life*, p. 48.
11. Strauss, *Life*, p. 84.
12. George Eliot, "R. W. Mackay's *The Progress of the Intellect*," pp. 268–85 (*Essays* 268–9).
13. See Erdozain, *Soul*, pp. 212–20.
14. Philip Davis's incomparable study, so aptly named *The Transferred Life of George Eliot* (Oxford: Oxford University Press, 2017), might be read as one long answer to the question of "why fiction?"
15. Marilyn Orr beautifully describes this incarnational mode in Eliot's writing in her study *George Eliot's Religious Imagination: A Theopoetics of Evolution* (Evanston, IL: Northwestern University Press, 2018), pp. 11-32.
16. See Redinger, *George Eliot*, pp. 110-115, for her account of the relationship with the Sibrees.
17. Mary Ann used that freedom to the fullest in her letters, discussing D'Israeli's theory of 'races' and herself asserting that "extermination up to a certain point seems to be the law for the inferior races—for the rest, fusion both for physical and moral ends" (GEL 1: 246). She describes the "negroes" as "too important physiologically and geographically for one to think of their extermination," yet unlikely to "fuse" with other races because of mutual "repulsion" and rejects all of Jewish culture but Hebrew poetry, saying, "much of their early mythology and almost all their history is utterly revolting.... Everything *specifically* Jewish is of a low grade" (GEL 1: 247). While she would later revise her assessment of Jewish culture, she does not reconsider the racial prejudice in regret or self-questioning. To my mind, these are the most disturbing sentences in the whole of her letters.
18. See Barbara Hardy, *Novels of George Eliot: A Study in Form* (London: Athlone Press, 1963), pp. 189–200.
19. Davis's tracing of Eliot's "transferred life" attunes us even further to the centrality of "trans" actions in the novelist's imagination.
20. In her important study *Before George Eliot: Marian Evans and the Periodical Press* (Cambridge: Cambridge University Press, 2013), Fionnuala Dillane describes the arrival of the "we" not exclusively as a feature of Eliot's fictional moralizing but also as a feature she learned as a writer for a range of periodicals, all of which were corporate productions that asked of their writers to recognize and participate in the particular "periodical's overarching brand voice" (p. 81).

4
"This Fuller Life," 1849–1854

Mary Ann left for the Continent with the Brays, travelling through France and Italy to Geneva, where the Brays left her when they returned to England at the end of July 1849. Her father had left her £2000 as a trust and approximately £100 in cash. With constant care not to "exceed [her] means" in paying for room, board, piano, newspapers from England, lessons, and lectures, Mary Ann would stay on in Geneva until March 1850, first in a pension and then as a boarder with the artist D'Albert Durade's family (GEL 1: 305).

Interest in her new surroundings and the various other boarders permeates her letters: "It jumps admirably with my humour to live in two worlds at once in this way. I possess my dearest friends and my old environment in my thoughts, –and another world of novelty and beauty in which I am actually moving" (GEL 1: 302–3). Mary Ann enjoyed meeting the friends of the Durades, participating in regular musical evenings, attending lectures in physics, and attending church, too, which reminded her of an "independent chapel at home" (GEL 1: 294). She observed the differences between Genevan and English practices, from the singing of hymns ("respectable though dronish") to a devotion to country ("even before devotion to the church"), to the energy of the sermons ("very superior in its tone") (GEL 1: 294). Throughout her life, Mary Ann would be sensitive to the potential of sermons to inspire their listeners and the frequent disappointment of preachers to reach their audience.[1] These sermons stood out to Mary Ann for their eloquence and delivery: "I go to the Genevese churches every Sunday and nourish my heterodoxy with orthodox sermons. However there are some clever men here in the church" (GEL 1: 330–1).

Yet for all the beauty of the environs and the novelty of experience, the period was also marked by anxiety at not hearing from her family, by illness and headache that made it impossible for her to continue the translation she had begun of Spinoza's *Tractatus Theologico-Politicus* (1670), and by her uncertain future. Writing to the Brays, certainly hoping for their reassurance, she expressed her sense of superfluity perfectly: "I am a sort of supernumerary spoon, and there will be no damage to the set if I am lost" (GEL 1: 322). The return to an England without her father loomed before her so vaguely and unspecifically that geography became all metaphor: "It looks to me like a land of gloom, of ennui, of platitude, but in the midst of all this it is the land of duty and affection, and the only ardent hope I have for my future life is to have given to me *some* woman's duty, some possibility of devoting myself where I may see a daily result of pure calm blessedness in the life of another" (GEL 1: 322).

Caring for her father had given her a devotional, daily purpose like none she had ever experienced. Her actions had been met with immediate, visible confirmation and gratification, unlike long-term projects of anonymous translation, which regularly made Mary Ann deeply anxious that all the work might in the end be for naught. With no one to say to her the words she had written to John Sibree—"Only persevere –be true, firm and loving –not too anxious about immediate usefulness to others—that can only be a result of justice to yourself"— she found herself in an anomalous position, expressing hope that a generic, as yet unidentified, female duty might land upon her and she would again be able to partake of "pure calm blessedness."

Leaving Christian orthodoxy as a *woman*, and most particularly as a single woman, exerted its own costs and challenges for self-definition. Mary Ann's turn to such religiously inflected language (without any characteristic hint of humor or irony) when she considered her future illuminates just those costs and challenges. We can see her struggling— and not genuinely succeeding—to find a formula by which an unbelieving, unattached female intellectual might live an ethically recognizable life. She had few models. Harriet Martineau, seventeen years older than Mary Ann, had been raised a Unitarian and successfully pursued an independent writerly and intellectual life, contributing articles (and much-needed funds) to *The Westminster Review*, among other publications. Yet Martineau, an agnostic who in 1851 aligned herself with atheism, was distinct from Mary Ann in two fashions: first, her interests turned as much on the practical pursuit of reform, including feminist reform, as they did on writing, giving her both a path and a language to articulate her female identity; and second, Martineau came of a powerful intellectual family. Until their break in 1851, all her intellectual projects were pursued with her brother James's support and interest. By contrast, Mary Ann had neither a supportive family base nor a clear political program that could be allied with her sense of herself as a woman.

Her path needed a different narrative. Upon her return to England, Mary Ann visited her siblings. From her brother's home at Griff, she wrote quickly to Sara Hennell to inquire about lodging in London. She requested details regarding John Chapman's large house at 142 Strand, the home from which he would manage *The Westminster Review* from 1851, let rooms, and live in the kind of permanent intellectual bustle and romantic conflict that he thrived on. In the fall, Mary Ann met Chapman and R. W. Mackay at Rosehill and then made an initial trip of two weeks to London. By January 1851, when her major review on Mackay came out, Mary Ann was settled at 142 Strand. There, Mary Ann fell into the opposite of "pure calm blessedness," navigating the webs of complication between Chapman, his wife, his live-in mistress, and herself, the newest object of desire, suspicion, envy, and unclarity. Kathryn Hughes has convincingly argued that Mary Ann was sexually intimate with John Chapman.[2] Painful chaos in the household resulted in Mary Ann returning unhappily to Coventry late in March, where she stayed until Chapman came seeking her in May after he had acquired *The Westminster Review*. Aware that he needed someone with more intellectual discrimination than he possessed, not to mention someone who could really *write*, Chapman turned to Marian, who had altered her signature that April at the bottom of a cool letter to him. Recognizing that a woman at the helm would not advance the journal's prospects, Marian and Chapman agreed that Marian would edit the review anonymously, for room and board, and Chapman would let it be known that he employed an editor upon whose judgment he relied thoroughly. Their pledge to a non-sexual business partnership was a renunciation that sent Marian back to *The Imitation of Christ*, recommending to Chapman that he read it, too.

Editing *The Westminster Review* in the attempt to make it the leading journal of progressive thinking posed enormous practical and intellectual challenges. Marian, who, we need recall, might have failed from any number of causes, succeeded brilliantly, seeking out the best writers for articles that she carefully commissioned and then coached into being, attending to all the details of production, from layout to proofing, aware all the time of the text as a commodity. As Fionnuala Dillane has argued, in her capacity as editor Marian revealed her interest in cultivating as broad an audience as possible, educating while also entertaining, expanding readers' horizons particularly in the Contemporary Literature section that she inaugurated and the newly defined reviews of national literatures.[3] Under her hand, the Prospectus (first hastily and unimpressively drafted by Chapman) described the journal as guided by its recognition of the Law of Progress. Its attempts at reform would be made by the editors' "steady comparison of the actual with the possible, as the most powerful stimulus to improvement," tempered by the recognition that the "institutions of man, no less than the products of nature, are strong and durable in proportion as they are the results of a gradual development" (*Essays* 4). Targeted areas of reform were legal process and ecclesiastical revenue, expansion of the vote, national education and higher education that did not discriminate on the basis of sect, local governments in the colonies that would yet serve interests of empire, and entirely free trade. Meanwhile, the journal's "constructive religious philosophy" was based upon its conviction that religion played an essential role in the human life and thus it would not disappear with progress, but "will only discard an old form to assume and vitalize one more expressive of its essence" (*Essays* 7). In this way the editors assumed a position of reverential sympathy for "cherished associations" and simultaneous commitment to freedom of inquiry with respect to all religious matters (*Essays* 7).

Marian defined the new *Westminster* and the *Westminster* defined Marian. From her anonymous but powerful platform, she encountered and helped confirm the status of the mid-century's most central thinkers in science, religion, philosophy, sociology, and art. Nearly immediately after assuming her new role, Mary Ann wrote to the Unitarian James Martineau to commission from him an essay on "Christian Ethics and Modern Civilization," in which she asked him to consider how far

Christian ethics were "available for our actual wants and in accordance with our highest conceptions," yet also to define "what we really owe to Christianity as a stage in the religious development of the race" (GEL 8: 27). If, as she contended, "the faith and life of the early Christians were entirely based on the idea of the special and the exceptional, whereas the essence of modern advancement is the recognition of the general and invariable," could Christian ethics thus offer an "effective religious and moral theory" (GEL 8:26)? Laying out exactly what she wanted the essay to cover, Marian's mastery of this field and her sense of the parameters of its necessary conversations allowed the *Westminster* to find the right people—"amongst the world's vanguard"—for the right essays and to guide them into their best possible form (GEL 2: 49).

Now, the woman who had spent her second and third decades reading ceaselessly in the Midlands; seeking out from Griff and Foleshill the books she saw advertised in periodicals; learning languages; keeping up with an extraordinary range of intellectual developments and challenges; and reviewing what she read for the benefit of only her intimate correspondents: became a cultural force, with authority to bring to the attention of the English reading public the work *she* judged worthy. As her past had prepared her for this editorial task, now this task prepared her for a novelistic future. Carrying particular responsibility for the review of literature published in America and on the Continent, Marian surveyed hundreds of books for each of the ten issues of the *Westminster* that she edited, learning the scope of the fictional field before she would enter into it as a wholly original voice.

The Westminster Review's commitment to reform, on one hand, and to gradualism, on the other, suited the Marian Evans we know from the letters, politically, spiritually, morally, and intellectually.[4] Already in 1843 she had written to Sara Hennell, reflecting on her holy war, that the "only safe revolution" for individuals, as with nations, "is one arising out of the wants which their *own progress* has generated" (GEL 1: 162). In other words, social change could not be imposed from outside or above; it could only arrive safely and permanently if it was felt to be imperative by those living its implications. Change needed to satisfy a peremptory need, in the same way that the relief of the answer to a burning question could only be felt by those who had burned with the question in the first place. For those minds at the vanguard, who might be tempted to "proselyt[ize] as fast as our zeal for truth may prompt us," Mary Ann had written, time would reveal that it was the "quackery of infidelity to suppose that it has a nostrum for all mankind, and to say to all and singular, 'Swallow my opinions and you shall be whole'" (GEL 1: 162). While such an approach reflected an elitism that distinguished more advanced minds from slower or less discriminating ones, it was also arguably a genuine recognition of human diversity from someone who could appreciate a range of dispositions and talents: "Ought we not on every opportunity to seek to have our feelings in harmony though not in union with those who are often richer in the fruits of faith though not in reasons, than ourselves?" (GEL 1:162)

Perhaps because of her own gradualism, Marian could appreciate the ways that England was changing. Reviewing W. R. Greg's *The Creed of Christendom* in September 1851 for the radical weekly *The Leader*, which had been founded the year before by Thornton Hunt and G. H. Lewes, Marian noted the favorable reception given to a work that followed in the footsteps of Charles Hennell's important and personally beloved *Inquiry*. In 1838, Hennell's strengths had been acknowledged in England only privately and, even after its second edition in 1845, *Inquiry* had been greeted publicly with censure. Yet, "in this *annus mirabilis* of 1851," Marian noted drily, Greg's arguments against the doctrine of inspiration both on historical counts and on the basis of conscience received a fair reading (*Essays* 296). Greg did not hold back from exploring the incompatibility of Christian creed with what he saw as more advanced moral truths. He criticized credal appeal to the selfish motives of reward and punishment (a serious sticking point for many Victorian critics of Christian orthodoxy), the negative moral influences of doctrines of repentance and conversion that sidestepped or refused the law of consequences, and the explanation of human suffering as specially ordained for human benefit. Without agreeing with him wholesale, Marian saw Greg as a powerful voice among those "pioneers of the New Reformation" who "protest[ed] against the current faith, because they would substitute for it one purer and more influential": "if our population is to be Christianized, religious teaching must be conducted in a new spirit and on new principles," she wrote (*Essays* 286). For so many of Marian's freethinking contemporaries, the aim was not unbelief but a religion worthy of the era.

1851, the year of the Great Exhibition, was to be an *annus mirabilis* in a number of ways. In October, Marian met G. H. Lewes, the vibrant, unusually wide-ranging intellectual who would become her partner in love and work. He had admired her essay on Greg when it came out in September, but it was not until after Marian's intense and painful relationship with Herbert Spencer in 1852 that Lewes and Marian recognized each other. Spencer, like Marian, was self-taught, born to Midland Dissenters, agnostic, and would come to be considered one of the most powerful intellects of his generation. His groundbreaking *Social Statics* had come out in 1850 with Chapman, and he worked as subeditor for *The Economist* opposite Chapman in the Strand, easily enabling a friendship with Marian. They shared a love for theater and opera, which they attended together regularly thanks to Spencer's work as arts critic for *The Economist*.

Spencer ranged in his thought from evolutionary biology to political economy to ethics, and he linked those studies to the nascent fields of sociology and psychology. The two intellects were natural partners in conversation. Marian's letters, and later her novels, test and play with Spencer's theory that evolution was a process leading from homogeneity toward ever more heterogeneity and differentiation. Marian also shared his commitment to empiricism and identified deeply with his interest in the analogy between social and natural life, seeing both as engaged in slow evolution driven by identifiable laws. Yet Marian would also push back against Spencer's totalizing theories, and against theory as the frame through which social reality was apprehended. As Marian drew nearer to her work as a novelist, she became more and more convinced that generalizations could not account for the nuanced differences of human circumstance. Perhaps that conviction more than any other pushed her—an intellectual who could easily have spent her career theorizing in various forms of nonfiction—into the writing of fiction.

In a period in which disciplines were only just emerging and differentiating into separate spheres of professional inquiry, Spencer reflected the tendency of Victorian thinkers to favor synthetic theories. There was something deeply humane about the linking together of political economy, ethics, biology, and religion, for example; about seeing the implications of one field for another and of engaging with questions of knowledge as well as policy, without sidelining any of their dimensions. The freedom to range among what we now see as distinct disciplines, with their own dedicated vocabularies and conceptual frameworks, cultivated an openness and creativity among the best of the era's thinkers. No wonder Marian enjoyed Spencer's conversation. Yet she would later reflect on the personal and intellectual risks of seeking grandiose theories to provide, as she so memorably named it in *Middlemarch*, the "Key to all Mythologies." Any single key was unlikely to unlock *all* knowledge; and mythologies were what any single theory wound up *producing*, not only investigating. Theory could also become desiccating; it could force life into its own preconditions or explain away conflict as a matter of law and, just as often, confuse people's understanding of what was closest at hand.

As Marian and Spencer drew nearer in the spring of 1852 and could be seen regularly together, enjoying each other's company, Spencer clarified to Marian that his interest in her could never develop into romance or marriage because his admiration for her was purely intellectual and moral. In other words, she was not beautiful. He explained, in a preponderance of abstract nouns, that his "fatal" lack of attraction was a situation of "instincts [that] would not respond," hinting at an evolutionary excuse (GEL 8: 42–3). Though Spencer located the flaw in Marian's physiognomy, in the end Spencer's theory pushed up against the finding that it was Spencer who could find no female ideal in life, while Marian, beautiful or not, knew a fully realized love with Lewes.

The episode of a few intense months, which ended in August 1852, was a battering one for Marian, perhaps especially on the heels of the abortive relationship with Chapman. Modern biographers have explored it at length, noting the way in which Marian appeared to lower herself, begging Spencer (in letters that remained private until long after their deaths) simply to grant her the crumbs of his attention and friendship because she could not imagine life without him: "I suppose no woman ever before wrote such a letter as this—but I am not ashamed of it, for I am conscious that in the light of reason and true refinement I am worthy of your respect and tenderness, whatever gross men or vulgar-minded women might think of me" (GEL 8: 57). Marian promised Spencer that she could do with "very little," and affirmed, "I do not ask you to sacrifice anything" (GEL 8: 57). In a sense, what she was proposing to Spencer was his own theory of political freedom; she offered him "the right of every man to do whatsoever he wills provided he does not infringe the equal freedom of any other man"; what she willed was merely the freedom to be near him, making no demands on him.[5]

But this language of relational freedom was really not native to her. Her language of human relations tended to exalt that most Christian ideal of "sacrifice," while tempering it with the wholly personal question of "worthiness": was the sacrifice worth the cost it would exact? This question of personal self-sacrifice would recur in her novels and had already recurred in her letters with respect to the matter of her single marriage proposal, her translation, and the novel *Jane Eyre* (while caring for her father, she had written to Charles Bray, with perhaps unwitting relevance, "all sacrifice is noble but one would like it to be for a better cause than a putrefying carcase" [GEL 1: 268]). When it came to Spencer, Marian did not give her own sacrifice the scrutiny it deserved. Was the one-sidedness of the sacrifice she was offering justified by the worth of the *relation* that would emerge on those terms? At the very heart of her long concluding sentence—"for I am conscious that in the light of reason and true refinement I am worthy of your respect and tenderness"—we can see Marian distinguishing between historically situated gender norms and social shame, on one hand, and enlightened personal rectitude and self-worth (channeling Spinoza's "light of reason") on the other. She emerges, as usual, defiant and correct. But in her care for her own embattled image she neglects to assess the *relationship*.

The give and take of her love with G. H. Lewes, its non-sacrificial mutuality, would be its most astounding feature. Unlike her relation to her father, who threatened to deprive her of home over her apostasy, or to her brother, who would break relations with her for decades over her non-legal union with Lewes, acknowledging her only when she had legally married John Cross, the relation to Lewes, while occasioning scandal, was no sacrificial offering.

Marian was at a moment in her life when a role stood to be filled, that vague female duty she had written about still hovering unspecified. For a time, Spencer had stepped into the central space that the terms of her partnership with Chapman had left empty: "But for him [Spencer], my life would be desolate enough now, with poor Mr. C. so occupied and so sad," Marian wrote in May 1852 (GEL 2: 29).

Yet Marian, in the kind of blindsidedness that would afflict her heroines, had mistaken Spencer, casting him in the wrong role. "Those who have known me best," she had written to him, "have always said, that if ever I loved *anyone* thoroughly my whole life must turn upon that *feeling*. You curse the *destiny* which has made the *feeling* concentrate itself on you" (GEL 8: 57, my emphases). Spencer was the "anyone" that destiny had selected as the object of that free-floating, intense "feeling." Many years later, as George Eliot, Marian Lewes would write the following extraordinary observation, in which her own wise eye, now as subject, supplanted the "anyone" she had mistaken, as object, in 1852:

> Anyone watching keenly the stealthy convergence of human lots, sees a slow preparation of effects from one life on another, which tells like a calculated irony on the indifference or the frozen stare with which we look at our unintroduced neighbor. Destiny stands by sarcastic with our dramatis personae folded in her hand. (*MM* 85)

It was to be Lewes, who had gone unappreciated when Marian first met him alongside Spencer, who would emerge as the man Marian could "love thoroughly"; it was to be her feeling for Lewes, not Spencer, upon which her "whole life" would "turn." Destiny had cast Marian and Spencer for a friendship; fortunately for all, one that could survive this irony. Spencer became a regular private guest of Lewes's and Marian's, one of their very few confidants when she began to write fiction, and one of the last people to whom Marian wrote before her death.

The question of projection—of where the self begins and ends, of the moral and mental capacity of the self to recognize in another anything genuinely different than its own contents—preoccupied the novelist George Eliot over the course of her career. Marian had cast Herbert Spencer for a role he could not play because her own feeling was seeking a place to settle. Chapman had cast Marian in a role it would have been deadly for her to play too long. Within her own family, her father and brother could only tolerate Marian within the categories they understood. Over a life's work of novels, Marian would ask whether human beings could ever dislodge their own ego in such a way that they might imagine the world from another's perspective.

Could human beings ever see each other clearly, fairly recognizing flaws or quiet heroism, without recruiting the other to the needs of their own stories about themselves? Or even more consequentially, without recruiting the other's life to the unfolding plot of their own lives? How could human beings recover from discovering truths about another that they had consciously or unconsciously avoiding confronting?

In 1853, Marian considered the great questions of human identity and projection via Ludwig Feuerbach's *Das Wesen des Christentums* (*The Essence of Christianity*). Written in 1841, it was recognized in Germany (as it could never have been among the English, Marian claimed) as "*the* book of the age" (GEL 2: 137). Marian translated it for Chapman's Quarterly series, worrying the entire time that he would not have the courage to keep his word and bring it out. He had agreed at the same time to publish another prospective work of Marian's, *The Idea of a Future Life*. In the end, half the promise was kept and Feuerbach was published under Marian's own name in June 1854. It remains the authoritative English translation.

The translation served as a measure of what had changed and what had not since the Strauss translation. Marian had labored over the Strauss while still living in the Midlands, the daughter of an ailing father, with a social world dependent on Rosehill, bounded by Coventry. Strauss's science had depressed her over two and a half years of uncertain progress. Now, in 1853–4, Marian had established her reputation as the translator of Strauss; she lived independently in London, where her exposure to the intellectual and cultural world was thorough and full. Though Sara Hennell was still her most regular and trusted help in the Feuerbach translation, Marian now had a broad base of colleagues and friends who knew and respected her. Though she was again convinced that no one would read her translation and that she might be laboring for naught, she had succeeded unquestionably at *The Westminster Review* (GEL 2: 152). The *Coventry Herald*, which she still read, also helped her mark the difference between the audience she had cultivated for the *Westminster* and the "Coventry people," for whom Charles Bray's article on the liberal theologian F. D. Maurice she judged "rather strong meat" (GEL 2: 125).

From Strauss to Feuerbach a dramatic leap had been made. While Strauss attempted to trace the historical processes by which the figure of Jesus had become the repository of myth, where Mackay wanted to consider how religion developed in history to suit the needs of successive ages, Feuerbach described his work as an anthropology exalted into theology. He was a kind of poetic preacher himself, seeking to understand the human origins of the Christian religious impulse. He imagined God something like the critic Matthew Arnold would describe culture itself in 1869, as "the best which has been thought and said in the world."[6] In Feuerbach's words, God was the collective "commonplace book in which [man] registers his highest feelings and thoughts, the genealogical tree on which are entered the names that are dearest and most sacred to him" (*Essence* 64). Feuerbach created a circuit from theology to anthropology back to theology, "very much as Christianity, while lowering God into man, made man into God; though, it is true, this human God was a by a further process made a transcendental, imaginary God, remote from man" (*Essence* xviii).

For Feuerbach, the religious impulse was fundamentally one of projection, and his task was to reveal the true processes that were obscured by the series of projections. Human beings projected the highest human values onto God and then proceeded to worship human nature, but only once it was construed as divine. In the long process of human development, Feuerbach argued, religion was a childhood in which human beings named what was *outside* themselves before recognizing its location inside themselves (*Essence* 13). Feuerbach's project was to awaken *"religion to self-consciousness,"* so that instead of mystifying human nature as divine, human beings could accurately perceive the divine as a human creation (*Essence* xxi). Feuerbach thus saw himself as the truth-teller of religion's essence: religion "not in intention or according to its own supposition, but in its heart, in its essence, believes in nothing else than the truth and divinity of human nature" (*Essence* xvi).

Why was it necessary to trace the circuits of projection, to make theology once again anthropology, to call a thing by its name? Feuerbach argued that the misrecognitions of religion—the exaltation of God—resulted in the degradation of man within a framework in which "sin" could only be atoned for by supernatural divine sacrifice: "To enrich God, man must become poor; that God may be all, man must be nothing" (*Essence* 26). Thus the radical corruption of the human being in relation to the goodness of God. In this dualistic framework, the individual sinner was left alone, with no recourse to efficacious natural means. If the essence of religion was revealed, then, human beings who had not realized their full selfhood—had sinned—could turn instead toward the collective human species. The species could serve as a kind of redemptive mirror, an "objective conscience," reflecting in aggregate the most fully realized human selfhood: "in the moral as well as the physical and intellectual elements, men compensate for each other, so that, taken as a whole, they are as they should be, they present the perfect man" (*Essence* 158, 156). Then sin functions not to stymie human beings but as a goad to realize higher human possibilities: "while I blame myself, I acknowledge what I am not, but ought to be.... But when I acknowledge goodness as my destination, as my law, I acknowledge it, whether consciously or unconsciously, as my own nature" (*Essence* 28). Feuerbach's aim was to "reunite" man with humanity and to dispel the profound alienation effected by religion-as-preached-and-practiced.

Though G. H. Lewes would call Feuerbach "a bombshell thrown into the camp of orthodoxy," Marian's feeling on reviewing the proofs in May 1854 was pleasure: it "opens up afresh to me what there is of truth and beauty in the book" (GEL 2: 155).[7] A great change had transpired in her life in the months before the translation. In October 1853, she had left 142 Strand for private lodgings and had told Chapman that she was ready to move on from the editorship of the *Westminster*, which dismayed him. From January to May 1854 she translated, her daily life transformed by an intimacy with Lewes and the space in which to conduct it. This relationship had been unfolding for a year already. In March 1853, she had written to Sara Hennell that, "in spite of [her]self," Mr. Lewes had "quite won [her] liking"; that in society, he is "as always, genial and amusing" (GEL 2: 94). To Cara, she wrote in April 1853: "People are very good to me. Mr. Lewes especially is kind and attentive and has quite won my regard after having a great deal of my vituperation. Like a few other people in the world, he is much better than he seems—<human as [?]> a man of heart and conscience wearing a mask of flippancy" (GEL 2: 98).

It is striking that Marian emphasized her overcoming of initial disinclination to Lewes and the fairly slow process of coming to see him in truth rather than in error. Her letters, though not very revealing, suggest a year in which she was spending increasingly more time socializing with him and coming to know his intellectual and literary style (important in a culture where people's work was often unsigned; Lewes's work ranged widely, too, from staged dramas to sociology to literary review, biography, and biology). In both her letters, Marian describes Lewes as having "won" her liking and regard, which suggests Lewes's sustained attempt to appeal to Marian, flipping the relations she had known previously.

But most important, the period of "vituperation" and "in spite of myself" confirms outright that Marian recognized in real time that she had misjudged the man who would be the central love of her life and had chosen to reverse herself; what an important finding! George Henry Lewes was different than he seemed and, in relation to him, Marian Evans learned the flexibility of an empirical observation that did not bend the reality to the theory, as she had accused Spencer of doing, but humbly watched and adjusted its own assessment accordingly, without ego or will in the way. Marian reaped the extraordinary rewards of looking closely at Lewes and setting aside even his own convincing self-craft. If most people spent their lives masquerading to appear better than they were, Lewes eluded the conventional narrative of hypocrisy exposed. A joke-telling, prank-playing, insatiably curious, lively atheist, he was a man of deep feeling, alive to duty and, in the simplest terms, reliably kind, attentive, genial. Later, in October 1856, Marian would confess to her married friend Cara, "It is a great experience—this marriage! And all one's notions of things before seem like the reading of a mystic inscription without the key. I can't tell you how happy I am in this double life which helps me to feel and think with double strength."[8] The "key" was not a theory at all. It was experience.

Being with Lewes, Marian found an amplified, shared humanity which did not mean the unity of two identical human beings. Their very real differences were bridged in a delight at the diversity and complementariness of individuals proceeding in an enriched double life. The individuality that confined a person to his or her own resources was not "sin" to Marian, but it was often suffering. Something in the love with Lewes was "human nature purified, freed from the limits of the individual man" (*Essence* 14).

Notes

1. In an 1869 letter to her friend Harriet Beecher Stowe, Marian thanked her for Henry Ward's sermon: "The great vocation of the preacher, which in your brother's case is, I believe, eminently effective, has a melancholy emptiness among us. My soul is often vexed at the thought of the multitudinous pulpits, which are such a vantage ground for teachers, and yet are for the most part filled with men who can say nothing to change the expression of the faces that are turned up towards them" (GEL 5: 72). She went frequently to hear preachers in London with her friend Barbara Bodichon.
2. Hughes, *George Eliot*, p. 145.
3. Dillane, *Before*, pp. 23–63.
4. Dillane reminds us that, like novels, articles and editing acts were highly mediated by genre, audience, and market constraints. I have attempted to keep in mind that Evans created personae as editor, reviewer, and writer for the *Westminster*, and to avoid assuming total consonance between her opinions and those seemingly expressed in her periodical work.
5. Herbert Spencer, *The Principles of Ethics* (Indianapolis: Liberty Fund, 1978), Vol. 2, p. 272.
6. Matthew Arnold, *Culture and Anarchy*, ed. Samuel Lipman (New Haven and London: Yale University Press, 1994).
7. George Henry Lewes, *Letters of George Henry Lewes*, Vol. 3, ed. William Baker (Victoria: ELS Editions, 1999), p. 165, n. 3.
8. Lewes, *Letters*, p. 38.

5
"A Heathen and an Outlaw," 1854–1856

Marian's "double life" began in earnest in July 1854, when she and George Henry Lewes took the dramatic step of setting out together for Weimar, he intending to work on his major study, *Life and Works of Goethe*, and Marian having left the editorship of *The Westminster Review* for freelance journalism. In the end, she would also take over Lewes's contract to translate Spinoza's *Ethics*. Yet the trip was notable mainly for the significant personal change it effected. Lewes had separated from his wife, Agnes Jervis Lewes, and moved out of their joint home in the summer of 1852, twelve years after they married and approximately two years after Agnes had given birth to the first of four children that would be fathered by Lewes's friend and partner, Thornton Hunt. Lewes claimed all of these children, granting them legal legitimacy. In addition to his four sons with Agnes (three of whom survived to adulthood), Lewes would support all of them financially, later bolstered considerably by Marian's income.

While Lewes chose to affirm the familial status quo and acknowledge Hunt's children as his own rather than sue for divorce at the time or after the passage of divorce reform in 1857, there is little evidence that he saw his wife's long-term affair as simply an exercise of free love, compatible with the terms of their marriage.[1] To his own great mentor, Thomas Carlyle, Lewes wrote from Weimar that the entire experience nearly broke him: "At various epochs I have explicitly declared that unless a change took place I would not hold out. At last—and this more because some circumstances...happened to occur at a time when I was hypochondriacal and hopeless about myself, fearing lest a chronic disease would disable me from undertaking such responsibilities as those previously borne—at last, I say, the crisis came" (GEL 2: 177). The crisis had not been precipitated by Marian, Lewes stated explicitly. The scandal that was to settle on her, as having stolen another woman's husband, had no basis in truth. In any case, Marian would have to bear the punishing double standard that worked against women's sexual freedom, condemning them, without recourse, as fallen women if they had public liaisons outside marriage. But if scandal inevitably attended Marian's choice to live with Lewes, it was still critical to both of them to separate truth from falsehood.

While Marian would never be legally married to Lewes and while Lewes would always remain legally married to another woman, both came to see the union as their true marriage. Marian adopted Lewes's name, signing with it from 1857, and Lewes referred to her as Mrs. Lewes to others. They referred to each other as wife and husband, and both referred to Lewes's sons as "their boys." As Nancy Henry has noted, in spite of the sexual double standard for women, bigamous and adulterous relations were more widespread than divorced couples in this period, in which highly restrictive divorce laws had not yet been reformed. In some cases of adultery or bigamy, children of different mothers or of different fathers did not always know their true relations to siblings or parents.[2] Additionally, second marriages following early deaths exerted their own effect on family structure, rendering notions of parenthood and sibling relations more flexible than we might have expected. Marian herself was the daughter of a second wife to her father, who had remarried after his first wife's death, with close relations to her half-sister, Fanny.

Yet, distinct from the social context, within the narrative of Marian's own life this union echoed most her decision of January 1842 not to attend church. As Marian had marked her gradual and mostly internal process of separating from Christian orthodoxy with the visible and costly testimony of not going to church, her attachment to Lewes and her willingness to dispense with marital orthodoxy found expression in the visible and costly testimony of leaving the country with him to live as a couple. As in the former case, she consulted with almost no one about her decision, informing in advance and at Lewes's request only two close male friends, Charles Bray and John Chapman, both of whom enjoyed sexual freedom in their own marriages and were acquainted with her financial affairs. (She may have informed two newer female friends, Bessie Parkes and Barbara Leigh Smith.) Yet she maintained silence with her closest and longest-standing female friends, the sisters Sara Hennell and Cara Bray, who surely deserved her confidence. Perhaps Marian sought to shield them from the condemnation that could spill over onto her friends. Yet, given the parallel with the holy war, it seems that Marian knew no way to incarnate a new stage of her mental and spiritual existence while maintaining continuity with the major figures of the stage she needed to end. Further, she knew no path to freedom of expression and self-development that did not articulate itself through sacrifice. As with her father, she would eventually come to see that she had imposed upon herself an unnecessary sacrifice of intimates.

The holy war did not only pose a parallel in behavior to the surprise union with Lewes but reprised an intersection of concerns: the original holy war of 1842 had intersected with the problem of marriage for Marian. In declaring her rejection of Christian dogma, she had also foreclosed conventional marital prospects. Her brother and father—not incorrectly—read her apostasy as a social and possibly political radicalization that would make it impossible for her to find a suitable mate outside the Rosehill group (GEL 1: 157). As a result, her father had threatened to remove himself and Marian from Foleshill altogether, given that he had rented a home there expressly to better his daughter's prospects. Marian's long epistolary response to him insisted that bowing to convention for the sake of such material advantage was impossible for her. While she agreed to return to church attendance, it was critical to her that her attendance not be understood as a bid for a conventional marriage partner. Religious freedom, on one hand, and female autonomy, on the other, were related causes, if not complementary ones. This was made exceedingly clear not only by Marian's male relatives in 1842 but also in 1854 by her close colleague George Combe, the phrenologist and financial supporter of the *Westminster*, when he expressed his outrage over the scandal which he saw as having "inflicted a great injury on the cause of religious freedom" (GEL 8: 129).

Thus, Marian's union with Lewes extended the holy war over her identity and her virtue, a virtue increasingly distinct from doctrines of any kind, religious, sexual, or social. Though her father was no longer alive to pick up the battle, her brother certainly was. Yet Marian was not courageous enough to announce her new union to Isaac Evans before it was tested and found as solid as necessary, and she held off letting him know of her "change [of] name" and her "husband" until 1857 (GEL 2: 331). In Isaac's place, she erected the unfortunate substitutes of Sara Hennell and Cara Bray as those figures whose love and friendship she would need to sacrifice in order to realize her own truth.

Cast into relief by this second episode in her holy war, Marian's deep attachment to the Christian ideal of sacrifice becomes visible as a shaping force in her life and in her self-narration. It is hard to overstate how central this ideal was for educated mid-Victorians, from atheists to evangelicals to Anglo-Catholics, as it came down in general cultural terms from such ubiquitous verses as Matthew 16:24–5: "Then said Jesus unto his disciples, If any man will come after me, let him deny himself, and take up his cross, and follow me. / For whosoever will save his life shall lose it: and whosoever will lose his life for my sake shall find it." Such teaching was particularly emphasized in *The Imitation of Christ*, the text that was precious to Marian throughout the whole of her life. The cross would become an emblem that made its way into her fictional oeuvre as a sign of the deepest human suffering. Meanwhile, suffering, inextricable from love, would become the mark of shared humanity. In Marian's novels the experience of suffering baptized people into new and higher selves. Suffering divided experience, making a break between their past and their present.

Marian's need to hallow her powerful relationship with Lewes must have been intensified by the impossibility of finding any cultural, let alone religious, form that could grant it any sacred public dimension. The positivist Auguste Comte (1798–1857) (upon whose early work Lewes had published a series of articles and then a book, *Comte's Philosophy of the Sciences* [1853]) had delineated a Religion of Humanity in his work *The System of Positive Polity* (1851–4). Marian was sympathetic to Comte's notion of "living for others," and developed a close friendship with Maria and Richard Congreve, as well as Frederic Harrison, who became deeply devoted to spreading Comte's thought in England, and interested in Comte's attempt to instill ritual into his religion of humanity, via calendar, festivals, and liturgy. Yet such invented religious forms were not the sort Marian could adopt (GEL 6: 387).

The lack of such forms was precisely the pain of living without creed or ritual and, especially, living *against* creed or ritual; yet sacrificial thinking survived where creed and ritual did not. In 1842, Marian had established her rejection of the doctrine of atonement: the notion that Christ died to save a sinful humanity and that only through the grace of his gift were true Christians redeemed from the debt they otherwise owed. Once she had rejected the redemptive force of that originary, inimitably efficacious sacrifice, the imperative for imitative self-sacrifice among human beings did not diminish, as Feuerbach noted. Even when translated into purely anthropological terms, sacrifice held its value; to suffer for another was divine (*Essence* 60). Marian could not construe the highest form of love without sacrifice, nor a worthy sacrifice without such love; it is hard to imagine a greater, specifically Christian inheritance than this thought structure. Just as years earlier she had rejected the prospect of marriage with the unnamed painting-restorer after finding unacceptable the cost of the "sacrifice" that he posed to her own life hopes, and just as she had offered Spencer the freedom to sacrifice nothing, because she would bear all the sacrifice of their relationship, so now, with Lewes, she hallowed the value of their love by deeming it worthy of sacrifice. The higher a cost that Marian could pay for the union and the greater her self-sacrifice, the more sacred was the union.

For Marian, the sacrificial, measuring habit of mind was the most readily available way to grant value to actions that otherwise threatened to be denied positive meaning and to be debated, misinterpreted, and criticized. Thus, while social reality dictated that Marian certainly would pay a price for her refusal to live by its norms, her adoption of the keywords of loss, pain, and sacrifice at this time signify beyond that reality. To Charles Bray she wrote about her eloping that she was "quite prepared to accept the consequences of a step which I have deliberately taken.... The most painful consequence will, I know, be the loss of friends" (GEL 2: 179). To John Chapman she wrote, "I am not mistaken in the person to whom I have attached myself. He is worthy of the sacrifice I have incurred and my only anxiety is that he should be rightly judged" (GEL 8: 124–5). Like the young evangelical she had been, decrying the pleasures of music if not for religious purpose, whatever granted her especial joy became justifiable and possibly sacred to the extent that it exacted a cost. How could her own joy or ease be justifiable when posed against all the suffering that characterized this world? Later, she would address just this anxiety when she wrote to Cara about herself and Lewes: "We are leading no life of self-indulgence, except indeed, that being happy in each other, we feel everything easy" (GEL 2: 214).

Indeed, for years to come Marian would focus on the work and responsibility she and Lewes embraced, as another proof of sacrifice: "We are working hard to provide for others better than we provide for ourselves, and to fulfil every responsibility that lies upon us" (GEL 2: 214). Describing themselves habitually as "hard workers," needing to provide for a family of young boys and to compensate for those who refused to meet their obligations, Marian came to insist that they not only met moral standards but exceeded them (GEL 2: 333). In her letter to Charles Bray from Weimar, Marian refuted the scandalous rumors that Lewes had abandoned his family. She reported that he was "in constant correspondence with his wife; she has had all the money due to him in London; and his children are his principal thought and anxiety" (GEL 2: 178). He had never understood a separation to release him from responsibility to her: "on the contrary he has been anxiously waiting restoration to health that he may once more work hard, not only to provide for his children, but to supply his wife's wants so far as that is not done by another" (GEL 2: 178). She maintained to Charles Bray that Lewes's correspondence with Agnes "has assured me that his conduct as a husband has been not only irreproachable, but generous and self-sacrificing to a degree far beyond any standard fixed by the world" (GEL 2: 179). Meanwhile, already in April 1854 before their departure abroad, Marian had taken over Lewes's writing and proof-reviewing commitments to *The Leader* as his health plummeted under stress, beginning the decades-long support of his family that she would shoulder. The "works" dimension of their partnership was very real, in material terms, yet Marian's frequent recourse to it as evidence for their virtue determinedly recruited it for sacrificial, justificatory purposes.

Sacrifice was so natural a mode of thinking to Mary Ann/Marian Evans, and so much about the Christian agent herself, taking up her cross, that it surprised her when outsiders reminded her that her own sacrifices, denials, and renunciations involved *them*.[3] To prove both her love and Lewes's worth, she set out to sacrifice the next most valuable thing in her life; hence her letter to Sara Hennell, in which she described the friendship of the Hennell sisters as the best thing she knew *outside* the love she now knew with Lewes: "while I retain your friendship I retain the best that life has given me next to that which is the deepest and gravest joy in all human experience" (GEL 2: 182). The ambiguity here—"best" versus "deepest and gravest"—and "next to"—adjacent, alongside versus not quite reaching the measure of—marks the inequality at the heart of sacrificial thinking: one gives up something of extremely high value for the sake of a second thing, which is of even higher spiritual value.

Yet Marian's need to spell this out to Sara and Cara reflects the way in which her readiness to sacrifice them, under the flag of self-sacrifice, had not affirmed their high value but had cast it instead as negligible. As Marian would go on to explore in her novels, sometimes it was extremely difficult to choose among competing claims. Yet in this case Marian had not needed to set up the claims as a choice. In the end, both Hennell sisters remained her friends and accepted her relationship with Lewes. But at this point Marian seems not to have been able to imagine a great joy or pleasure that came without personal sacrifice at its most painful pitch, from her closest intimates: "From the majority of persons, of course, we never looked for anything but condemnation" (GEL 2: 214).

Here, as with her father, Marian's own sacrificial thinking took to heart Christian teaching and then sought to incarnate it in a world that, on one hand, enshrined and hallowed such thinking and, on the other, often abandoned it when it came into conflict with the motives of personal advancement and happiness. Yet even to focus on this failure, this professing of Christian belief without living up to it, was itself part of the Christian narrative that Marian had internalized. Rather than showing up the insufficiency of the religious model, Marian embraced its call. In spirit, she would be the truest Christian, as countless sermons defined it: the unworldly one. Marian's love for Lewes would reflect his true, but almost universally misunderstood, character (even she had at first misjudged him). As for marriage itself, Marian wrote, "Light and easily broken ties are what I neither desire theoretically nor could live for practically. Women who are satisfied with such ties do *not* act as I have done—they obtain what they desire and are still invited to dinner" (GEL 2: 214). This last early-censored, now much-quoted statement bristles with worldly intelligence, even as it rejects just such intelligence as a guide for living. Marian knew the codes; she simply refused them. In doing so, she claimed a truer understanding and respect for the essence of marriage than those who lawfully married in accordance with expectations or those who paid obeisance to the codes publicly, but privately indulged themselves.

Again, Marian drove a wedge between dogma and essence. Like Marian's relation to religion, her relation to the institution of marriage was driven by her awe for its genuinely elevated and sacred dimension, and reshaped for her purposes by her intense drive for a living truth and self-expression. The awe for the potentially sacred made what we might call "nominal" marriage—for financial security, social sanction, or other worldly interests—of no interest to Marian, just as nominal Christianity had not appeared to her as any sort of viable option when she was younger: "it is the duty of Christians...not to take the low ground of considering things merely with relation to existing circumstances, and graduating their scale of holiness to the temperature of the world; but to aim as perseveringly at perfection as if they believed it to be soon attainable" (GEL 1: 9). Just as Marian could not spurn the essence of religion, even at her most rejecting moments, neither could she degrade or desecrate the essence of marriage. When it came to "marriage *laws*," Marian believed intelligent people could differ with equal sincerity and earnestness, yet when it came to marriage itself, in its essence, "if there be any one subject on which I feel no levity it is that of marriage and the relation of the sexes—if there is any one action or relation of my life which is and always has been profoundly serious, it is my relation to Mr. Lewes" (GEL 2: 214, 213).

Marian's non-legal marriage to Lewes was a sacred tie and, like other experiences of the deepest order, it seems to have cast her back upon her most authentically religious language and thought, which she then altered to her purposes, as in a letter of June 1857 to her old friend Mary Sibree Cash:

> I am very happy—happy in the highest blessing life can give us, the perfect love and sympathy of a nature that stimulates my own to healthful activity. I feel, too, that all the terrible pain I have gone through in past years...has probably been a

preparation for some special work that I may do before I die. That is a blessed hope—to be rejoiced in with trembling. But even if that hope should be unfulfilled, I am contented to have lived and suffered for the sake of what has already been.
(GEL 2: 343)

Returning to the habit of weaving Scripture into her letters, Marian invoked Psalms 2:11, "Serve the Lord with fear, and rejoice with trembling," as she meditated on blessing (granted now by life rather than God), on pain and suffering as preparation for a special work (rather than acts of providence), on consecrated hope and its possible fulfillment (but not prayer), and on the profound consciousness of death hovering and its prompting to evaluate the life thus far lived (with no rewards beyond the grave and no eternity). The only terms that break up this religious meditation—"nature," "stimulates," "healthful activity"—may merge Spinoza, as we will see, with the reformed language of Marian's early piety.

Even while negotiating from a distance the fallout of their departure, Marian and Lewes spent their weeks in Weimar reveling in their freedom to socialize, to sightsee, to walk, to enjoy music, and to read aloud together as they would do over the course of their lives together. The comparative acceptance of unmarried couples was especially welcome, and Marian's love and appreciation for the musical genius of Franz Liszt was enhanced for her by his own unmarried liaison. As Lewes interviewed people who had known Goethe personally and composed what would become his major biography, Marian turned to journal writing, from which she composed "Three Months in Weimar" for *Fraser's Magazine* (June 1855). She began to take interest in writing about female intellectual life on the Continent as compared to England. In an essay for the *Westminster*, she hazarded a theory for the greater contribution of French women to the national literature. While she was writing long review essays for the *Westminster*, she simultaneously contributed short pieces to *The Leader*. Between 1855 and 1857, she would take over the Belles Lettres section of the *Westminster* in a moment that allowed her to comment on some of the greatest writers of her day, including the poets Alfred, Lord Tennyson, and Robert Browning.

Much of the time abroad, from November 1854 when the couple reached Berlin, was dedicated to translating Spinoza's *Ethics*, which

Marian first took on in the attempt to help Lewes, but then assumed independently. Practically speaking, Marian was seeking steady employment with the promise of publication. But Marian was part of an intellectual generation that was, as Clare Carlisle puts it, "ready for Spinozism" and its moment had come: "Although there was plenty of religious dogma in George Eliot's England, God and the human relation to God had finally become an open question."[4] Lewes's own strong interest in Spinoza dated back to an 1843 essay he had written for the *Westminster* as "the first attempt to vindicate the great philosopher before the English public," as he put it (*Ethics* 17). Marian had also first read Spinoza in 1843, turning to translate the *Theologico-Political Treatise* in the period following her father's death in 1849 but putting it aside after some months due to her poor health (GEL 1: 321). In putting it aside, Marian had written to the Brays that a literal translation would not suffice to make Spinoza "accessible to a larger number"; that it was necessary to effect a second, "yet more difficult process of translation," "to study his books, then shut them and give an analysis" that would constitute a "true estimate of his life and system" (GEL 1: 321).

Yet by 1854, with both Feuerbach and Strauss behind her, perhaps Marian felt differently about translating the philosopher who had laid a basis for their works. In July 1855, as Marian was more than halfway through her translation, J. A. Froude published a long, important essay on Spinoza in the *Westminster*, a further testament to Spinoza's increasing relevance for their generation, one that had been led by Carlyle and Coleridge to a deep encounter with German thought but would not find in Romanticism enough solidity to steady a milieu roiled by religious doubt.[5] Spinoza, born Jewish in seventeenth-century Amsterdam, excommunicated for heresy, a member of no Church, a celibate and solitary spectacle-maker, decried as an atheist in spite of his claim that God was the immanent cause of all things, had become the special province of thinkers such as Froude, Lewes, and Marian, and the circles that extended beyond each of them, from *The Westminster Review* in London to Rosehill in the Midlands, to the Continental society they encountered in extended travel, particularly in Germany.

Though in 1854 Marian found herself translating the *Ethics*, the *Theologico-Political Treatise* seems likely to have spoken powerfully to her in its division between philosophy and faith: "Philosophy has no end in view save truth: faith...looks for nothing but obedience and piety" (*TTC* 189). Notably, obedience and piety would not be dismissed in her future novels but posed as genuine human goods. Her question would be how to identify the time for sacred rebellion, which we might affiliate with truth. For Spinoza, one arrived at truth through the "the natural light of reason which is common to all" (*TTC* 119). Granting human beings the "supreme right of free thinking, even on religion," Spinoza stated that it was "in every man's power to wield the supreme right and authority of free judgment...and to explain and interpret religion for himself" (*TTC* 119) The rule for the interpretation of Scripture was reason, "not any supernatural light nor any external authority" (*TTC* 119). Yet the "aim and object of Scripture" itself, "is only to teach obedience" (*TTC* 183). "To love God above all things, and one's neighbor as one's self" was its essence (*TTC* 172). Beyond that, all dogma and ritual drawn out from a humanly authored, transmitted, and corrupted Scripture was non-binding. The sectarianism that Marian herself had reacted against so strongly before her apostasy was anathema to Spinoza as well: "they are the true enemies of Christ," wrote Spinoza, "who persecute honourable and justice-loving men because they differ from them, and do not uphold the same religious dogmas as themselves: for whosoever loves justice and charity, we know, by that very fact, to be faithful" (*TTC* 185).

As Marian and Lewes believed, it was the progressive work of human beings to perceive more and more fully the system of natural laws by which nature and social life were governed. Spinoza, too, insisted on the "fixed and unchangeable order of nature or the chain of natural events," yet he called this the divine law: "to say that everything happens according to natural laws, and to say that everything is ordained by the decree and ordinance of God, is the same thing" (*TTC* 44, 45). While the masses, he argued, thought of miracles as extraordinary exceptions from natural order, and "imagine[d] two powers distinct one from the other" with "the power and providence of God" prevailing over nature, it was, in fact, the opposite: the laws of nature themselves revealed God's nature and existence as infinite, eternal, and immutable (*TTC* 81, 86). Further, it was not phenomena which *eluded* human understanding that attested to God's power; it was those "phenomena that we clearly and distinctly understand which heighten our knowledge of God, and most clearly indicate His will and decrees" (*TTC* 86). Ignorance and superstition refused the tracing of cause and effect that reason revealed.

Marian's novels would pick up the gauntlet, seeking to trace cause and effect, and to demonstrate that human beings could attain greater freedom when they gained greater understanding of the relations of causality that determined their own and others' actions. While Marian understood human freedom to be dramatically curtailed by all kinds of limiting factors, she never came to Spinoza's absolute terms: "we act solely from the will of God" (*Ethics* 158); "There is no absolute or free will in the mind, but [the mind] is determined to will this or that by a cause which is also determined by another cause...and so on *in infinitum*" (*Ethics* 152).

At the same time, Spinoza emphasized the human receptivity to influence. The *Ethics*, in particular, outlined the way in which human minds and bodies formed habits of thought and action through interaction. Human beings, who were highly complex and differentiated, could be affected in a proportionally great number of ways. This capacity for being affected by ideas adequately cognizant of their causes was, for Spinoza, the measure of power. Of particular relevance for Marian was Spinoza's definition of the terms of pleasure and pain in ways that moved them far away from their Christian and derivative moral associations. In defining the emotions, Spinoza laid out the propositions that "Pleasure is the transition of man from less to greater perfection" and that "Pain is the transition of man from greater to less perfection" (*Ethics* 314). In healthy environments, as the Spinoza scholar Hasana Sharp has explained, "we will be drawn to those ideas that enable us to think effectively, to persevere with more vitality and joy. In the most amenable situations, our ideas would reflect fewer of our reactive, anxious, and fearful passions."[6] Suffering, especially mental suffering, thus becomes not a path to greater knowledge or capacity but instead a hindrance to it: "The more perfection any being has, the more it acts and the less it suffers" (*Ethics* 314).

While Marian would never lose her belief that suffering essentially defined human life and singularly deepened human knowledge and connection, at the same time the idea of health—of appreciation for all "stimulus" to "healthful activity," as in her letter to Mary Sibree Cash—seems to sit beside her commitment to sacrifice and suffering, as a countercheck. Spinoza, German culture, and Lewes himself all brought her away from the world she had grown up in. Weimar, she noted wryly, in her essay for *Fraser's*, gave space to rationalism and to pleasure: "from princes down to pastry-cooks, rationalism is taken as a matter of course"; "Unlike our English people, they take pleasure into their calculations.... It is understood that something is to be done in life between business and housewifery."[7]

Yet the return to English business and housewifery awaited. In March 1855, they left Berlin, Lewes traveling to London to see Agnes and then to find himself and Marian lodgings, while Marian remained in Dover for six weeks. In the summer of 1855, settled with Lewes in East Sheen, Marian continued her translation of Spinoza, working on Part IV of the *Ethics* while writing a major article for the *Westminster* responding to eight texts of the popular evangelical Rev. John Cumming, minister of the Scottish National Church in Covent Garden. The move from Spinoza's logical propositions that sought to make of ethics a science no less exacting than geometry likely contributed to Marian's ire when she turned to Cumming's jumbled productions, prompting the most scathing of her reviews.

With the term "perversion" peppering her paragraphs (it appears nine times in the essay), Marian argued that when dogma was accorded "the place and authority of first truths," intellectual dishonesty resulted: "So long as a belief in propositions is regarded as indispensable to salvation, the pursuit of truth *as such* is not possible" (*Essays* 44, 45–6). Her next move was to argue that intellectual dishonesty could not be separated from moral failing. Cumming exemplified for her the "alliance between intellectual and moral perversion" (*Essays* 53). He exercised the privilege of the clergyman boasting "a smattering of science and learning," to "riot in gratuitous assertions, confident that no man will contradict him; he may exercise perfect free-will in logic" (*Essays* 38, 39). Marian then argued for intellectual rigor not solely on its own terms but by appealing to moral virtue: "A distinct appreciation of the value of evidence – in other words, the intellectual perception of truth – is more closely allied to truthfulness of statement, or the moral quality of veracity, than is generally admitted" (*Essays* 44). Dogma led to complicated fallacies which led to falsehood; inquiry led to direct forms of evidence which led to truthfulness (*Essays* 45). Recognizing the contradictions the pious regularly experienced between dogma and morality, she proposed a solution: to teach "that the free and diligent exertion of the intellect, instead of being a sin, is a part of their responsibility – that Right and Reason are synonymous. The fundamental faith for man is faith in the result of a brave, honest, and steady use of all his faculties" (*Essays* 67). If all this sounds fairly commonplace, its radical import lies in the fact that Marian was articulating an ethical claim independent of a basis in Christian revelation (even Spinoza acknowledged the need of common men for revelation). Intellect could ground ethical responsibility.

Cumming was a natural target for Marian because he seemed practically to insist upon an opposition of religious and moral convictions, in a way that Christopher Herbert has argued was not an outlying tendency but a mainstream feature of much evangelical thought in the nineteenth century.[8] Rather than foster human morality, rather than foster an expansive love, he seemed invested in hatred, egoism, and persecution of the enemy as signs of true piety. Cumming had two categories of character: Christians who acted for the glory of God versus sinners (heretics and Catholics) who were God's enemies, agents of Satan, destined for hellfire. The Calvinist code that had troubled Marian since 1842, that "the greater proportion of the human race will be eternally miserable," seemed to delight Cumming. He had no ability to envision that there might be a third path upon which human beings motivated to relieve want might operate not for God's glory but simply to aid their "fellow sinners and sufferers," with no personal interest at stake (*Essays* 59).

Indeed, by preaching the glory of God as the primary motive, Marian argued, Cumming retarded the moral development of his own followers rather than advancing it. There was "no perversion more obstructive of true moral development than this substitution of a reference to the glory of God for the direct promptings of the sympathetic feelings," she declaimed (*Essays* 66). "All these natural muscles and fibres are to be torn away and replaced by a patent steel-spring," called "the glory of God" (*Essays* 65). Here we can see Marian insisting, first, upon a wider, more universal human basis for fellowship *sans* reward, and second, upon an alliance, rather than an unnatural opposition, between moral virtue and Christian piety. The only Christianity she could genuinely understand as religion was one that "extend[ed] and multipli[ed]...the effects produced by human sympathy" in the "idea of a God who not only sympathizes with all we feel and endure for our fellow-men, but who will pour new life into our too languid love, and give firmness to our vacillating purpose" (*Essays* 66).

Finally, Marian sought to cast down Cumming's straw-man versions of scholars of the higher learning and of freethinkers, exposing them as stereotypes both outdated and mischaracterized: "The only type of 'infidel'' he recognizes is

> that fossil personage who "calls the Bible a lie and a forgery." He seems to be ignorant—or he chooses to ignore the fact— that there is a large body of eminently instructed and earnest men who regard the Hebrew and Christian Scriptures as a series of historical documents, to be dealt with according to the rules of historical criticism, and that an equally large number of men, who are not historical critics, find the dogmatic scheme built on the letter of the Scriptures opposed to their profoundest moral convictions. (*Essays* 49)

The essay on Cumming was crushing, but it is worth noting that Marian was preaching to the choir, particularly on the last point of redrawing the image of freethinkers; among the regular consumers of *The Westminster Review* in 1855, who was likely to have to revise dramatically their views of Cumming, or of historical criticism, after reading the review? Yet Marian gave the essay all her rhetorical force and sought to protect its legitimacy by hiding her authorship. Responding to Charles Bray in October 1855, after those at Rosehill had guessed she had guessed its authorship, Marian wrote: "it *is* mine, but... [I] beg that you will not mention it as such to any one.... The article appears to have produced a strong impression, and that impression would be a little counteracted if the author were known to be a *woman*" (GEL 2: 218).[9] A few months later, anticipating the publication of *Ethics* (which did not come to pass due to a dispute with the publisher, Henry George Bohn), Marian again asked Charles Bray to avoid mentioning her name "in connection with it. I particularly wish not to be known as the translator of the Ethics, for reasons which it would be 'too tedious to mention'" (GEL 2: 233).

While gender was a real handicap in nonfiction (the following year, she and Lewes would advise Sara Hennell in no uncertain terms to publish as S. S. Hennell [GEL 2: 283]), at the same time Marian had felt sufficiently confident to have the Feuerbach translation come out under her own name. Yet that had been right before she and Lewes left England; she had caught the slightest mercy with timing. Now, however, gender was not her only handicap. She was a woman living outside marriage with a man unfaithful to his legal wife; most thought of her as Lewes's mistress. As such, her views on such subjects as morality and religion, however smartly expressed, were likely to meet with dismissal if not mockery. Spinoza's reputation for atheism would not be assisted by Marian's own reputation. Even among the freethinking set, most women would not come to call upon Marian Evans Lewes until her reputation as the great novelist George Eliot was well entrenched. When the late Charles Hennell's wife, Rufa, whose wedding Marian had attended years earlier, called on them "very kindly and nobly" in April 1855, Marian wrote that it was a "good action" (GEL 2: 199–200).

Yet even while obscuring her authorship, Marian was broaching consequential dimensions of her life as a writer: the questions of audience and medium, and the related questions of labor in relation to income. In the convergence between the essay on Cumming, written to the converted as a tour de force of victorious argument, and the translation of Spinoza, written for the highly educated with all the technical precision of philosophical logic, Marian may have reached a turning point with the boundaries of audience and the constraints of genre. The novels she was soon to begin writing would break out well beyond the few thousands of the *Westminster* readership and exponentially beyond the readership of Spinoza; her income from fiction would also rise exponentially in comparison with that of journalism. While it would take another year until Marian began work on her first piece of fiction, the reviews she wrote in 1855–6 are marked by various articulations of ethical and aesthetic preoccupations. These preoccupations turned to convictions, as she set them out first in sharply negative terms that fiercely undercut lesser thinkers and writers, and then positively, as a program that she would soon take up in fiction. Fiction would offer Marian multiple viewpoints that could be entered into, analyzed, tested by imagined encounters and influences, and reflected upon by an observing narrator, with humor, sympathy, irony, intelligence, and personal distance. Mathematical logic and triumphalist critique would be set down. Stories would bring the readers.

Notes

1. See Henry, *Life*, pp. 97–100, for her important revisionary account of the contemporary legal considerations. Henry convincingly argues that Lewes could later have sued for divorce regardless of having acknowledged Edmund, but that the prospect of public court cases would likely have seemed dissuasive for all the adults and children involved, "not to mention the new author George Eliot, who came into being the same year as the Matrimonial Causes Act of 1857" (p. 100). In other words, Lewes and Eliot were not wholly victims of Agnes, the law, or their own generosity, but chose their status from the available options.
2. Henry, *Life*, p. 81.
3. See Ilana M. Blumberg, *Victorian Sacrifice: Ethics and Economics in Mid-Century Novels* (Columbus: Ohio State University Press, 2013), especially pp. 139–72. See also Jan-Melissa Schramm, *Atonement and Self-Sacrifice in Nineteenth-Century Narrative* (Cambridge: Cambridge University Press, 2012).
4. Clare Carlisle, "George Eliot's Spinoza: An Introduction" (*Ethics* 1–60, 27). On Eliot and Spinoza, see also Isobel Armstrong, "George Eliot, Spinoza, and the Emotions," in *Companion*, ed. Anderson and Shaw, pp. 294–308.
5. Carlisle, "Introduction," pp. 29, 55.
6. Hasana Sharp, "The Force of Ideas in Spinoza," *Political Theory* 35.6 (2007), pp. 732–55, p. 746.
7. "Three Months in Weimar," *Fraser's Magazine*, Vol. LI (1855), pp. 699–706, *George Eliot Archive*, https://georgeeliotarchive.org/items/show/85, pp. 704, 706.
8. Herbert, *Evangelical*, pp. 1–10.
9. Haight's critical edition of the letters notes that six words are then deleted.

6
"We Mortals," 1856–1857

Writing in January 1856, about six weeks before she finished translating the *Ethics*, Marian reviewed the novel *Rachel Gray* for *The Leader*. The novelist had found "really a new sphere for a great artist who can paint from close observation, and who is neither a caricaturist nor a rose-colour sentimentalist"; this sphere was "that most prosaic stratum of society, the small shopkeeping class."[1] However, the novelist had failed to offer an honest portrayal of her subjects. "Our own experience of what piety is amongst the uneducated," wrote Marian, with the authority of her Midlands youth, "has not brought us in contact with a Christianity which smacks neither of the Church nor of the meeting-house, with an Evangelicalism which has no *brogue*."[2] That George Eliot insisted on realism in art is widely known; yet it is equally important to note that her commitment to literary realism was first articulated as a commitment to a realist depiction of *religious* life among the emerging middle and industrial classes, the farming and artisan classes, and the gentry in rural England and its provincial towns. The period 1856–7, leading up to Marian's first work in fiction, was a period of intensive, significant journalism which rewards close attention. Influenced by John Ruskin's *Modern Painters* (1843–60), Marian insisted on what she saw as an ambitious standard of realism for great contemporary art: "to exhibit men and things as they are" (*Essays* 149). For both thinkers, realism was an ethical as well as an aesthetic program. Just as she had argued in her essay on Cumming that intellectual truth-seeking and direct forms of evidence bred moral habits of veracity, Marian argued that in art, too, the moral emotions of sympathy or fellow feeling could arise only from seeing clearly what was before one, without shaping it to preconceived ideals or inherited prejudices; one needed to avoid "the spectacles... of the doctrinaire or the dreamer" (*Essays* 127).

Marian's demand for honest, comprehensive representation may have been more indebted to her scriptural education than previous assessments of her realism have acknowledged. In her biting essay for the *Westminster*, "Silly Novels by Lady Novelists," of October 1856, Marian's intense objections to the "want of verisimilitude" argued, first, against the narrow social range of characters represented (*Essays* 142). Most novels were set in "very lofty and fashionable society," in which no economic strain, or even activity, was evident: the "working-day business of the world" was "somehow being carried on," but it was not the novel's subject matter (*Essays* 141). In her other major review essay of the period, on Wilhelm Heinrich Riehl's *The Natural History of German Life* (July 1856), she had expanded the claim from her short review of *Rachel Gray* and focused intently on the need for broader representation of the social classes, and particularly of the need to bring to those outside the working classes "concrete knowledge" of "the real characteristics of the working classes"—the small shopkeepers, artisans, and peasantry—through "direct observation" rather than "the influence of traditions and prepossessions" (*Essays* 108). Marian delineated the following subjects of inquiry: "the degree in which they are influenced by local conditions, their maxims and habits, the points of view from which they regard their religious teachers, and the degree in which they are influenced by religious doctrines, the interaction of the various classes on each other, and what are the tendencies in their position towards disintegration or towards development" (*Essays* 112).[3]

In this list of subjects, we can see Marian anatomizing categories of experience that required any aspiring writer to attend to and interact with "the People" themselves; her recommendation thus accorded a much broader range of human beings the dignity of interior and material lives worth narration. This was not Riehl's interest so much as her own. Bringing to mind the way that G. H. Lewes had sought out interviews with people who had come into actual contact with Goethe, Marian appreciated Riehl's travels, his "wandering over the hills and plains of Germany for the sake of obtaining, in immediate intercourse with the people, that completion of his historical, political, and economical studies which he was unable to find in books"

(*Essays* 127). In spite of his scientific bent toward abstraction, Riehl understood that detail was critical when it came to amassing the knowledge of society (*Essays* 130); the various social ranks each had their own natural history and none was interchangeable with any other (*Essays* 129). As if laying out the players in that vague "working-day business of the world" so little taken note of in silly novels, Marian enumerated with instructive specificity: "The landholder, the clergyman, the mill-owner, the mining-agent, have each an opportunity for making precious observations on different sections of the working classes" (*Essays* 112). The problem was that their experience and their form of expression rarely made it into print.

If the direct observation Marian recommended was necessary for the purposes of "the social and political reformer" who was concerned with correct policy, Marian herself would recruit such accuracy and honesty for artistic purposes (*Essays* 112). Here, as she set out an artistic program, her language shifted to the "sacredness of the writer's art" and its greatest purpose, the extension of human sympathies (*Essays* 161, 109). While Marian believed in this great ethic universally, she articulated it in a very particular form for the elite readers of the *Westminster*: as an education of the higher classes who bore a particular ignorance when it came to those beneath them. Art was singularly effective, on her view, in allowing those with more material wealth to recognize the shared humanity of those with less: "more is done towards linking the higher classes with the lower, towards obliterating the vulgarity of exclusiveness, than by hundreds of sermons and philosophical dissertations. Art is the nearest thing to life; it is a *mode of amplifying experience* and *extending our contact* with our fellow-men beyond the bounds of our personal lot" (*Essays* 110, emphasis mine).

In shifting in the second sentence to Spinozan terms, Marian called upon the notion that ideas were "more or less powerful by virtue of their life force"; Hasana Sharp has argued that this equation of power with vitality entails "a collective rather than an individual struggle for thinking and living well": "given that we are beings that belong to a power of thought that far exceeds our mind," according to Spinoza, in order to "live as powerfully and joyfully as possible," there are "collective dimensions of thinking life...a transpersonal accumulation of ideal power" that need cultivation.[4] We can see Marian here calling upon art rather than data, theory, or dogma to unite as many people as possible in expanding the sort of powerful knowledge that contributed to health and freedom.

False ideas troubled her. The "idyllic" style of portraits of the peasantry in art and literature did active harm by romanticizing poverty, want, and hard labor. Calling all art sacred but singling out the artistic task of "paint[ing] the life of the People" as "all the more sacred," Marian wrote:

> It is not so very serious that we should have false ideas about evanescent fashions – about the manners and conversations of beaux and duchesses; but it *is* serious that our sympathy with the perennial joys and struggles, the toil, the tragedy, and the humour in the life of our more heavily-laden fellow men, should be perverted, and turned toward a false object instead of the true one. (*Essays* 109)

Marian's objections were not only to unrealistic portraits of the working classes. She objected to all idealization. She was particularly incensed by religious heroines who were "amazingly eloquent" and "amazingly witty," "perfectly well-dressed and perfectly religious; she dances like a sylph and reads the Bible in the original tongues" (*Essays* 140). Perhaps one reason why such idealized religious heroines specially offended Marian was that it meant the novels in which they figured could not chart moral development. While her own fictional plots were yet to unfold, they would come to be identifiable as "George Eliot" novels because of their narratives of revelation and change. Her characters underwent what she called "baptisms" of suffering that forced a profound ethical reorientation. Such crises often served as the dramatic climaxes of her novels. Yet such change, or even merely such glimmers of new, deeper understanding, could only come to pass in characters that were not perfect to begin with. This religious insistence was one of George Eliot's defining contributions to Victorian realism; she opened it from the psychological interior of a single character into a claim about the nature of the surrounding world and reality itself.[5]

In his classic study of Western modes of realist representation, Erich Auerbach defined the signal differences between Homeric and biblical narrative, arguing that a psychological "multilayeredness" characterized the human beings of the Hebrew Bible.[6] The unfolding present of the narrative in which characters acted was "fraught with background," testifying to a consequential accrual of personal history: "although they are nearly always caught up in an event engaging all their faculties, they are not so entirely immersed in its present that they do not remain continually conscious of what has happened to them earlier and elsewhere; their thoughts and feelings have more layers, are more entangled."[7] Auerbach pointed to such figures as David, Saul, Jacob, and Joseph, noting the extraordinary development of their personalities: "But what a road, what a fate lie between the Jacob who cheated his father out of his blessing and the old man whose favorite son has been torn to pieces by a wild beast!"[8]

Based on the evidence of her early letters, Marian seems to have been more powerfully moved by the New Testament than by the Hebrew Bible, with the figures of Jesus and Paul more frequently stirring her than any other. Yet Auerbach's description of the style of the Hebrew Bible is more strongly suggestive of her aesthetic than any other account of the scriptural influences upon the Victorian novel or the functions of the Victorian novel as secular scripture. In a social world that extends beyond the ruling class, characters "fraught with their own biographical past" emerge "distinct as individuals."[9] They lead no charmed lives; they are unprotected, "fallible, subject to misfortune and humiliation," even from positions of great elevation. Yet their individuality emerges from surviving such shifts: "precisely the most extreme circumstances, in which we are immeasurably forsaken and in despair, or immeasurably joyous and exalted, give us, if we survive them, a personal stamp which is recognized as the product of a rich existence, a rich development."[10] Auerbach's own shift here from third-person to first-person plural, to the "we," draws us forward from the biblical text to contemporary literature and psychological modernity; to my ear, he draws us into the realism George Eliot would define. Although, for Eliot, suffering was necessary to stamp her characters and Auerbach expands the frame of experience to all extremity, he claims further that just such a fulcrum of change defines realist literature. It is this "element of development" in character that separates narrative that reads as legendary from narrative that reads as historical, whether or not its events ever occurred.[11]

Setting her consequential dramas in the heart of the family, a marriage, or the parish, Eliot believed it unnecessary either to falsely elevate setting or to forcibly harmonize the basic units of social life. Her instinctive grasp of the fact that "the sublime, tragic, and problematic take shape precisely in the domestic and commonplace" (as opposed to Homer, in whose work "domestic realism, the representation of daily life, remains...in the peaceful realm of the idyllic") may be a scriptural or religious inheritance.[12] As Auerbach explains the theology that undergirds the Hebrew Bible's style of representation, "The sublime influence of God here reaches so deeply into the everyday that the two realms of the sublime and the everyday are not only actually unseparated but basically inseparable."[13] Eliot's realist novels both traversed the social classes and entered intensively into daily life; these features reflect the Protestant convictions that human exchanges may hallow (or defile) and that the realm of the everyday bears transcendent meaning.

Whether or however much Marian had absorbed from Scripture the appreciation for an unprettified depiction of character and a fearless willingness to follow characters into scenes and conditions hardly edifying, we can see her staunch alliance of narrative method with ethical meaning. Marian's opposition to the stasis of perfect heroines found a complement in her opposition to representing such heroines as the center around which everything else revolved. Later, George Eliot would become famous for refusing to ally all the narrative empathy with single figures, however winsome they might be. Distributing attention to even her "rayless" figures, as she put it in *Middlemarch*, she encouraged her readers to imagine the plot from other, passible human points of view (*MM* 191). By contrast, novels in which "all surrounding parties made the accompaniment of the heroine" "on her 'starring' expedition through life," "the final cause of their existence" practiced and encouraged egoism (*Essays* 141).

Finally, Marian took aim at novels that set out to advance a religious affiliation. Though she did not say it explicitly, she implied that the egoism of novels "intended to expound the writer's religious, philosophical, or moral theories," regardless of High Church, Low Church, or evangelical sympathies (*Essays* 148). It is not hard to see why it would have been unbearable to Marian to encounter novels in which the authors pronounced "opinion on the knottiest moral and speculative questions," abetted by "amazing ignorance" (*Essays* 149). But mainly, novels preaching what she derisively called "opinions" offended her conviction that art teaches by moving its audience, rather than by arguing or proclaiming. She saw a profound disconnection between the theology dropped as "medicinal sweetmeats" into such novels and the more pervasive preoccupation of the novels (*Essays* 156). In short, she did not judge them to be religious novels in spirit. She saw them as worldly tales, uninformed by powerful spiritual motives of any kind, in which clerical love interests and pulpit-stair settings were merely trappings that might have been exchanged for any other style (*Essays* 156–7). When it came to these avowedly religious novels, Marian expressed moral-religious displeasure at the hypocrisy of evangelicals who "gratuitously" sought their subjects "among titles and carriages" (*Essays* 157). Why did they accord honor to power and wealth?: "and are not Evangelical opinions understood to give an especial interest in the weak things of the earth, rather than in the mighty?" (*Essays* 157). And so, repeatedly, Marian circled back to the opening she was creating for her own art. An "abundance of fine drama" was lying in wait for the right novelist, who would be able to discern it among the lower and middle classes.

Yet beyond her Midlands roots, why was it that Marian was so adamant about the need to see represented the religious lives of the working and middle classes, or, as she put it in one formulation, "the operation of . . . religious views among people (there really are many such in the world) who keep no carriage . . . who even manage to eat their dinner without a silver fork"? (*Essays* 157). As a woman of unique intellect, surrounded most of the time by learned minds (from her twenties forward, nearly all her friends were authors or public figures in one field or another), why did she find herself so powerfully drawn, particularly in the early phase of her life as a novelist, to representing human beings who were by and large untaught and certainly unintellectual, and who predominantly ascribed to some sort of institutional Christianity? To put the point even more sharply, the milieu she set out to represent was often the sort she knew she could not tolerate personally.[14] She had moved to London to leave behind a narrow rural world in which an unusual woman like herself was unintelligible. Such communities lived by adherence to longstanding local custom and received knowledge, and had little capacity to understand or value original thought and action.

Perhaps she set out to write about this class of people because she knew she could cultivate a larger audience of readers in representing lives that were not defined, as her own was, by intellectual pursuit. (Later, intellectuals creep into her novels. They tend to be misunderstood, or somewhat lonely outliers, or defeated in more or less misguided pursuits.) Yet she may have been drawn to the working classes because there were dimensions of learnedness—false or superficial learnedness—that were deeply alienating to her and that she associated with bad religion. Chief among them at this time was the use of reason, indirect evidence, and belabored argumentation to do the work she believed direct moral emotion should do. In the best of cases, the absence of education allowed for that direct moral emotion to shine visibly. Marian had begun to explore this correlation between moral and intellectual faculties in her review of Cummings; in the fall of 1856, she wrote her first fiction, "The Sad Fortunes of the Reverend Amos Barton," set among the unlearned people of Shepperton, and in her review of January 1857 she made it the central dimension of her repudiation of the poet Edward Young, whom she had embraced in her youth.[15]

Marian's strongest moral objection to Young was that his religion was pure selfishness, "egoism turned heavenward" (*Essays* 206); relatedly, her strongest aesthetic objection was his didacticism. Young imagined that the only possible source of human virtue was a belief in immortality; what could motivate people to act virtuously if they did not believe there was divine reward? As a consequence of this failure of imagination, Young became didactic, suffering from an "unintermittent habit of pedagogic moralizing" (*Essays* 206). Rather than singing, "inspired by the spontaneous flow of thought or feeling," as Marian believed a poet should, Young insisted, and argued, and set out proofs (*Essays* 208). To Marian, all the insistence and argumentation signaled deficiency in direct moral emotion. He had no ready human sympathy and so needed to supplement it through "laboured obedience to a theory or rule" (*Essays* 206). By contrast, for Marian the sign of genuine moral emotion was its direct operation: "Love does not say, 'I ought to love' – it loves. Pity does not say, 'It is right to be pitiful' – it pities. Justice does not say, 'I am bound to be just'—it feels justly" (*Essays* 206).

In this major critique of religious culture embedded in the review of a single poet, Marian argued that creed stunted morality. Religious creed actually functioned to weaken moral emotion, to train human beings to say, "I ought to love," rather than to love. In moving the focus to immortality, religious teaching encouraged "impiety towards the present and the visible," and located its motives in the realms of "the remote, the vague, and the unknown" (*Essays* 213). Realism, by contrast, rooted itself in this world, in the particular and the immediate. As such, it was an aesthetic that encouraged direct moral emotion (here, we can understand why Marian was always gratified by reports that her novels had brought readers to tears), not a belabored rationale that appealed to human beings' lowest egoistic propensities to tease them into a semblance of virtue.

If the problem of a sufficient motive for virtue in the absence of immortality troubled some, for Marian the sober truth of common mortality presented itself as the most powerful motive. For her, common mortality had become a kind of deep knowledge, that sort that was "wrought back to the directness of sense," in this case, moral sense: "to us it is conceivable that in some minds the deep pathos lying in the thought of human mortality—that we are here for a little while and then vanish away, that this earthly life is all that is given to our loved ones and to our many suffering fellow-men—lies nearer the fountains of moral emotion than the conception of extended existence" (*Essays* 203). The "fountains," that scriptural reference of abundance that Marian had adapted for her own use, were fed by the pathos of human limits.

In a much less quoted passage than her famous pronouncements in the Riehl review, Marian laid out, in a nearly fictional first-person passage, what reads as the closest thing to a positive statement of her beliefs concerning religion at this time. As if writing back to Young, Marian assumes the voice of a man who does not believe in immortality yet believes in a great deal nonetheless:

> We can imagine the man who 'denies his soul immortal', replying, "It is quite possible that *you* would be a knave, and love yourself alone, if it were not for your belief in immortality; but you are not to force upon me what would result from your own utter want of moral emotion. I am just and honest, not because I expect to live in another world, but because, having felt the pain of injustice and dishonesty towards myself, I have a fellow-feeling with other men, who would suffer the same pain if I were unjust or dishonest towards them.... I am honest, because I don't

like to inflict evil on others in this life, not because I'm afraid of
evil to myself in another. The fact is, I do *not* love myself alone,
whatever logical necessity there may be for that in your mind.
I have a tender love for my wife, and children, and friends, and
through that love I sympathize with like affections in other men.
It is a pang to me to witness the suffering of a fellow-being, and
I feel his suffering the more acutely because he is *mortal*—
because his life is so short, and I would have it, if possible, filled
with happiness and not misery. Through my union and fellowship with the men and women I *have* seen, I feel a like, though a
fainter, sympathy with those I have *not* seen; and I am able so to
live in imagination with the generations to come, that their good is
not alien to me, and is a stimulus to me to labour for ends which
may not benefit myself, but will benefit them." (*Essays* 201)

For a writer who tended toward highly complex syntax and a wide-
ranging vocabulary, we can note here their absence. We encounter the
most basic diction; the simplest possible active verbs (have, am, feel,
see [recall, "Love does not say, I ought to love—it loves"]); clear posi-
tives and negatives (have/have not; because/not because), the straight-
forward cause-and-effect structure organized by the repetitions of
"because"; and finally, the most complex relation—the sympathetic,
imaginative work marked by the term "through." Living ethically in
this world involved extrapolating from one's own experience of feeling,
whether suffering or love.

This review could have served as a guide to any reader who was
unsure how to read Marian's first fiction, "Amos Barton." Perhaps the
key to that novella, as well as to the Young review, was the first-person
plural phrase, "We mortals," which sounds bland enough on its own,
perhaps simply another way of saying "the human condition," but
which, for Marian, was an intentional, if gently couched, claim for an
extensive, inclusive ethics based in mortality rather than immortality.
Marian began to write this first fiction on September 23, 1856,
encouraged by Lewes, who loved her simple, suggestive title, "The
Sad Fortunes of the Reverend Amos Barton." A few weeks earlier, she
had written to Sara Hennell about Sara's own work, "I like reading
what my friends write and finding out a great deal more about them
than one can ever know in any other way. We mortals have such a

knack of shutting up our best selves quite away from each other, as well as our worst" (GEL 2: 263). It is hard to imagine that the secret plan for fiction was not already coming together.

Once she was finished in early November, Lewes wrote on Marian's behalf to John Blackwood, the Scottish publisher of *Blackwood's Magazine*, proposing for the anonymous author a series of "tales and sketches illustrative of the actual life of our country clergy about a quarter of a century ago; but solely in its *human* and *not at all* in its *theological* aspect" (GEL 2: 269). Rather than joining the "abundant religious stories polemical and doctrinal," the author set out "his" (that is, her) objective, perhaps with some overstatement: "to do what has never yet been done in our Literature," at least for some decades, since Jane Austen and Oliver Goldsmith's very popular *The Vicar of Wakefield* (1766) (GEL 2: 269). The writer would represent the clergy "like any other class with the humours, sorrows, and troubles of other men," and promised a "sympathetic and not at all antagonistic" tone that was likely to appeal to Blackwood's conservative ethos (GEL 2: 269).

Marian Evans Lewes was certainly about to do something new in the history of the novel, though it was hardly described by the narrower aim of representing the clerical class as any other men. In the same letter to Blackwood, Lewes checked on his own proposal for an article about "Sea Anemones," which would ultimately become part of his volume *Sea-Side Studies* (1858) on the marine biology of Ilfracombe, Tenby, the Scilly Isles and Jersey. It is worth noting that Marian joined Lewes's zoological expeditions over the course of 1856 and 1857, observing up close not only the zoophytes and mollusks and annelids, but also participating in the physical work of scientific observation, "armed with chisels and baskets" (GEL 2: 318), tramping through dirt and damp in clothing suited to the task, bearing a crowbar to turn over heavy stones, seeking the optimal-height jars and the optimal earthenware pans, sharing Lewes's "passionate fondness for the work itself."[16] Lewes, writing what remains a genuinely delightful work meant for a wide audience, describes his encounter with the surrounding world: "Everything was new to me, so that every step was delightful. When I discovered what had long been known to others, the pleasure of discovery was something essentially different from that of mere learning."[17] Once specimens were collected, the microscope, he wrote, allowed him to see "things removed from us—kept distant by ignorance and the still more obscuring screen of familiarity."[18]

In the period that George Eliot was experimenting with removing screens of familiarity and ignorance in human life, Lewes reveled in "the great drama which is incessantly enacted in every drop of water, on every inch of earth."[19] In Lewes, we can see the way that mid-nineteenth-century science, from marine biology onward, was powered by a sense of dramatic discovery with great consequence for human self-understanding and positioning. As ignorance and familiarity yielded incrementally to knowledge and paradoxically heightened curiosity, science prompted human reorientation: "And if with this substitution of definite and particular ideas for the vague generalities with which at first we represented Nature –if with increase of knowledge there comes, as necessarily there must come, increase of reverence, it is evident that the study of Life must of all studies best nourish the mind with true philosophy."[20] Temperamentally, Marian and Lewes's shared association of knowledge with reverence—and reverence with joy—was ushering in an era of extraordinary productivity and contribution to what had never yet been done in literature.[21]

Notes

1. "Rachel Gray," *The Leader*, 5 January 1856, Vol. 7, p. 19, *George Eliot Archive*, https://georgeeliotarchive.org/items/show/125, p. 19.
2. "Rachel Gray," p. 19.
3. Dillane, *Before*, pp. 87–102, reads the Riehl review—which almost always is read by scholars as a direct transposition of Evans's beliefs—noting the distance Evans imposed between Riehl's and her own views; further, she demonstrates that Evans was especially unsympathetic to Riehl's tendency to totalizing theory. In spite of Dillane's reminder not to elide narrating persona with author, I focus here on passages that represent beliefs I can arguably identify with Evans, given their repeated presence across her journalism, letters, and subsequent fiction.
4. Sharp, "Force," pp. 750, 733.
5. One could argue that we see this in Jane Austen novels—for example, as Emma comes to see the folly of her ways. But Austenian transformation stops within the developing self-consciousness of the character. In Eliot's novels, I suggest, it pushes outward into a claim about the nature of reality itself.
6. Erich Auerbach, *Mimesis: The Representation of Reality in Western Literature*, trans. Willard R. Trask (Princeton: Princeton University Press, 1953), p. 13.

7. Auerbach, *Mimesis*, p. 12.
8. Auerbach, *Mimesis*, p. 17.
9. Auerbach, *Mimesis*, p. 17.
10. Auerbach, *Mimesis*, p.18.
11. Auerbach, *Mimesis*, p.18.
12. Auerbach, *Mimesis*, p. 22.
13. Auerbach, *Mimesis*, pp. 22–3.
14. See, for example, her letter struggling with the egoism she evinced by not going to live with her sister Chrissey at a time of crisis: "by renunciation of my egotism I could give almost everything they want. And the work I can do in other directions is so trivial!" Yet, "To live with her in that hideous neighbourhood amongst ignorant bigots is impossible to me, it would be moral asphyxia" (GEL 2: 97).
15. U.C. Knoepflmacher gives a braided reading of these texts in *George Eliot's Early Novels, The Limits of Realism* (Berkeley and Los Angeles: University of California Press, 1968), pp. 40–9.
16. G. H. Lewes, *Sea-Side Studies at Ilfracombe, Tenby, the Scilly Isles, and Jersey* (Edinburgh and London: Blackwood, 1858), *Google Books*, p. 36. See also pp. 17, 28, 33.
17. Lewes, *Sea-Side*, p. 35.
18. Lewes, *Sea-Side*, p. 54.
19. Lewes, *Sea-Side*, p. 55.
20. Lewes, *Sea-Side*, p. 55.
21. Highly relevant here is Amy M. King, *The Divine in the Commonplace: Reverent Natural History and the Novel in Britain* (Cambridge: Cambridge University Press, 2019) (I came to King only after completing this work). King helpfully places both Eliot's realism and her descriptive force in the context of "reverent natural history" writing, and convincingly argues for what she calls "paranaturalist realism": a "hybrid fictional style willing to use the capacious descriptive practices of reverent natural histories in the service of delineating a human community as well as natural scenes" (p. 169).

7
"A Divine Work to Be Done in Life," 1857

Much as Mary Ann's decision not to go to church had come after she had settled many things within herself, so that she could confidently articulate what she did and did not believe, the writer George Eliot came into life fully formed. John Blackwood responded to Lewes's proposal on behalf of his "friend" with interest and Marian's sketch of Amos Barton was sent to Edinburgh. As negotiations unfolded regarding "Amos Barton," and the succeeding two sketches, "Mr. Gilfil's Love Story" and "Janet's Repentance," George Eliot seemed very unlike a diffident new writer. Urged a few times by a generally approving Blackwood to make changes that would soften harsh dimensions of character, plot, or setting and set the audience a bit more at ease, the new author wrote back without an ounce of accommodation:

> I am unable to alter anything in relation to the delineation or development of character, as my stories always grow out of my psychological conception of the dramatis personae.... My artistic bent is directed not at all to the presentation of eminently irreproachable characters, but to the presentation of mixed human beings in such a way as to call forth tolerant judgment, pity, and sympathy. And I cannot stir a step aside from what I *feel* to be *true* in character. (GEL 2: 299)

Blackwood accepted his new author's credo, perhaps somewhat cowed by the absolute proclamation—"my stories always"—that in this case had not a smidgen of history to back it up. Blackwood, recognizing that it might "stimulate the author to go on with the other Tales with more spirit," had accepted "Amos Barton" for immediate publication, paid his unknown author a highly respectable fifty guineas (twice what she made for the *Belles Lettres* reviews of a hundred titles), and advertised it as the beginning of a series, purely on faith (GEL 2: 275). "Amos Barton" received pride of place, opening the first number of 1857. The experiment in fiction was an unqualified success, perhaps most importantly in securing George Eliot an intelligent, sympathetic, sensitive, and loyal publisher who would prove to be a personal and professional support for the rest of her career.[1]

All in all, *Scenes of Clerical Life* took approximately a year to compose. By March 1857, when Marian and Lewes set off for another seaside expedition, the first part of "Mr. Gilfil" was published and by October she had finished writing "Janet's Repentance." Marian was paid for her work in checks written to Lewes, with both eager to maintain the incognito so that her work would be judged by its own merits and not by her dubious reputation (GEL 2: 284). Additionally, she was not yet ready to cut away the security of a return to journalism. For all the artistic certainty she evinced in her proclamations to Blackwood, Marian was not professionally certain as a fiction writer: she told Blackwood she was "very anxious to maintain my incognito for some time to come" (GEL 2: 309). "If GE turns out a dull dog," she wrote, "and an ineffective writer—a mere flash in the pan—I, for one, am determined to cut him on the first intimation of that disagreeable fact" (GEL 2: 310).

Yet the success of these three works secured her in a different direction. Her marriage with Lewes thrived and with further children born to Agnes and Thornton Hunt, no questions lingered about the nature of any of the ties. On May 26, 1857, Marian elected to write to her brother Isaac and half-sister Fanny (and through them to Chrissey, whom Marian eagerly wished to assist financially and practically) to let them know of her marriage, emphasizing to them, as she had to the Hennells and Brays earlier, the "hard work" she and Lewes had taken on to support his sons and the character of the man whose name she had taken. From this point forward, Marian's personal letters were signed "Marian Lewes."

Isaac responded through his solicitor a few weeks later, hurt by his exclusion from any earlier communication of Marian's "intention and prospects" (GEL 2: 346). The solicitor requested details of the marriage, and Marian explained that the marriage was not legal, because Lewes was not divorced, though "long deprived of his first wife by her misconduct"; Marian declared that she and Lewes regarded the union as a "sacred bond," but that she had not informed her family for three years because, "knowing that their views of life differ in many respects from my own, I wished not to give them unnecessary pain" (GEL 2: 349). Isaac himself did not resume communication with Marian until the year of her death, upon the occasion of her legal marriage to John Cross. Less expectedly, Marian's sisters followed her brother's lead, in what was a deeply painful break with Chrissey, not to be repaired until the months in which she approached her death and resumed correspondence. In spite of this resumption, the two sisters did not meet. Likewise, Fanny briefly kept up her correspondence with Marian, only to cut her off soon after. Decidedly, the fiction-writing part of Marian Evans Lewes's life was a separate epoch from what had come before. In the absence of communication with her siblings, this early stage of writing, particularly while still incognito, threw Marian and Lewes upon each other as exclusive partners, sharing a powerful secret.

Although "George Eliot" had described his aim as the representation of clerical figures in their human rather than theological dimensions, Marian's first "scene of clerical life" offered a braided portrait, in its repudiation of a cleric who cannot see the human beings around him for his absorption in the empty and often self-serving forms of his office.[2] Amos Barton, an evangelical churchman with a smattering of theology from Cambridge, is drawn as a highly imperfect human being who is not a great preacher, not a great scholar, not a particularly good friend to any of his parish flock or clerical colleagues, nor any sort of moral model. He is, as the narrator tells us, "palpably and unmistakably commonplace," the "quintessential extract of mediocrity," with a "knack of hitting on the wrong thing" whether in clothing, grammar, or the attempt to share the gospel (*Scenes* 80, 85, 56). Possessed of "a natural incapacity for teaching" (*Scenes* 63) and a "deficiency of small tact," he alienates those he is meant to instruct, telling a woman in the poorhouse that just as she cannot locate snuff when she wants it in life, after death "you may have to seek for mercy and not find it" (*Scenes* 64); he threatens a small boy that "God can burn [him] forever" (*Scenes* 65).

Yet Amos's greatest culpability lies in his inability to recognize the great generosity of his wife, Milly, who quietly loves and provides for him and their many children under significant economic duress, as her own health declines without Amos even noticing; he haplessly fails to dispel an empty scandalous rumor circulating about him, thus isolating Milly and their family further from those who otherwise might have helped them. The story ends with Milly's death in childbirth and Amos's shocked recognition that he did not love or give enough while he could. When his parishioners witness his great human suffering, they open their hearts to him, but just when his ties to Shepperton become a genuine form of solace and meaning, Amos loses his curacy to nepotistic considerations outside his control. He is exiled from Shepperton and his proximity to his wife's grave, and relocated to a distant, dusty manufacturing town. "Thy will be done" is the passage inscribed on his wife's grave, appropriately enough in this intensely didactic story. Yet the coda, which would be a mode George Eliot used often to emphasize moral aftereffects, brings readers back to Milly's grave twenty years later, where Amos leans upon the arm of his attentive eldest daughter, who incarnates Milly's love: "Milly did not take all her love from the earth when she died. She had left some of it in Patty's heart" (*Scenes* 115).

This is an intense and ironic story, a darker critique of individual character and religious culture than it may have seemed to Blackwood. Amos is not really just mediocre; he is deeply unlikable. Self-deceived, doing more harm than good in every single detail the story provides, he rushes Milly to her grave by omission and commission. The Church and the gospel that are the tools of his trade have had no moral effect on him; George Eliot makes clear that he might have done more good in a secular path, like his father the cabinetmaker. Moreover, in an era of sectarian dispute Amos's tendencies to anger and disputatiousness find religious cover and outlet. His insistence on specific doctrinal adherence, whether to the innovations of singing hymns rather than psalms or to donations for church rebuilding, alienates rather than cultivates the souls in his cure.

George Eliot's first story was an indictment of a Christianity whose essence had been emptied out by its own all-too-human agents and whose institutions had offered no deep-reaching teaching or correction to its own teachers and correctors. The Church in this story advances no sacred goals, and often retards them. The ironic climax of the story comes when the figure who is meant to embody and spread the gospel becomes able to do so only once he has come up against newly felt knowledge—the reality of human mortality—that itself repudiates Christian teaching on human immortality and the comforts of eternity. When Amos is confronted with a dead Milly, and begins to understand she will never reawaken, the ironic mode of the story becomes even more pronounced: all his complex, ill-understood teachings on the doctrine of the Incarnation, of all doctrines, echo as ever more hollow. Whereas theology made no inroads in Amos's or his listeners' hearts, this story suggests that the recognition of God in man can be learned only by the emotional loss built in to our mortality: in short, "we mortals."

For the George Eliot of 1856, then, the gospel was made flesh only when the most ordinary, common human suffering, rather than any doctrinal claim, peremptorily demanded repentance for insensibility to human love and life. Repentance arrived as a result of confronting wrongs that could never be made right nor compensated in a world of time. The clergyman had denied the divine by looking away from the "sacred human soul," which, the narrator states, is "the divinest thing God gives us to know" (*Scenes* 111). Milly is both associated with and compared to angels repeatedly by the narrator: "Milly's memory hallowed her husband, as of old the place was hallowed on which an angel from God had alighted" (*Scenes* 111). When Amos cries out, "Milly, Milly, dost thou hear me?" at her grave, confessing, "I didn't love thee enough – I wasn't tender enough to thee – but I think of it all now" (*Scenes* 114–15), we can hear the echo of biblical figures seeking belatedly, upon waking from unconsciousness, to incorporate new knowledge: "And Jacob awaked out of his sleep, and he said, Surely the LORD is in this place; and I knew it not" (Gen. 28:16). Fellow sacred human souls prompt the regret and repentance that advance moral development.

What stands out in this first story? Perhaps not Amos, nor the flat and idealized Milly, nor the sentimental, predictable storyline (as U.C. Knoepflmacher long ago noted, George Eliot had not yet come to terms with the conflict between her idealism and her realism).[3] The signature of George Eliot in this story is, first, her focused depiction of Christian theology as irrelevant to the lives and experience of nearly everyone on her canvas, and second, her pointed disassociation of moral goodness and generosity from theological commitment. When it comes to the villagers of Shepperton, they are no better and no worse than their counterparts anywhere else in rural England. And even the most basic elements of theology elude many of them. In one comical example, old Mrs. Patten insists that she is no sinner: "When Mr. Barton comes to see me, he talks about nothing but my sins and my need o' marcy. Now...I've never been a sinner. From the fust beginning, when I went into service, I al'ys did did my duty by my emplyers. I was a good wife as any in the county.... The cheese-factor used to say my cheese was al'ys to be depended on" (*Scenes* 48). Granted, Mr. Hackit, who had "more doctrinal enlightenment," is "a little shocked by the heathenism of her speech," but Mrs. Patten's common sense tells her that original sin has no purchase on her (*Scenes* 48–9). She has met the standards she knows for correct behavior in this world: she has done her duty to her social superiors, she was a good wife, and she did her work well. Certainly, Eliot shapes Mrs. Patten's ignorance for comic effect, yet her common sense is also bracingly reasonable. As the doctrinally enlightened Mr. Hackit says later on, parsons can be "too high learnt to have much common-sense" (*Scenes* 85); he concludes daringly, "that's a bad sort of eddication as makes folks unreasonable" (*Scenes* 86). We can hear the narrator confirming that reason and common sense trump the torturous complexity of doctrine when it issues in no positive personal or communal effects.

In "Amos Barton," Eliot embodied the most positive of Christianity's effects in a single humble, humane clergyman: "The true parish priest, the pastor beloved, consulted, relied on by his flock; a clergyman who is not associated with the undertaker, but thought of as the surest helper under a difficulty" (*Scenes* 93). What distinguishes this teacher is that he "has the wonderful art of preaching sermons which the wheelwright and the blacksmith can understand...because he can call a spade a spade, and knows how to disencumber ideas of their wordy frippery. Look at him more attentively, and you will see that his face is a very interesting one—that there is a great deal of humour and feeling praying in his gray eyes, and about the corners of his roughly-cut mouth" (*Scenes* 93). Mr. Cleves, the narrator surmises, probably comes from the "harder working section of the middle class"; he gathers the working men weekly, "and gives them a sort of conversational lecture on useful practical matters, telling them stories, or reading some select passages from an agreeable book, and commenting on them; and if you were to ask the first labourer or artisan in Tripplegate what sort of man the parson was, he would say, — 'a uncommon knowin', sensible, freespoken gentleman; very kind an' good-natur'd too"' (*Scenes* 93–4). Here is George Eliot's endorsement of the only Christianity she could recommend in this first story: one utterly free of anything specifically Christian, but suffused with humanity. While her second scene of clerical life, "Mr. Gilfil's Love Story," stayed closer to the human rather than theological aspects of clerical life, her third story, "Janet's Repentance," returned to a braided portrait. This time, rather than distinguishing divine from human sympathy in favor of the latter, George Eliot took a painful story of marital abuse and a wife's turn to alcohol and redeemed her heroine's suffering with an earnest evangelical conversion. Janet is saved by the man her abusive husband has settled on as an enemy, the evangelical curate, Mr. Tryan. From his own life experience as a fellow sinner and sufferer, Mr. Tryan teaches Janet that only submission and obedience to the divine will can provide sinners with the grace that gives them superadded strength against temptation and hopelessness.

"Janet's Repentance" stages the belief that human sympathy is insufficient unless it leads to divine sympathy; the narrator tells us that Janet's confession to a receptive human being "prepared her soul for that stronger leap by which faith grasps the idea of the Divine sympathy" (*Scenes* 397). Fascinatingly, this story seems to move *away* from a purely humanist creed of kindness. Kindness is not powerful enough to save Janet from despair; only her belief in grace can do that work.[4] When Mr. Tryan is near death, at the story's end, he reassures Janet that she will be able to withstand temptation without him as well: "But you will not feel the need of me as you have done...You have a sure trust in God...I shall not look for you in vain at the last" (*Scenes* 410). And Janet affirms, "God will not forsake me," in an unsuperseded conversion that makes it very difficult to read this story as a secular tale in which human beings save each other outside the powerful forms of religious faith (*Scenes* 410).

Yet the story reads nothing like a religious novel of the 1850s, in spite of its lengthy inclusion of Mr. Tryan's teachings and the structure of Janet's sin, confession, and repentance. In continuity with Marian's convictions since the 1840s, the story targeted sectarianism, aligning it with the violence and abuse of its chief purveyor in the story, Janet's husband. Yet George Eliot did not see the story as anti-Anglican, in spite of its stark division between evangelical hero (Mr. Tryan) and Anglican villain (Janet's husband, Mr. Dempster). To Blackwood, she wrote on June 11, 1857: "The collision in the drama is not at all between 'bigoted churchmanship' and evangelicalism, but between *ir*religion and religion. Religion in this case happens to be represented by evangelicalism" (GEL 2: 347). This claim seems believable enough given that George Eliot both was working from a historical event and understood most sectarian identification to be inessential and circumstantial. In the increasingly divided town of Milby, George Eliot singles out old Mr. Jerome as her non-clerical hero precisely because he is least interested in sectarian identity. Mr. Jerome, to whom she devotes long description, is a retired cornfactor who recognizes the universal truth of human suffering, is catholic in his attempts to help sufferers, and appreciates all good teaching, no matter the source: "To a fine ear [his] tone said as plainly as possible—'Whatever recommends itself to me, Thomas Jerome, as piety and goodness, shall have my love and honour. Ah, friends, this pleasant world is a sad one, too, isn't it? Let us help one another, let us help one another'" (*Scenes* 305).

As we have seen, the heart of George Eliot's claim to a realism that had not yet been seen in "our literature" was her commitment to providing an inside view of English religious life and history among the working classes. She wanted a detailed realism that would range from style of speech to practices of food and clothing, to matters of belief and superstition, to annual and life cycle rituals, to relations among the youth and between the sexes, to the place of the cleric among them. In the extended, historically specific description of Mr. Jerome in the following passage, we can feel George Eliot distinguishing herself as natural historian–novelist, taking up in particular the matter of sectarian identification. Among "the People," she reported back to her readership, sectarian bias was mostly an effect of the chance of birth, upbringing, and surroundings; an autobiographical social and cultural identification, it bore inessential relation to matters of religious faith or doctrine:

> And it was entirely owing to this basis of character, not at all from any clear and precise doctrinal discrimination, that Mr. Jerome had very early in life become a Dissenter. In his boyish days he

had been thrown where Dissent seemed to have the balance of piety, purity, and good works on its side, and to become a Dissenter seemed to him identical with choosing God instead of mammon. That race of Dissenters is extinct in these days, when opinion has got far ahead of feeling, and every chapel-going youth can fill our ears with the advantages of the Voluntary system, the corruptions of a State Church, and the Scriptural evidence that the first Christians were Congregationalists. Mr. Jerome knew nothing of this theoretic basis for Dissent, and in the utmost extent of his polemical discussion he had not gone further than to question whether a Christian man was bound in conscience to distinguish Christmas and Easter by any peculiar observance beyond the eating of mince-pies and cheese-cakes. (*Scenes* 305)

In the best cases, sectarian bias began when a person recognized human agents worthy of love and reverence, and followed them in religious affiliation. "Opinion," a term almost always negative for George Eliot, did not pursue truth but fed conflict, as we can see in the adolescent contest between the "advantages" of one's own side against the "corruptions" of the other side, and again, the primacy and priority ("first") of one's own side. The specific matters of debate were dressing for the competitive urge to predominance.

Because affiliation was based mostly on a circumstantial rather than doctrinal basis, when circumstantial factors shifted, so could affiliation. Ideally, this allowed for sectarian divisions to soften and for people to seek out goodness and wisdom wherever it was found, going to multiple sites of worship, listening to sermons from any worthy preacher. More cynically, it meant that superficial commitments to doctrine were regularly trumped by convenience and self-interest in daily life: "It is probable that no speculative or theological hatred would be ultimately strong enough to resist the persuasive power of convenience: that a latitudinarian baker, whose bread was honourably free from alum, would command the custom of any dyspeptic Puseyite; that an Arminian with the toothache would prefer a skilful Calvinistic dentist to a bungler stanch against the doctrines of Election and Final Perseverance" (*Scenes* 317). In this detailed, humorous treatment of sectarian identification, George Eliot offered a central finding of her early fictive anthropological survey of English religion: much of religious identity had extremely little to do with what her readers—then or now—might have considered religion worthy of the name. Theology and doctrine played the weakest part in religious identification and motive.

Yet George Eliot did not discount religion where it existed. Among the lesser educated classes, from farmer to artisan to industrial worker to shopkeeper and sometimes all the way to the gentry, she characterized true religion as a way of being in the world (not unlike what we see in a thinker such as Charles Taylor—"the construal we just live in") and as a set of very general and often very vague but strong, ordering beliefs.[5] George Eliot was brilliant at showing the way such belief required ritualized, historical, and communal forms of expression. In "Mr. Gilfil's Love Story," the simple farmers sleep through the church service and then "[make] their way back again through the miry lanes, perhaps almost as much the better for this simple weekly tribute to what they knew of good and right, as many a more wakeful and critical congregation of the present day" (*Scenes* 122). In "Janet's Repentance," Janet's mother's faith sustains her in uncritical fashion as well:

> Mrs. Raynor had been reading about the lost sheep, and the joy there is in heaven over the sinner that repenteth. Surely the eternal love she believed in through all the sadness of her lot, would not leave her child to wander farther and farther into the wilderness till there was no turning.... Mrs. Raynor had her faith and her spiritual comforts, though she was not in the least evangelical and knew nothing of doctrinal zeal. I fear most of Mr. Tryan's hearers would have considered her destitute of saving knowledge, and I am quite sure she had no well-defined views on justification. Nevertheless, she read her Bible a great deal, and thought she found divine lessons there—how to bear the cross meekly, and be merciful. Let us hope that there is a saving ignorance, and that Mrs. Raynor was justified without knowing exactly how. (*Scenes* 291)

In George Eliot's fiction, a "saving ignorance" is the Christianity that settles on regular practices, in this case reading the Bible a great deal; that finds recurring solace in powerful images, in this case the lost sheep; and that personalizes practice and teaching (often in humorous or theologically unsound ways) to the particulars of the believer's immediate loved ones and circumstances, in this case from the "sinner that repenteth" to her child. Eternal love that allows always for the joyful return of the sinner is Mrs. Raynor's main theological conviction; her practical lessons from the Gospel are how to bear the cross meekly and how to be merciful. Here, we see George Eliot exploring where and how basic religious (usually scriptural) ideas genuinely shaped the experience of individuals among the rural English in the early nineteenth century.

While it is possible to feel that George Eliot condescends to these characters of simple faith, her humor and her particularization of individuals often mitigate that experience, not to mention her habitual irony at the expense of far more educated characters and her readers themselves. Even more important, it is worth contextualizing for a moment to note what she did *not* do with her simple, working, believing Christians. She did not use them to show the cleansing effects of poverty on the soul. She did not offer them sacrificially in fictional deaths to indicate that they were too good for this world or to affirm their rewards in another world, nor did she go to the other extreme and make them moral idiots in urgent need of religious discipline. Finally, she did not make them bland purveyors of ideologically coherent acceptance of their place in the class structure.[6] The status of ignorance in George Eliot's very learned novels would benefit from sustained critical treatment; but in terms of the intersection of ignorance with religious feeling George Eliot asserts that religious feeling can thrive independently of religious learning and that doctrinal or theological ignorance has no worse effects than any other form of ignorance.

Even as George Eliot tended to represent only a few basic tenets of Christian teaching as powerful personal and cultural forces, her fiction explored the unique contributions of different religious strains in English and Christian history. From her first fictions to her last, Eliot particularized a remarkable slate of religious movements at specific historical moments, from evangelicalism to distinct strains of Dissent, to Renaissance Catholicism, to a nationalist Judaism. In "Janet's Repentance," Eliot gave the evangelicalism in which she grew up its due. Setting the story twenty-five years before its writing, thus coinciding with her own formative years of adolescence and education in the 1830s, she described evangelicalism as a powerful moral force. Yet she was quick to emphasize that no religious "revival" has purely positive effects. "Religious ideas," she famously wrote,

> have the fate of melodies, which, once set afloat in the world, are taken up by all sorts of instruments, some of them woefully coarse, feeble, or out of tune, until people are in danger of crying out that the melody itself is detestable. It may be that some of Mr. Tryan's hearers had gained a religious vocabulary rather than religious experience; that here and there a weaver's wife, who, a few months before, had been simply a silly slattern, was converted into that more complex nuisance, a silly and sanctimonious slattern; that the old Adam, with the pertinacity of middle age, continued to tell fibs behind the counter, notwithstanding the new Adam's addiction to Bible-reading and family prayer. (*Scenes* 319–20)

Yet, she contended, a powerful religious movement, even when confronted by the hard resistance of human character, can at times make its way, whether floating in the air as melody or "gradually diffusing its subtle odour into chambers that were bolted and barred against it" (*Scenes* 319). The narrator readily acknowledges the imperfections of both evangelicalism and its preachers and practitioners but insists on its transformative evolutionary effects in a back-and-forth structure of assertion, qualification, assertion, qualification:

> Nevertheless, Evangelicalism had brought into palpable existence and operation in Milby society that idea of duty, that recognition of something to be lived for beyond the mere satisfaction of self, which is to the moral life what the addition of a great central ganglion is to animal life. No man can begin to mould himself on a faith or an idea without rising to a higher order of experience: a principle of subordination, of self-mastery, has been introduced into his nature; he is no longer a mere bundle of impressions, desires, and impulses. Whatever might be the weaknesses of the ladies who pruned the luxuriance of their lace and ribbons, cut out garments for the poor, distributed tracts, quoted Scripture, and defined the true Gospel, they had

learned this—that there was a divine work to be done in life, a rule of goodness higher than the opinion of their neighbours. (*Scenes* 320)

Unlike her contemporary Dickens (who greatly admired *Scenes of Clerical Life*), she did not depict evangelicalism as defined by Calvinism. The worst she was willing to say of evangelicalism here was that it might be mere dressing and not deeply transformative of its adherents. (Mrs. Linnet, for instance, reads spiritual biographies now that evangelicalism has come to town, but only their secular parts!) Eliot never gives a behavioral justification for the ceaseless cries of "hypocrisy and cant" that assail Mr. Tryan. She leaves largely unrepresented Calvinist expressions regarding predestination and the salvation of a small group of the elect, ideas which she thought were likely to push flawed believers into worse versions of themselves. Meanwhile, the plot of "Janet's Repentance" shows us Mr. Tryan sacrificing his life in works of charity and goodness.

Thus, in "Janet's Repentance" evangelicalism is not singled out for any of the incisive critique Marian had levelled in her *Westminster* reviews of Young and Cumming. It is one historical melody among others. It may be that the narratorial perspective Marian assumed in "Janet's Repentance" and "Amos Barton," of a man looking back at his childhood, and particularly at his sensory experiences attending church in his childhood, accounts for a certain softening nostalgia. Yet even this nostalgia for the mystery, the liturgy, the bread and butter in the hand of the nurse, and the church architecture of the past alternates with the narrator's more ironic, even sardonic, treatment of the moral and intellectual limitation of the church- and chapel-goers. To the extent that we can read *Scenes of Clerical Life* autobiographically, it is not in the shape of embrace or rejection.

When we consider the spiritual tenor of this first collection of fiction, more than an embrace of evangelicalism or a critique of institutional affiliation, the stories of clerical life can be described as a direct reckoning with death. Each of the novellas is organized by the deaths of major characters: the death of Amos Barton's wife; the death of Mr. Gilfil, upon which the novella opens, and the premature death of Tina, the love of his young life; the death of Janet's abuser, Mr. Dempster, and her savior, Mr. Tryan. The novellas are also dotted with the deaths of minor characters. It makes good sense that George Eliot would open her fictional career with these stories shaped by suffering and death. It is also noteworthy that she chooses not to end any of these stories upon the momentous deaths narrated. Each novella takes the reader beyond the life-changing death to witness the day after, the years after, to take the measure of the remaining lives that must continue the struggle to make something of their own mortal lot.

These simple plot structures of life and death, loss and aftermath, posed some of the most intense, uncomfortable questions for a novelist who no longer believed in eternity and immortality as a solace for the absence of loved ones; nor in providential reward and punishment as a rationale or impetus for morality; nor in incarnation, atonement, and resurrection as a holding framework for human limitation, regret, or repentance. In these initial stories, Eliot boldly confronted the hardest problems facing religiously unorthodox moral thinkers in the mid-nineteenth century, as if expressly not to shy away from them; as if to say, realist novels will take up the greatest problems of life's meaning, posed in the harshest relief, or such novels will be worth nothing at all.

In this grouping of sudden deaths and deathbed scenes, of graveyard gatherings, recitations of "I am the Resurrection and the Life," stone inscriptions of "Thy will be done," private cries and public mourning; in these scenes of death, interspersed with scenes of life, clerical and non-clerical alike, Eliot testified to mid-Victorian forms filled with the breath and substance of a wide variety of faiths. These faiths were not all reconcilable. Thus these early stories sometimes reveal the desire to dramatize mimetically one thing while preaching elsewhere another thing. Yet George Eliot had successfully formulated her abiding belief in a human unity that precluded sectarian difference:

> Yet surely, surely the only true knowledge of our fellow-man is that which enables us to feel with him —which gives us a fine ear for the heart-pulses that are beating under the mere clothes of circumstance and opinion. Our subtlest analysis of schools and sects must miss the essential truth, unless it be lit up by the love that sees in all forms of human thought and work, the life and death struggles of separate human beings. (*Scenes* 322)

In this passage, in which we can hear echoes of Feuerbach, of Comte, of evolutionary thought, and of Marian Evans the essayist, a narrator emerged who rejected the dividing force of opinions and made knowledge a realm not of intellect but of feeling. This feeling could unite, through love, all human forms as evidence of separate but species-wide, shared struggles that were to be the main matter of the realist novel.

By the end of summer 1857, as the last of the three stories was appearing in *Blackwood's Magazine*, both Marian and Lewes were already speaking of her need for a "larger canvas," which meant to them the move from short story to novel (GEL 2: 378). While Marian now knew that her ties to her siblings were cut, including her ability to assist Chrissey financially, Lewes eagerly maintained his loving yet distant relations with his sons. The three would come to play an important emotional role in Marian's life as well, and Lewes's burden of support would be eased dramatically by Marian's earning power as a popular author. At the end of August 1857, Lewes traveled on his own to Hofwyl for ten days in order to visit the boys there, writing joyfully to Blackwood of "the greatest pleasure a father's heart can feel, in seeing my boys robust in health, greatly improved, and perfectly happy" (GEL 2: 380). Immediately upon Lewes's return, Marian submitted the final installment of "Janet's Repentance" to Blackwood and announced to him on September 5, 1857: "I have a subject in my mind which will not come under the limitations of the title 'Clerical Life,' and I am inclined to take a large canvas for it, and write a novel" (GEL 2: 381). This would be *Adam Bede*.

Notes

1. Only *Romola* was not published by Blackwood. Blackwood died approximately a year before Eliot, after publishing what would be her final work.
2. Simon During, "George Eliot and Secularism," in *Companion to George Eliot*, ed. Amanda Anderson and Harry E. Shaw (Malden, MA: Wiley-Blackwell, 2016), pp. 428–42. During notes the unusual mixes that arise in Eliot's "particular mode of secularism" that simultaneously "aims to disseminate an elevated natural spirituality against the Christian faith" even as it is interested in the Anglican Church as a secular institution, "historically and socially" (pp. 429–30).

3. Knoepflmacher, *Early Novels*, p. 32. See also George Levine's brilliant description of Eliot's realism and her idealism as it evolved through her career in *Realism, Ethics and Secularism: Essays on Victorian Literature and Science* (Cambridge: Cambridge University Press, 2008), pp. 25–50.
4. See Ilana M. Blumberg, "Sympathy or Religion?: George Eliot and Christian Conversion," *Nineteenth-Century Literature* 74.3 (2019), pp. 360–87.
5. Taylor, *Secular*, p. 30.
6. Deaths in George Eliot's work can be debated, but even "Amos Barton"'s Milly does not play this sort of role. Amos learns his lesson through her death, but her death offers a realist picture of women's hard lives.

8
"Harvest Time," 1858–1859

In January 1858, John Blackwood brought out the first edition of *Scenes of Clerical Life*, by "George Eliot," and Marian set to earnest work on the project that would catapult her from the phase of "literary" to "popular" success, as Blackwood put it (GEL 2: 433). The writing of *Adam Bede* was buoyed by holding in her hands the "handsome" two volumes of *Scenes* (the material form of her books was deeply important to Marian over the course of her life) and by their reception among readers and reviewers (GEL 2: 418).

To appreciate fully Marian Evans Lewes's writerly experience in 1858 requires recognizing the exclusivity of her relation to Lewes. There is a pathos to the fact that, with the publication of her first volumes of fiction, she sent not a single copy "on private grounds," as she put it to Blackwood, noting that only when she chose to give up her incognito would she take "a few intimate friends into her confidence" (GEL 2: 419). In other words, while she requested that professional copies be sent to nine readers, including Dickens, Ruskin, and Froude, Marian sent no copy to the Brays or to Sara Hennell, none to any family member, none to Spencer or Chapman or any colleagues or fellow thinkers and writers from the *Westminster*, and none to either of her closest newer friends, Bessy Rayner Parkes and Barbara Smith Bodichon.[1] It took until February 1858 for Marian and Lewes to divulge her identity even to her great supporter John Blackwood (though it was not a surprise to him). In spite of dropping hints and clues about her new, demanding occupation to friends and editors who sought to commission articles, Marian zealously kept her secret. Only under the increasingly problematic consequences of false claims to her work by a Joseph Liggins did Marian and Lewes unveil the secret in the summer of 1859.

Sharing with Lewes alone the "rigid secrecy as to authorship," as Lewes put it, settled him at the heart of the fiction-writing enterprise, well beyond the practical managing of affairs with Blackwood (GEL 2: 429). The secret was likely a necessary one; in 1858, Marian's status as a non-legal wife and an unbeliever posed serious risks to popular success, and Marian confided to Charles Bray in March 1858 that she was keeping her work a secret not on a whim but in the "solid interest" of very necessary income (GEL 2: 444). Yet the secret made Lewes alone Marian's testing board. She read her work aloud to him; she considered his suggestions as she refused to consider anyone else's; and she depended on his strong, well-considered belief in the range of her abilities. In May 1859, she related to Barbara Bodichon, who alone among her friends had been certain about Marian's authorship, "He is the prime blessing that has made all the rest possible to me – giving a response to everything I have written, a response that I could confide in as a proof that I have not mistaken my work" (GEL 3: 64).[2] As if there could not have been one without the other—George Eliot without George Henry Lewes—Lewes's entrance into Marian's life and her entry into fiction writing were together what the narrator of *Adam Bede* would call the abundant "harvest time" that could come only after seed time. Marian first encountered this metaphor as a scriptural one, rooted in verses such as "They that sow in tears shall reap in joy" and "Make us glad according to the days wherein thou hast afflicted us" (Psalms 126:5; 90:15). Making the agricultural metaphor central to the pastoral *Adam Bede* allowed Eliot to meditate on the relationship between suffering and joy just as she was living its transition in her own life.

Maintaining her tradition of marking birthdays and the new year by reflection in her journal, on January 2, 1858, Marian marked a shift in her life so new that it was still difficult to count on. She described Lewes taking a copy of *The Times* out of his pocket, upon his return from London, to show her an early review of *Scenes*, and meditated, "I wonder how I shall feel about these little details ten years hence, if I am *alive*. At present I value them as grounds for hoping that my writing may succeed and so give value to my life—as indications that I can touch the hearts of my fellow men, and so sprinkle some precious grain as the result of the long years in which I have been inert and suffering. But at present fear and trembling still predominate over hope" (GEL 2: 416). Fiction writing might redeem the long, painful years of her past by allowing her to give something valuable to a community well beyond her circle of intimates. Value might come of suffering; perhaps suffering had indeed been seed time.

Scenes had given Marian ground to wrestle with the pain of death in a world where the belief in eternal life in Christ could no longer guarantee its meaning. *Adam Bede*, a novel that embodied Marian's perseverance and continued life and a possible future of more writing ("ten years hence"), gave her ground to wrestle with human suffering in a world she saw as ordered by natural law alone, without the guarantee of providential reward and punishment; Christian atonement and salvation could no longer assure all human beings that their suffering bore purpose or was reckoned. The novel also constituted the beginning of a career-long inquiry into conscience, the will to do right in spite of its difficulty, absent a belief that the divine gift of Christian grace was available to beat temptation and avoid sin. Yet no other novel in the oeuvre of George Eliot would deal so directly and intensively as does *Adam Bede* with human suffering: its apportionment (who suffers? who suffers more? who suffers most?); its reason (why does it happen?); its effects (can good come out of evil?); and its meaning for human relations (what is the relationship between suffering and love?).

Marian's novel allowed for multiple responses to these questions, given that her characters in this newly wide canvas spanned the simplest laborers, educated Anglican gentry, pious dissenting artisans, and various clerical figures. As Sean Gaston describes it, many of her characters "believe, to varying degrees of fervour, certainty and doubt, in a divine agency."[3] Is there a way to identify what the novelist was preaching? Or what the novelist believed? It is easier to identify what troubled her, what questions held her fast, as she searched for provisional grounds for living. As she would do in her novels, Marian divided her own life into "epochs"; in 1858 it was clearly her union with Lewes that divided between her past and present. Marian understood her past as one of intense suffering. Interestingly, her present—in which she was cast away from her family and largely rejected by respectable society—appeared to her a time in which she had no cause for complaint. As she finished *Scenes*, in June 1857, she wrote to Cara Bray from the Jersey shore: "I never have anything to call out my ill-humour or discontent...and I have everything to call out love and gratitude" (GEL 2: 340).

Marian's narration, of past suffering and present ease or enjoyment, was not strictly chronicle, but a thought structure: while her past had not been luxurious, she had never suffered material hardship. She experienced school as painful, though she found there beloved, long-lived mentors and a few intimate friends. She lost her mother at a young age, a loss she rarely wrote about explicitly but that was nonetheless profound; and she tested the bounds of her father's love with painful results when she chose to separate from the Anglican Church.[4] Still, she was able to tend to him with a sense of great love and purpose at the end of his life, as she wished. As a young woman, she had the freedom to read and learn with great energy and enthusiasm, for many years supported financially and thus at least tacitly approved by her father. At all phases of her life, she was greatly fortunate in her friends, emotionally and intellectually. When she gave up Christian certainty, a tremendous loss of moorings, those friends were her companions as she set out in search of intellectual and professional independence. Her achievements and opportunities were extraordinary and rare.

Throughout, she suffered from the ill health of regular headaches, toothaches, and, most of all, anxiety and mental anguish. The mental anguish that attended all these phases was the primary suffering to which she attests; in an early letter she suggests that "those who know much of mental conflict" would prefer "external trial" in its place (GEL 1: 17). Until she and Lewes found each other, her loneliness and worry as to her place in the hearts of her friends, and her place in the world, nagged at her ceaselessly. Thus while her headaches and tendency to great anxiety and self-doubt never abated, she described her life with Lewes as one of joy and even ease, the ease that comes of happiness in one's hard work. Suffering had preceded love; love could not be fully appreciated without having suffered. By the time Marian wrote *Adam Bede*, she could see the task of making the right choices when they were most difficult and lonely, as the work of youth, of seed time.

As a young woman in her early twenties up until her apostasy, Marian had valued suffering so much that she described herself to Maria Lewis as being "in danger of failing in sympathy for those who are experiencing it" (GEL 1: 15–16). Whether or not this statement was tongue-in-cheek, Marian truly saw suffering as central to the human experience and fully accommodated by Christian faith. Suffering was humanity's lot since the biblical Adam had been told, "In sorrow thou shalt eat" (Gen. 3:17), and the Gospel was clear that the true Christian would endure suffering beyond the "worldling," but also enjoy the "special blessings derived from that endurance," as Mary Ann put it in an adolescent letter (GEL 1: 16). Suffering, she wrote, functioned as a way of drawing close to and imitating Christ; "to pass through life without tribulation...would leave us destitute of one of the marks that invariably accompany salvation, and of that fellowship in the sufferings of the Redeemer which can alone work in us a resemblance to one of the most prominent parts of His Divinely perfect character" (GEL 1:95). Chillingly, even the death of Chrissey's one-year-old daughter brought forth thanks for "one of the beauties of this earth," which Marian specified as a gift to spectators who could witness "the meltings of sorrow" functioning to "subdue[e] and refin[e] the spirit," especially of the "harder sex" (GEL 1: 140). She did note the pain to the "poor parents" (GEL 1: 140).[5]

For Marian, faith in the uses of suffering—its refining and purifying effects, its subduing of the will—were inseparable from its promised rewards. Her letters from this period abound with such pronouncements: when a friend suffered the loss of her fourteen-year-old sister to tetanus, Marian expressed her faith that "The sweet uses of adversity will compensate to her for these sad days" (GEL 1: 141). To the pressing problems faced by the single, working Franklin women and Maria Lewis Marian affirmed God's attention and purpose in extending their suffering: "The refiner and purifier of silver must see His own likeness in the metal ere he ceases the purging process. He will then make you glad according to the years wherein you have known adversity" (GEL 1: 114). God, continued Marian, makes "the tearful sowing a prelude even to a rich harvest of peace and comfort on earth" (GEL 1: 114). To another friend: "I will pray...for an abundant harvest of joy after this seed-time of tears"; "it is but part of the dower to which you are entitled as one of His family" (GEL 1: 56). The promise of suffering's fruit was more frequently expressed in Marian's letters than any other religious tenet.

There is no question that the sheer abundance of untreatable illness and early death in Victorian experience encouraged the centrality of a theodicy that could square the prevalence and intensity of innocent suffering with a personal God of mercy. Marian also described a God who did not delight in the suffering of human beings but "who has seen it requisite unwillingly to wound" (GEL 1: 49). At irregular intervals, a hint of doubt may be visible in Marian's sureties: "trial," she wrote to an acquaintance, "*if not futile*, operates according to God's gracious design on the soul"; "we are awakened...to a consciousness of our real position, that of beings whose eternal weal or woe is pending, and may be decided in a moment" (GEL 1: 149, emphasis mine). If not futile, trial can bring "the satisfaction of having partially set our feet on the firm foundation of truth" and offer the "peace" that comes from the grasp of eternal truth (GEL 1: 49).

All these reflections on the uses and rewards of suffering enter into the weave of *Adam Bede*. The events narrated in the novel make it difficult to see it as anything but a tragedy, yet the novel resists that definition. Deeply sensitive to the agricultural rhythms of English farm life, the novel also requires a "harvest time" beyond a simple coda or narratorial pronouncement, and thus, after a gap of eighteen months, dramatic action resumes in Book Six and readers witness a new equilibrium, established in the wake of tragedy. Yet for five books, readers are immersed in events that grow increasingly more dire. The novel opens with Adam, the intelligent, strong, honest rising carpenter, who has set his heart on Hetty, the beautiful, ignorant, and egoistic young niece to the farming Poyser family. Yet Hetty's affections are stolen by the kind-hearted, but weak-willed, heir to the estate, Arthur Donnithorne. When Adam catches the two kissing, he abandons class constraints and confronts Arthur, whom he has known and loved since childhood, but Arthur does not own up to the seriousness of the liaison, claiming falsely that he has done nothing but flirt with Hetty. When Adam pushes Arthur to disabuse her of the idea that he can ever marry her, Hetty, all her fantasies crushed and her private thoughts a secret to all who surround her, eventually agrees to marry Adam out of hopelessness. Adam, transfixed by her childlike beauty, imagines nothing beyond caring for and protecting her, and fails to fathom her desires or her character. As the wedding approaches,

Hetty runs away in desperate search of Arthur, to no avail, and Adam soon learns from the trusted parish rector, Mr. Irwine, that she has been apprehended for the crime of infanticide.

Asked by Blackwood for a précis of the story, Marian had replied that she could not give him the plot because it would tell him nothing; all meaning, she argued, lay in the "treatment" (GEL 2: 447). Seduction, pregnancy, infanticide, not to mention a violent struggle between an estate heir and a working man: none of these sensational plot features promised moral uplift. Yet at the center of this story were the existential and historical problems of a world shrouded in moral mystery, in which innocents could suffer without reward or even respite, and powerful people could imagine escaping the costs of wrongdoing. In a world not ruled by justice, often untouched by mercy, was it morally acceptable to enjoy any happiness? Was it possible to separate such happiness from others' suffering?

As readers, we follow Adam's painful discovery of Arthur and Hetty's liaison and we are privy to all the honest, earnest man's outrage at Arthur's weak will and his sense of freedom to do casual wrong without the fear of consequences. Arthur's deepest lesson is that there are misdeeds that are truly irrevocable. Yet his life has tended to show him otherwise. Arthur has grown up protected from consequences, cushioned by his hereditary expectations. From his own largesse and an innately kind disposition, he has been happy to dispense whatever is at his disposal to others. But his wealth prevents him from understanding what the poorer man knows: that not everything can be bought or redeemed or repaired by money:

> Arthur's, as you know, was a loving nature. Deeds of kindness were as easy to him as a bad habit: they were the common issue of his weaknesses and his good qualities.... When he was a lad of seven, he one day kicked down an old gardener's pitcher of broth. From no motive but a kicking impulse, not reflecting that it was the old man's dinner; but on learning that sad fact, he took his favourite pencil-case and a silver-hafted knife out of his pocket and offered them as compensation. He had been the same Arthur ever since, trying to make all offences forgotten in benefits. (*AB* 356–7)

But the gardener cannot eat the pencil case or knife for dinner. There are damages that cannot be managed with money; there are non-fungible values. There is loss. Arthur comes up against the sorrowful knowledge of evil on the long-awaited day he inherits the estate and simultaneously learns that Hetty has been charged with infanticide.

In this primitive plotting, Eliot sets up a Nemesis perfectly timed and targeted to illustrate as vividly as possible the law of consequences; in so doing, she risks the realism of a non-providential universe. Yet her realism is embedded not in plot but in character portrayal; here, the unlikely convergence of events divulges Arthur's sense of himself as above the law and Nemesis comes to reveal his subjection to it. Arthur has thought that he has narrowly escaped; that the world, conveniently arranged for him, will allow him to elude the natural laws of sex and the moral consequences of dishonesty. All along he has imagined, from his place of privilege, all the good he will bestow upon Hetty once he comes into the estate, so that what was once a source of pain to her will ultimately be a great aid: perhaps hereafter he might be able to do a great deal for her, and make up to her for all the tears she would shed for him. She would owe the advantage of his care for her in future years to the sorrow she had incurred now. "So," says the narrator ironically, in response to his sophistical thinking, "good comes out of evil. Such is the beautiful arrangement of things!" (*AB* 358). Arthur's theory of seed and harvest is not natural nor Christian but self-serving utilitarian sophistry.

Yet, in spite of the perfectly timed Nemesis, Eliot stops short of setting up her own providential universe. She does not offer us a plot in which Arthur is taught a lesson as he and Hetty face carefully apportioned lots of punishment. She does not save the blameless Adam from suffering. Eliot chooses not to make a world that minimizes or reverses harm so long as regret is evident. Even in a world where the consequences of natural and moral law do enforce some order, justice is impossible to achieve or even to define. Eliot's most complicated and radical suggestion in the novel is that personal suffering can come in unjust allotment and remain never adequately redeemed, not by a second chance nor even by granting the sufferer powerful new knowledge and sympathy. Some suffering simply must be suffered.

As if in renunciation of all the tidy, religiously hopeful, letters of Marian Evans in her early twenties, the novel rejects and refutes compensation, justification, and the glorification of suffering. Through the figure of Adam, the readers confront the intolerable attempt to compensate for others' suffering after having caused it, as well as the attempt to justify it with its positive outcomes for others. Adam fires upon Arthur for trying to deny the harsh truth that "Evil's evil and sorrow's sorrow, and you can't alter its nature wrapping it up in other words. Other folks were not created for my sake, that I should think all square when things turn out well for me" (*AB* 573). Later, when a friend hesitatingly suggests that Adam may perhaps be better off never having married Hetty and that the tragedy at least prevented this mistake, Adam refuses it all: "Good come out of it!... That doesn't alter th' evil; her ruin can't be undone. I hate that talk o' people, as if there was a way o' making amends for everything. They'd more need be brought to see as the wrong they do can never be altered. When a man's spoiled his fellow creature's life, he's no right to comfort himself with thinking good may come out of it: somebody else's good doesn't alter her shame and misery" (*AB* 504).

Marian maintained throughout her life a profound, unshakeable belief that suffering was morally transformative for the sufferer, that there were lessons of sympathy and charity that could be learned only through suffering. Yet by the time she wrote *Adam Bede*, she had lived long enough to see that much suffering came out of unequal gender and class relations. Thus she greeted suffering more hesitantly, with an all-important caveat: it is possible to "pay" with one's own pain for the personal benefit of increased awareness, greater knowledge, and greater power, in Spinozan-influenced terms; yet one may never affirm the value of someone else's suffering, especially if one reaps its benefit. It is this blurring that Adam hears in Arthur's desire to make things right, in any words of consolation urging him to see the prevention of his marriage as a gift of any kind. Adam remains focused on the distinction between persons: Hetty has suffered and nothing can change her suffering; it is irreducible. Even though Adam is incorrect that she is entirely innocent, he is correct that she bears the burden of all the misdeeds, misprisions, and injustices laid bare in the novel, among them the fact that her own family feels shame and betrayal more than the desire to protect her. And she is sentenced to death in all her ignorance, for all her ignorance.

This is a terrible impasse in a novel seeking to represent its people's pastoral life in its true colors. And, one might reasonably ask, given George Eliot's intense commitment to a delineation of the effect of religious ideas and practices on the "people," as she articulated in the review essay on *The Natural History of German Life* and elsewhere, where are Christian faith, community, and teaching in this story? Is there any way to avoid reading Hetty as a sacrificial function, one that allows everyone but herself atonement and salvation and shores up the conventional Victorian sexual standard that punished women far more severely than men, thus indicting rather than glorifying the central Christian narrative?

Indeed, Adam's adamant and lengthily developed refusal of Hetty as sacrifice is the main indicator that George Eliot rejected such a function for her. Perhaps we might read Hetty instead as an effect of failed Christian culture, rather than its apotheosis. She knows no doctrine and she holds no belief in powers of any kind. The moral teachings of the Gospel have eluded her entirely: duty has no hold on her. She bears no natural emotional attachment or gratitude toward the family that took her in after her own parents died. All ego, Hetty is the first of many Eliot antiheroes to be driven to very bad ends by unrestrained ego rather than by innate evil. Animated by the animal force to survive and live, her actions are guided by an aversion to pain and an attraction to pleasure.

But it is not only the untaught who grow up untouched by the Gospel. In spite of Arthur's status and education, George Eliot ascribes to him not a single thought or consideration connected to any Christian teaching. Arthur's beloved tutor, the parish rector Rev. Irwine, is not shaped by the deep awareness of the possibility of sin or the necessity for grace to overcome the temptations and incentives to wrong doing in this world. The narrator describes Mr. Irwine as thoroughly worldly, in this way overlapping with Arthur and Hetty: "epicurean, if you will, with no enthusiasm, no self-scourging sense of duty" (*AB* 111). Yet, perhaps as a result of his early enthusiasm for poetry and ethics, Mr. Irwine has become a man of great compassion, humility, sense, and duty. He is a man "of a sufficiently subtle moral fibre" that he is "tender to other men's failings, and unwilling to impute evil" (*AB* 111, 113); this quality the narrator unequivocally names "charity," with all its Christian resonance (*AB* 113). Yet Mr. Irwine's commitments are all funneled through practical, humanist teachings rather than Christian doctrine or belief in the divine.

Mr. Irwine's genuine, generous, and tolerant care for his parishioners does not extend to "serious alarms about the[ir] souls," and he sees religious custom rather than doctrine, or even basic belief, as meaningful in their lives: "If he had been in the habit of speaking theoretically, he would perhaps have said that the only healthy form religion could take in such minds was that of certain dim but strong emotions, suffusing themselves as a hallowing influence over the family affections and neighbourly duties" (*AB* 112). In a complicated combination of class privilege, the idiosyncrasies of personality, and historical circumstances, Mr. Irwine's predominating trust in human character, instead of the Christian minister's respect for the strength of sin, plays a painful role in allowing the tragedy to unfold.

The villagers of Hayslope, those for whose souls Rev. Irwine cares, are nominal Anglicans. They go to church weekly, many of them read the Bible, and they feel those "dim but strong emotions" of which their rector is aware. Adam's aged mother, for instance, when led in prayer after her husband's death, "without grasping any distinct idea, without going through any course of religious motions," feels "a vague sense of goodness and love, and of something right lying underneath and beyond all this sorrowing life" (*AB* 159). "Vague," "dim," "something," "a sense": such is the intangible Christian culture Eliot ascribes to the world in which she grew, made material by repeated practices and the continuity of generations in one place. Reminding us that Marian Evans's own father and brother were buried in the parish where they lived and married, Rev. Irwine sees the church's benefits to the peasants who stay rooted in the same parish where their "fathers worshipped...and the sacred piece of turf where they lay buried" (*AB* 112).

The narrator expresses strong appreciation for the specific religious forms in which human relations are expressed and through which human beings find aid. Such relations cease to be sustained or threaten to weaken considerably without the historical customs that embody them; at times, the aid can be found in no other way. Rather than Rev. Irwine's sense that attending church or residing in the parish exert beneficial effects, Eliot focuses upon an active religious practice, confession, to contend against its dangerous absence. Unsurprisingly, she is less interested in rituals of absolution than in the capacity of the human being to articulate their experience, to take responsibility for it within a monologue that is then answered, at length, by another passible human voice. This person is not necessarily an intimate, but someone brought close at that moment as a fellow human being embroiled in the same "troublous medium," as she would put it years later in *Middlemarch*.

At the beginning of his involvement with Hetty, Arthur wants moral aid; he knows that what he is doing is wrong yet his will fails him whenever he encounters Hetty. Arthur decides to confide in Mr. Irwine in order to safeguard himself against further wrong, and he sets out to breakfast with the rector. The narrator has his own ironic thoughts about the combination of breakfast and confession in the modern age:

> The progress of civilization has made a breakfast or a dinner an easy and cheerful substitute for more troublesome and disagreeable ceremonies. We take a less gloomy view of our errors now our father confessor listens to us over our egg and coffee. We are more directly conscious that rude penances are out of the question for gentlemen in an enlightened age, and that mortal sin is not compatible with an appetite for muffins. (*AB* 207)

In the novel's turning point toward tragedy, Arthur cannot go forward with his resolution to confess and receive the aid he needs to steel his will. The narrator comments not on Arthur's weakness of will here, but on the absence of forms:

> Still, there was this advantage in the old rigid forms, that they committed you to the fulfilment of a resolution by some outward deed: when you have put your mouth to one end of a hole in a stone wall, and are aware that there is an expectant ear at the other end, you are more likely to say what you came out with the intention of saying. (*AB* 207)

Religious rituals can be more than rote activities. They can materialize intention so that human beings can more easily envision a standard beyond their own desires and satisfy an acknowledged duty.

Whereas Arthur has no religious lexicon, Adam possesses a conscience inseparable from his religious orientation. Adam, clearly drawn from Marian's love for her own father, is described as an unusually talented workman, disciplined, curious, with joy in his work, which he sees as part of God's world:

> there's the sperrit o' God in all things and all times – weekday as well as Sunday – and i' the great works and inventions, and i' the figuring and the mechanics. And God helps us with our headpieces and our hands as well as with our souls; and if a man does bits o' jobs out o' working hours – builds a oven for 's wife to save her from going to the bakehouse, or scrats at his bit o' garden and makes two potatoes grow istead o' one, he's doing more good, and he's just as near to God, as if he was running after some preacher and a-praying and a-groaning. (*AB* 53–4)

Adam understands his vocation and his talents as God's gifts and he sees God's will put into action by good work of all kinds. At the same time, he is drawn to the teachings of the Gospel. The religious forms which nurtured him develop into the channel for his deepest feelings and his voice bursts out in hymns because he can't help himself. The church service, which "was a channel to him.... its interchange of beseeching cries for help, with outbursts of faith and praise – its recurrent responses and the familiar rhythm of its collects, seemed to speak for him as no other form of worship could have done" (*AB* 245). Yet the narrator suggests that these forms may be interchangeable, rather than carrying eternal value; Adam's attachment comes from having woven these particular rhythms into himself over years: "the secret of our emotions," comments the narrator, "never lies in the bare object but in its subtle relations to our own past" (*AB* 245).

Quite different is the approach the novel represents in its compelling Methodist preacher, Dinah, a figure based upon a dramatic story of sin and prison conversion told to Marian Evans by her Aunt Evans in her youth. To Dinah, the Gospel is eternal truth, not the moral channel for individuals living at particular moments in history, as the narrator hints. On the strength of her vocation and her fervent belief, Dinah, who is Hetty's cousin, saves a mute Hetty from facing death utterly alone and heals the family's and community's wounds. Dinah links the novel back to the time of John Wesley when, the narrator says, "a crowd of rough men and weary-hearted women drank in a faith which was a rudimentary culture, which linked their thoughts with the past, lifted their imagination above the sordid details of their own narrow lives, and suffused their souls with the sense of a pitying, loving, infinite Presence, sweet as summer to the houseless needy" (*AB* 81–2). It is precisely this education of culture, this imaginative work forging a link to the past and a link to others, a sense of something beyond self, however intangible and amorphous and unknown (a "sense," again), that Hetty lacks.

Dinah's profound gifts as a preacher come from her deep desire to share the good she has found in the Gospel, in the idea of the savior Jesus as suffering man and as powerful Son of God. She asks the simple, forceful questions that link religious ideas to the experience of living: "Will God take care of us when we die? And has he any comfort for us when we are lame and sick and helpless? Perhaps, too, he is angry with us; else why does the blight come, and the bad harvests, and the fever, and all sorts of pain and trouble? For our life is full of trouble, and if God sends us good, he seems to send bad too. How is it? how is it?" (*AB* 70). These questions are articulated early in the novel and their simple language and syntax stand out, as they remain for the reader the most forceful formulation of the questions of theodicy driving the novel. The novel's people of faith can say only, as Adam does, "I'm not th' only man that's got to do without happiness i' this life.... It's God's will, and that's enough for us: we shouldn't know better how things ought to be than He does, I reckon, if we was to spend our lives i' puzzling" (*AB* 371), which is not too different than his pious Methodist brother Seth's belief that "we've nothing to do but to obey and to trust" (*AB* 81). Yet no one says that the suffering is welcome, that it promises reward, that being its spectator is one of earth's beauties.

Dinah, with her powerful prayer, faith, and love, is the only figure who can save Hetty.[6] At the story's darkest moment, Dinah comes to Hetty in her jail cell, as she awaits execution (which is commuted to transportation at the last moment). Dinah refuses to accept Hetty's silence out of fear for the latter's soul, the fear Mr. Irwine constitutionally cannot feel. She prays with Hetty and tells her that she must confess what took place so that Jesus will be her friend and she will not be alone when she dies: "God's love and mercy can overcome all things – our ignorance, and weakness, and all the burthen of our past wickedness – all things but our wilfil sin; sin that we cling to, and will not give up" (*AB* 495). All the trouble this realist novel has recorded is here laid upon God's mercy. Dinah redirects human relations to human–divine relations, as if in the reverse of Feuerbachian anthropology: "She cries to me.... Saviour! It is a blind cry to thee," and, in the end, Hetty confesses (*AB* 495).

Once Hetty begins to speak, she tells her long, harrowing tale without stopping, reinforcing the novel's suggestion that religious channels can enable otherwise impossible human growth. Hetty describes her situation: impossible to return in abject shame to Hayslope, unable to find Arthur, burdened by an unwanted baby whose cries nonetheless pierce her, she buried the baby with a light cover of grass and chips, hoping someone might hear the cries and rescue the child. She returned to the spot, pulled by the cries still ringing in her ears, and the baby was gone; at that, she says, "My heart went like a stone," the scriptural metaphor for impenetrability (*AB* 500). What are the effects of this confession? First, Dinah has helped to exonerate Hetty somewhat; in spite of having offered no self-defense at the trial, Hetty is no hardened killer. Additionally, Hetty's long speech softens her heart. With Dinah's aid, Hetty becomes capable of seeing not only herself but those others who until now have been entirely outside her ken. She apologizes to Adam; she sends a message to her family; she tries to find forgiveness for Arthur so that God will forgive her too (*AB* 506). Dinah concludes that "the brethren sometimes err in measuring the Divine love by the sinner's knowledge," marking the ignorance that characterizes not only Hetty but so many of the Hayslope villagers, living in a veritable absence of informing ideas (*AB* 502).

If Hetty reaps any benefit whatsoever from the tragedy of her life, it is in her tiny steps beyond egoism, toward a child's vision of Jesus, as guided by Dinah. Yet in a novel that underscores the short-term effects of religious teaching on the country folk, it is difficult to take Hetty's conversion as a lasting benefit, especially given that she is cut off from Dinah and from everything and everyone familiar when she is transported. Hetty's sentence allows for no effects of her confession nor her repentance, and no reintegration with her family. Then report comes that she has died at the end of her sentence, on the eve of her return to England, cementing the tragedy at the center of the novel and reasserting Arthur's lesson: that there are evils with no redress. Meanwhile, Arthur, chastened and weakened by suffering, but perhaps purified and refined, too, bears the possibility of reintegration years hence. In the novel's most redemptive act, Adam and Dinah ultimately marry after the passage of time. Only Hetty suffers without any benefit.

The end of the novel is preoccupied with harvest: personal happiness in a world of suffering others. First, Dinah must face the thorny problem of seeking her own happiness rather than living for others; she must begin to believe that her marriage is God's will for her rather than selfish promptings. Then both she and Adam must be able to distinguish between the irreducible suffering of Hetty and their own new, deeper love that the scenes of suffering prepared. Rev. Irwine is content to think, "what better harvest from that painful seed-time could there be than this? The love that had brought hope and comfort in the hour of despair, the love that had found its way to the dark prison cell and to poor Hetty's darker soul—this strong gentle love was to be Adam's companion and helper till death" (*AB* 578). But Eliot could not fully accept this metaphor herself because of its unspoken costs, and so she has Dinah and Adam wrestle a new truth out of their inherited teachings.

Remarkably enough, Eliot located this new truth—this new relation between love and suffering—in the figure of Jesus Christ and allowed Dinah to preach it. Dinah understands love to be made of sorrow: the Man of Sorrows takes up the cross of sin and suffering out of Infinite Love; thus in the human world "our love is one with our sorrow.... Surely it is not true blessedness to be free from sorrow, while there is sorrow and sin in the world: sorrow is then a part of love, and love does not seek to throw it off" (*AB* 374). If love and sorrow were separable, then love might be egoism, might allow others' pain to pay for it. Scriptural seed time and harvest raised ethical problems that the Calvinist Mary Ann Evans had not found troubling: George Eliot, by contrast, reached for a model of simultaneous, eternal, and universal joy and suffering. Joy would never displace suffering, not even for the most faithful Christian, because such was not the nature of human existence.

Mature joy could now be refigured as love that held sorrow at its heart. George Eliot described it as a gift. The gift was not being exempt from all the burdens and griefs of life, but *bearing them alongside a beloved other*. Dinah puts it like this: paired with Adam, she feels the "fulness of strength to bear and do our heavenly Father's will, that I had lost before" (*AB* 576). Marian described her life with G. H. Lewes likewise, reflecting on the reality of effort and continued struggle, but describing it as transformed and made endurable by love: "We are leading no life of self-indulgence, except indeed, that being happy in each other, we feel everything easy" (GEL 2: 214). The love she had found with him, she wrote, was simply the "deepest and gravest joy in all human experience" (GEL 2: 182).

Adam Bede may have challenged orthodoxies in its questions, but it is hard not to feel its author's pull toward religious resolutions, even if they required de-emphasizing some doctrines and employing others in their place. In *Adam Bede*, the deepest Christianity is shown to hold sufficient experiential answers for its believers. Yet the novel's most fluid religious affirmation may well be its description of divine gifts, of those talents and tendencies experienced as coming from beyond the self. The gift of speaking well, whether preaching genuinely, confessing, confiding, comforting, learning: its source is simply the "Unknown." As the narrator puts it, "After our subtlest analysis of the mental process, we must still say, as Dinah did, that our highest thoughts and our best deeds are all given to us" (*AB* 159). The way lives unfold is equally mysterious. In the same way that water cannot be told to "Flow here but flow not there," that you cannot "lecture the trees for growing in their own shape," Dinah, like Adam, sees God's spirit informing the developmental processes of each human life (*AB* 134, 136). As she puts it, "we are led on, like the little children, by a way that we know not" (*AB* 135). Dinah waits, at all turning points, to determine as best she can what God wills for her.

In a way, Dinah's model—waiting for "a leading"—could not be farther from the life Marian led, as she broke from the Church and united herself with Lewes. And yet, there is a deep resonance: Marian could hardly have predicted her path when she first addressed the experience of human suffering in the letters of her early twenties. She could hardly have predicted her path when she became a translator and then an editor, reviewer, and journalist. She could hardly have predicted her path when a series of possible loves failed to answer her needs. Yet she followed a strong internal directive, striving, when she could, to set aside her fear. In Lewes she found a man who would help her realize her gifts. And in Blackwood she found extraordinary faith. Before she put pen to paper to begin *Adam Bede*, Blackwood wrote her: "In continuing to write for the Magazine I beg of all things that you will not consider yourself hampered in any way. Of course I will say when I think you are failing to produce the effect you intend or otherwise missing the mark, but unless you write entirely from the bent of your own genius or knowledge or observation it would not be worth my while to make any comments at all" (GEL 2: 352).

Blackwood's carte blanche told George Eliot that he, too, believed she should trust herself and she did, disregarding convention and circulating-library principles in life and writing alike. To Charles Bray she wrote, "There is no one who is in the least likely to know what I can, could, should or would write" (GEL 2: 444). In April 1858, two months after Blackwood had come to know precisely who George Eliot was, Marian and Lewes left for Germany, where she would continue work on *Adam Bede*. In July, in Dresden, where she and Lewes were satisfied to seek no society but that of the great painters in the galleries, she described herself writing "uninterruptedly and with great enjoyment in the long, quiet mornings" (GEL 2: 504). For both of them, joy was at hand.

Marian had followed the bent of her own branches, the flow of her own stream. The wrestle and anguish of her past was changing form:

> It would be a poor result of all our anguish and our wrestling if we won nothing but our old selves at the end of it—if we could return to the same blind loves...the same feeble sense of that Unknown towards which we have sent forth irrepressible cries in our loneliness. Let us rather be thankful that our sorrow lives in us as an indestructible force, only changing its form, as forces do, and passing from pain into sympathy—the one poor word which includes all our best insight and our best love. (*AB* 531)

Marian's best resolution to the problem of egoism, of the displacement of others' suffering with one's own joy, was to rededicate herself to sharing the word.

Notes

1. In her journal of January 8, 1858, she listed: "Froude, Dickens, Thackeray, Tennyson, Ruskin, [the scientist Professor Michael] Faraday, the author of "Companions of My Solitude" [Lewes's dear friend Arthur Helps], [the mountaineer and entertainer] Albert Smith, and Mrs. [Jane] Carlyle (GEL 2: 418).

2. Another example: "Under the influence of the intense happiness I have enjoyed in my married life from thorough moral and intellectual sympathy, I have at last found out my true vocation, after which my nature had always been feeling and striving uneasily without finding it" (GEL 3: 186).
3. Sean Gaston, "George Eliot and the Anglican Reader," *Literature and Theology*, 31.3 (2017), pp. 318–37, doi:10.1093/litthe/frw026, p. 320.
4. It is noteworthy that her mother's death is never referred to explicitly in any extant correspondence. See Davis, *Transferred Life*, pp. 23–4, who writes especially sensitively about the transmutation of that loss in the fiction.
5. On the monstrosity of the redemption of suffering, and its conflict with the ethics of sympathy, see Herbert, *Evangelical*, pp. 173, 194. At the same time, Mary Ann's pious expressions at such deaths were not exceptional among Victorians.
6. Kreuger, by contrast, sees Eliot as maintaining an "ironic distance" from Dinah, refusing to "align herself with that [preaching] power, just as she declined direct involvement in the public crusades of her day, particularly feminist ones" (*Repentance*, p. 255).

9
"Pilgrims on Earth," 1859–1860

It was only a matter of months between the completion of *Adam Bede* and the beginning of *The Mill on the Floss*, Marian's first novel to be set before a public aware of its author's controversial identity. *The Mill on the Floss* was exposing in other ways at well. It is considered the most autobiographical of George Eliot's novels, with its long, detailed representation of childhood and early youth, the life of family and clan, in provincial England.[1] Yet it is worth focusing here not only on its function as autobiographical memory but on its place in George Eliot's unfolding career in the early 1860s and her aim to offer a picture of the people's lives, particularly at the intersection of socioeconomic experience and religious faith and practice.

The unstated element of that otherwise well-articulated project was gender: what difference did it make to be female? Having found a solid partner in Lewes, perhaps Marian could depict now with greater security and sympathy the first in a series of distinct female protagonists united by their earnest striving and their lonely suffering, blighted mostly by their ignorance of the collective human knowledge so effortlessly gleaned over the centuries but making no part of a girl's experience. As in *Adam Bede*, we can see George Eliot honing her representation of a working and agrarian England barely touched by Christian faith, with the result that many of her characters have to "mak[e] out a faith" for themselves from the materials that fall to hand; then, the more fully they believe, the less they fit into a world shaped by Christian custom and calendar but not in the least informed by what Eliot saw as the higher claims of "religion": "something, clearly, that lies outside personal desires, that includes resignation for ourselves and active love for what is not ourselves" (*MOF* 386).

The Mill on the Floss is a hard book, its heroine absorbed by the difficulty of facing what its author described as the greatest problem of human life, "the shifting relation between passion and duty," with only the chanciest of company and no tools (*MOF* 627). Maggie is passionate, imaginative, compassionate in all directions, eager for love and recognition. Yet she is terribly limited by circumstances, by lack of education (her far less intellectually able brother, Tom, gets the private classical education she might have benefited from), by a dearth of books and society of cultured minds. When Maggie's loving, yet proud and impetuous, father loses the family mill to processes of law and power he cannot fathom, Maggie must leave school. Tom must leave school as well, yet his gender allows him entry to a broader world, while Maggie is confined at home, comforting her bewildered parents and whiling away time in empty, repeated activity.

The narrator imagines that the reader will feel the lack Maggie can barely name: the need for some idea to lift her above the sordid facts of her life, the need for a theory that might grant an ethical meaning or counterpoint to rigid custom and habit, and an explanation for suffering and privation. We are meant to recognize how intensely Maggie needs not only the theory, "this wide hopeless yearning for that something, whatever it was, that was greatest and best on this earth," but the light and ingenuity by which to apply a general idea to the specific, complicated trials of her own anomalous life, her "burthen of larger wants than others seemed to feel," and decidedly more than her brother feels (*MOF* 381).

The abiding emotional conditions of the novel—the lonely longing within narrow horizons of time and space (childhood and provincial life)—clearly resonate as autobiographical, as do the strained relations between brother and sister. Yet it is striking that critics tend not to point out how much this novel *departs* from autobiography in its depiction of its heroine's material and external conditions. Mary Ann belonged to a family whose economic standing rose over the course of her youth, affording her an increasing sense of material security, not to mention as many books as she liked, first from the library of Arbury Hall, opened to her expressly by its mistress, and later, those she ordered on her father's account with a local bookseller. The young Mary Ann Evans thus had access to a world of accumulated knowledge and adopted for herself theory, code, and explanation in evangelical Christian faith and Calvinist doctrine.

Then, too, Mary Ann had interlocutors: Maria Lewis; her school friend Martha Jackson; her Aunt and Uncle Evans; and parish figures in Chilvers Coton. Maggie's journey is far more difficult and lonely than Mary Ann's in all these ways. Even more notable, Mary Ann's work as she approached adulthood was to claim independence from the strictures of Christian teaching, rather than to turn toward it as Maggie does, in an act of independent, thoroughly countercultural self-formation. Perhaps Mary Ann's reverse move had been possible precisely because of the material ways she differed from a Maggie Tulliver.

In limited autobiographical and mostly counter-autobiographical ways, then, *The Mill on the Floss* returns us to Marian Evans's desire for a natural history of English Protestant life. In other words, we need to read this novel not only, or even primarily, as a return to Mary Ann Evans's childhood but as part of an adult novelist's program to consider faith under conditions of relative poverty, and a lack of culture and education. Maggie becomes representative of what the narrator tells us was called at the time "emphasis," or "emphatic belief," and which belonged to the poor far more than to "good society" (*MOF* 385). Maggie, in her spiritual need, represents for the narrator full classes of laboring human beings who survive without most physical comforts, let alone luxuries, and "have absolutely needed an emphatic belief, life in this unpleasurable shape demanding some solution even to unspeculative minds" (*MOF* 385). Yet the narrator does not leave it there, where such an analysis might suggest that the laboring classes take up religious belief dumbly or desperately; that its truth is negligible; and that if only they did not have material need, they would see their way clear to abandoning it. Nor does the narrator suggest that religious belief is fed to the laboring classes by masters seeking to strengthen the status quo of society's hierarchical structure.

Instead, the narrator describes a suffering majority that enables the powerful minority to enjoy its privileges. Chief among the privileges of "good society" is the absence of any need for "principles and beliefs" beyond those of "an extremely moderate kind"; even those moderate beliefs are "presupposed," but never discussed, because the only eligible subjects are those which "can be touched with a light and graceful irony" (*MOF* 385). How is this light irony and high living—velvet carpets, claret, opera, thoroughbred horses, ballrooms, celebrity intellectuals and clergy—to be maintained? On the backs, says the narrator, of a "wide and arduous national life" (*MOF* 385). This life is "condensed in unfragrant deafening factories, cramping itself in mines, sweating at furnaces, grinding, hammering, weaving... or else, spread over sheepwalks, and scattered in lonely houses and huts on the clayey or chalky cornlands" (*MOF* 385). Often, "it spends its heavy years often in a chill, uncarpeted fashion amidst family discord unsoftened by long corridors" (*MOF* 385).

As in *Adam Bede*, here, too, George Eliot makes the inequality of lots a central ethical and social problem. Maggie's existential need—and the need of many struggling human beings—emerges in a social system that is not equitable. While in *Adam Bede* this inequality displayed itself mainly in the vestiges of feudal relations, in *The Mill on the Floss* the scene shifts to the incursion of industrial and commercial relations where agrarian ones had previously held sway. Like the other massively popular mid-century novelist, Charles Dickens (the only person to whom Eliot requested that a presentation copy of the novel be sent), George Eliot was committed to exposing the social relations shaping individual lives; unlike Dickens, however, Eliot was drawn to representing the interaction and often the ill fit between broad, external conditions and special, internal experience (GEL 3: 279). Maggie is nothing if not isolated by the broad social conditions within which she lives.

Maggie, who is seeking an illumined, unified life, lives among nominal Christians for whom "church was one thing and common sense another," as the narrator puts it, capturing an entire mode of folk consciousness in the phrase (*MOF* 366). The town of St Ogg's has long been insulated from the Gospel: "One aged person remembered how a rude multitude had been swayed when John Wesley preached in the cattle-market; but for a long while it had not been expected of preachers that they should shake the souls of men" (*MOF* 184). Maggie has no sectarian church which might provide "some warmth of brotherhood by walling in the sacred fire" (*MOF* 372). In one of the most polemical moments in the novel, the narrator describes the utter failure of the parish priest, Dr. Kenn, to influence his parishioners toward charity and mercy by noting that the residents of St Ogg's have ignored more powerful teachers than Dr. Kenn:

> they maintained [their views] in opposition to a higher authority, which they had venerated longer. That authority had furnished

a very explicit answer to persons who might inquire where their social duties began, and might be inclined to take wide views as to the starting-point. The answer had not turned on the ultimate good of society, but on "a certain man" who was found in trouble by the wayside. (*MOF* 637)

Referring to Luke 18:35, when Jesus restores sight to a blind man whom the multitude tries to silence from calling out to him, George Eliot describes the people of St Ogg's as lacking the basic capacity to respond to human need. Maggie cannot turn to her neighbors in trouble, because the deepest Christian ethics of "discipline and fraternity" are not widely shared (*MOF* 625).

Alone, Maggie finds her ballast in critical years, between the time she is thirteen and fifteen, in a religious text that was precious to Marian over her entire lifetime: *The Imitation of Christ* by Thomas à Kempis. Marian read in this book during the composition of the novel and throughout her life; near her death, she gave it as a gift to her second husband, John Cross (GEL 3: 205). Even in the heat of her early apostasy, Mary Ann could distinguish between "what [she] believe[d]" to have been the "moral teaching of Jesus himself," which she "admire[d] and cherish[ed]," and the doctrines that succeeded his life (GEL 1: 130). She honored the teaching with a lifelong devotional reading practice of *The Imitation of Christ*, a book that was predicated upon a person "taking her stand out of herself, and looking at her own life as an insignificant part of a divinely guided whole" (*MOF* 384). However much Marian's own adulthood repudiated many of the severe asceticisms taught by *The Imitation of Christ*, some of which she practiced in her evangelical period, she nonetheless never trivialized nor doubted her lifelong inquiry into the dangers of egoism or her concern over the questionable ethics of personal happiness in a world of widespread and unevenly experienced suffering. Likewise, her ambivalence about the limits of obedience to authority and the claims of duty took force precisely from the *seriousness* she accorded those values, clearly articulated in *The Imitation of Christ* (GEL 3: 231).

Maggie encounters *The Imitation of Christ* at a point of despair. She has lost all her childhood books in the sale of the family's possessions. The few books remaining seem thin to her; she perpetually wishes for books "with *more* in them" (*MOF* 379). She enters a crisis in which "[s]he rebelled against her lot, she fainted under its loneliness";

she feels "fits even of anger and hatred towards her father and mother who were so unlike what she would have them to be" (*MOF* 380). Searching with little hope for "some key that would enable her to understand and, in understanding, endure, the heavy weight that had fallen on her young heart," she turns listlessly to the string of books brought to her one day by the heroically kindhearted packman, Bob Jakin, who seeks to comfort her for those she lost (*MOF* 379). Maggie opens *The Imitation of Christ* and begins to read the fourteenth-century text, guided by the voice of the monk and the markings of an earlier reader: "some hand, now for ever quiet, had made at certain passages strong pen and ink marks, long since browned by time" (*MOF* 382). The sudden textual presence of an anonymous, wise guide and companion, all the more present for his bodily absence, allows Maggie a place in a chain of transmission that feels to her intensely personal.

The reader of *The Mill on the Floss* is tossed into this chain of transmission as well, mediated for us by George Eliot's selective quotation from Thomas à Kempis. Nowhere else in the works of George Eliot do we encounter such extended quotation from a single text. "Know that the love of thyself doth hurt thee more than anything in the world," Maggie reads, with all the intensity of a first meeting of foreign ideas bracingly relevant to her own life. Here, in its most unadorned form, readers, too, encounter this early expression of the fight against egoism that shaped all the work of George Eliot and that, as Stefan Collini has described, shaped the dominant moral sensibility of the Victorian educated classes.[2] As Collini argues, an "obsessive antipathy to selfishness" and a "constant anxiety about apathy and infirmity of the will" dogged Victorian intellectuals when they considered the moral obligations incumbent on individuals in society.[3] Yet Collini does not explore what Eliot so successfully captures: the revelatory aspect that moral teaching could assume for the young or less educated. The priority of concern and duty to others before the self could be experienced not only as a burden but also as opening onto new consciousness, at times, greater freedom, and, certainly, greater spiritual satisfaction.

The monk and the earlier reader speak to Maggie across history, "testif[ying] to the sameness of a human soul's belief and experience" lived "under the same silent far-off heavens, and with the same passionate desires, the same strivings, the same failures, the same weariness"

(*MOF* 384–5). This repeated "sameness" is not mill-like monotony, though, but the fellowship of shared passibility: the "we mortals" so central to George Eliot's consciousness. Maggie takes the book to herself and over the course of two years reads in it devoutly, alongside the Bible and John Keble's *The Christian Year*. "They filled her mind with a continual stream of rhythmic memories" (a phrase recalling *Adam Bede*), training her from the inside in their lessons of renunciation, their stress of obedience above understanding, their refusal of pride over others, and their cultivation of humble self-criticism (*MOF* 387). The novel's final crisis will confirm the value of teachings so fully integrated that they alone survive when crushing loss allows the personality access only to its automatic resources.

From the intensity of her loneliness, young Maggie feels saved: "Here, then, was a secret of life...here was insight, and strength, and conquest, to be won by means entirely within her own soul, where a supreme teacher was waiting to be heard" (*MOF* 383–4). *The Imitation of Christ* in fact alternates among narrating voices, from the voice of the Disciple to the voice of Jesus, "the Beloved," to the voice of God. Some chapters are organized not as monologues but as dialogues between the Son and the Father. Consequently, "thee" and "thou," shift from referring to the reader to Jesus, to God, asking the reader to inhabit different positions in relation to both speaker and addressee. "We" often functions as the speaking subject in sentences that vary from descriptive (and often psychological in their interest) to prescriptive, suggesting that this may be an unacknowledged tonal point of origin for George Eliot's characteristic narratorial "we."

As Maggie reads the sentences organized by that inclusive "we," she finds herself: "God has thus ordered it, that we may learn to bear one another's burdens; for no man is without fault; no man but hath his burden; no man sufficient of himself; no man wise enough of himself; but we ought to bear with one another, comfort one another, help, instruct, and admonish one another."[4] Maggie adopts Christian renunciation out of her shapeless suffering, seeking "Something that will present motives in an entire absence of high prizes, something that will give patience and feed human love when the limbs ache with weariness and human looks are hard upon us" (*MOF* 386). Maggie trains herself in such teachings as, "When one temptation or tribulation goeth away, another cometh," which recalls one of the most powerful metaphors of *The Mill on the Floss*: Maggie's "life-struggles," which "had lain almost entirely within her own soul, one shadowy army fighting another, and the slain shadows forever rising again" (*MOF* 405).[5]

The Mill on the Floss might be read as Eliot's historically emplotted, gendered version of *The Imitation of Christ*, in its most tragic face. Temptation figures centrally in the novel, replacing the multiple facets of desire with all its worst consequences. Maggie's vitality, her love of this world, concentrate themselves into the passionate wish for human understanding and companionship, innocent enough desires in themselves. Yet repeatedly the figures who might meet that need double as dangerous, forbidden objects of temptation, as if to say that desire is inherently dangerous; that all love threatens to reveal itself as self-love; and that all self-love will ultimately take multiple, innocent others as its cost.

Like an early Christian, Maggie's devotion to the ascetic teaching she adopts for herself leads to the Cross. Revealing both the deep inroads made by specific Christian ideas in English minds—sin, temptation, punishment—and the failure of the Christian ethics of fellowship and charity to inform English social practice, *The Mill on the Floss* illuminates the binds a thinking, poor girl living in the Midlands around the 1820s might find herself in.

In an early scene in which Maggie explains to Philip, the sensitive, artistic, wealthy son of her father's enemy, that she cannot maintain their friendship, she timidly suggests that a certain freedom may come from renunciation. She tells Philip that she has been "a great deal happier,"

> ...since I have given up thinking about what is easy and pleasant, and being discontented because I couldn't have my own will. Our life is determined for us – and it makes the mind very free when we give up wishing and only think of bearing what is laid upon us and doing what is given us to do.   (*MOF* 397)

While Philip contests Maggie's claim by saying "we can never give up longing and wishing while we are thoroughly alive" (*MOF* 397), Maggie embraces the passivity of obedience, clearly learned from such teachings as "It is much safer to obey, than to govern"; "It is a blessed simplicity when a man leaves the difficult ways of questions and disputings, and goes on forward in the plain and firm path of

God's commandments"; "If thou intend and seek nothing else but the will of God and the good of thy neighbour, thou shalt thoroughly enjoy internal liberty."[6] The dangers of choice were apparent to the young Mary Ann Evans, who wrote in a letter of 1839 that her wish for "any cross but" the one God had chosen for her was a clear proof that no other trial would answer the purpose: "What a curse it would prove for us to have our own way" (GEL 1: 31). She contended that God had arranged things in precisely the way each person needed. Further, she found herself troubled by the possibility of "leisure and self-direction to an extent that involves fearful responsibility" (GEL 1: 109).

The anxiety over choice and responsibility, and the wish for clear purpose and action, recur throughout the novels of George Eliot, well exceeding questions of passive obedience to God's plan. Perhaps this is why George Eliot focuses Philip's objections in this novel to address primarily what Philip calls Maggie's turn to "narrow asceticism" (*MOF* 402). In a debate that animates the novel and reignites between them over the course of a year, Philip tries to induce the new Maggie to return to her love for "poetry and art and knowledge," arguing that they are "sacred and pure" (*MOF* 402). Her answer is so truthful that it makes her astonishingly vulnerable, were Philip listening fully. She says, "'it would make me in love with this world again, as I used to be; it would make me long to see and know many things – it would make me long for a full life"' (*MOF* 402). A year later, in the reprise of this debate, she clarifies: "I was never satisfied with a *little* of anything. That is why it is better for me to do without earthly happiness altogether" (*MOF* 428). (Recall even her desire for books with "*more*" in them.)

Underappreciated by Philip, Maggie has arrived at a tentative, perhaps flawed, but nonetheless articulate and autonomous self-assessment: her hungers are too great, her "wants" are "illimitable" (*MOF* 425). She cannot imagine desire under control, enjoyment that is moderate or temperate enough not to unsettle her life. Perhaps this is what the young Mary Ann Evans was getting at when she wrote in far more self-protective circumlocution:

> I do not deny that there may be many who can partake with a high degree of zest of all the lawful enjoyments the world can offer and yet live in near communion with their God; who can

> warmly love the creature, and yet be careful that the Creator maintains his supremity in their hearts; but I confess that in my short experience and narrow sphere of action I have never been able to attain this. (GEL 1: 6)

Total abstinence, she added, was much easier than moderation.

Yet Philip does not understand such abstinence as resignation, which he defines as the "willing endurance of a pain that is not allayed – that you don't expect to be allayed" (*MOF* 427). Instead, he sees abstinence as the opposite of resignation. To him, it is attempted escape, a secret form of flight:

> you are shutting yourself up in a narrow self-delusive fanaticism which is only a way of escaping pain by starving into dullness all the highest powers of your nature.... it is stupefaction to remain in ignorance – to shut up all the avenues by which the life of your fellow-men might become known to you. (*MOF* 427)

Philip understands Maggie to have made a rule of something that he sees as limited by time and circumstance: he argues that she "will not always be shut up in [her] present lot,"' but he cannot see that in order to maintain her ties to her family, to survive the weariness and discontent and poverty, to survive the "arduous national life" that Philip has never taken any part of, she must not allow herself to want (*MOF* 402).

Philip is speaking a discourse of self-development, of flourishing, while Maggie is speaking one of survival; he speaks of alternating periods of fortune, while she attempts to grasp something about the nature of human existence. "I used to think I could never bear life if it kept on being the same every day, and I must always be doing things of no consequence, and never know anything greater," says Maggie; "But...is it not right to resign ourselves entirely, whatever may be denied us?" (*MOF* 426–7). While Philip is concentrated on grabbing whatever happiness there may be for himself and for Maggie, Maggie is busy teaching herself not to expect anything in this world: we mortals are only "pilgrims on earth," as *The Imitation of Christ* teaches: "It is vanity to mind only this present life, and not to foresee those things which are to come. It is vanity to set thy love on that which speedily passeth away, and not to hasten thither where everlasting joy abideth."[7]

Alarming Maggie considerably, Philip turns the tables and argues tactically that "It is mere cowardice to seek safety in negations. No character becomes strong in that way. You will be thrown into the world some day, and then every rational satisfaction of your nature that you deny now, will assault you like a savage appetite" (*MOF* 428–9). Here, we might recall Marian's great fear after her father's death that in his absence she would have no restraining force on her appetites, that she would become "earthly sensual and devilish for want of that purifying restraining influence" (GEL 1: 284).[8] Desire was closely linked to wrongdoing and even monstrosity.

Indeed, the novel proceeds in such a way that readers might judge Philip's words to be confirmed. Later, after the death of their father, forbidden by Tom from communication with Philip and working under hard conditions as a teacher, Maggie returns to St Ogg's for a visit. In the home of her devoted, generous cousin, Lucy, Maggie encounters the first sexual temptation of her life in the person of Stephen Guest, who is all but engaged to Lucy. Stephen and Maggie fall passionately in love, and in spite of their efforts to maintain their pledged loyalties, they ultimately betray all their ties, leaving St Ogg's together in an unplanned elopement. Maggie stops the elopement and separates from Stephen before any sexual consummation, but not before the world's opinion is set against her, and not before Lucy and Philip (at this point, Maggie's betrothed) learn of the flight. Tragically, the marriage to Stephen that would exonerate her in the world's opinion, as well as reconcile her brother to her, is the very thing she feels she must shun, in spite of its hypnotic attractions. Although she has succumbed to the temptation of hurting Philip, Lucy, and her family members, Maggie finally refuses to put the "shadow of a wilful sin between [her]self and God" (*MOF* 603). She cannot, she tells Stephen, "consent" with her "whole soul" to feast in joy on others' misery (*MOF* 606).

It is at this plot twist—Maggie's hunger for Stephen and her transgression against her own ethics and society's norms—that Philip may appear to have been correct: perhaps Maggie's natural appetites, too long denied, overwhelm her. Astute critics side implicitly and explicitly with Philip's judgment, suggesting that perhaps *The Imitation of Christ* sustains Maggie briefly, but ultimately it cannot but fail her because its wisdom is flawed.[9] Yet, given Marian's lifelong devotion to *The Imitation of Christ*, it seems unlikely that she would have agreed with such an interpretation of her novel. As Philip later notes in a letter of loving forgiveness to Maggie, she has *not* allowed savage appetites to prevail, not even those society condones because they are conventionally dressed. On the contrary, Maggie turns back at the least opportune moment in this-worldly terms: she is too late to save her reputation, she has likely lost her friends and family, and she refuses the very step she might take to restore her reputation and indulge her passion for Stephen.[10]

In short, Philip acknowledges that he has been only partially correct in his assessment of Maggie and the value of her self-discipline. It is true that she has denied the force of her own discontent; that her "rebellious murmurings," like the children of Israel's, persist; that her desires cannot be rooted out. But none of this marks a failed attempt at self-discipline. In fact, when her temptations rise up against her most forcefully, she is able to overcome them precisely because of the training she has given herself, in practice and doctrine: the world was not made for her pleasure; natural impulses are not to be valorized but effortfully disciplined; the Cross is everywhere.

Against Stephen's arguments and his visible suffering, Maggie's discipline wavers, but eventually re-establishes itself. Maggie regains hold on the single clarity she possesses: "if the past is not to bind us, where does duty lie?" (*MOF* 601–2). True, she has not had the strength to withstand all temptation, but "there was at least this fruit from all her years of striving after the highest and the best – that her soul, though betrayed, beguiled, ensnared, could never deliberately consent to a choice of the lower" (*MOF* 597). When temptation resurfaces in the shape of a letter from Stephen begging her to reconsider and to join him, only the accumulated power of Maggie's years of spiritual practice can sustain her. Even prayer is unattainable: "She sat quite still...without active force enough even for the mental act of prayer" (*MOF* 648). As she sits in silent crisis, "the long past came back to her and with it the fountains of self-renouncing pity and affection, of faithfulness and resolve" (*MOF* 648). And finally, the words "rushed even to her lips... 'I have received the Cross, I have received it from thy hand; I will bear it, and bear it till death, as thou hast laid it upon me'" (*MOF* 648).

From her recitation of verses, Maggie can then initiate her own prayer, one that is non-formulaic and dynamic. Because her religious life has been nearly entirely solitary, her prayer is not composed of religious ideas, as Dinah's prayers are in *Adam Bede*. She has never prayed in the company of a religious mentor, as Janet does alongside Rev. Tryan in "Janet's Repentance." Maggie's aching cries and her natural prostration do not leave her in place but move her forward to new understandings and desires. This is prayer as action:

> "How shall I have patience and strength? O God, am I to struggle and fall and repent again? – has life other trials as hard for me still?" With that cry of self-despair, Maggie fell on her knees against the table, and buried her sorrow-stricken face. Her soul went out to the Unseen Pity *that would be with her to the end*. Surely there was something being taught her by this experience of great need.... "O God, if my life is to be long, let me live to bless and comfort." (*MOF* 649, emphasis mine)

Beginning in despair, Maggie expresses disbelief that she can survive the trials that may yet await her. Her prayer reacts to the pain of the present and the fear of the future; she is overcome by the sharp understanding that this world is defined by the repeating cycle of temptation, sin, and return. Here, Maggie simply falls to her knees, a physical expression of her inability to go on. Now, the narrator tells us, "her soul [goes] out to the Unseen Pity that would be with her to the end," a phrase as unclear and abstract as the table against which she falls is concrete.

But her soul's appeal to a force characterized by its invisibility, its pity, and its company to and through death brings her to a new thought: there must be a lesson in what she suffers. If God is present as pity, suffering cannot be for nothing. It must yield some good. From this realization a thoroughly new prayer leaps from her: "let me live to bless and comfort." Maggie's prayer is a description of spiritual work: she moves her focus from herself to the Unseen Pity, to suffering others. She emerges from her prayer in a different consciousness. As a very young woman, Mary Ann Evans had written: "*I want to feel* what St. Paul so strikingly expresses—that they who live should not henceforth live unto themselves but unto Him who died for them and rose again" (GEL 1: 32, emphasis mine). Eliot allows Maggie that hard-earned feeling.

Whatever meaning one makes of Maggie's death by flood—perhaps she is a martyr, perhaps she is a victim, perhaps death punishes her, or perhaps it offers mercy (as her publisher, John Blackwood, thought)—by the judgment of George Eliot Maggie achieves a painful spiritual victory before the flood. The victory, as Paul Yeoh has pointed out, is not limited to her, which also indicates its importance.[11] Her life, as evidenced by the visitors to her tomb—Philip, Lucy, and Stephen—is sanctified by the knowledge she has painfully gained, but also shared, through her example. In the moments of the flood, some truth of Maggie's struggle and her strength is transmitted to Tom, as well. As the flood rises, Maggie jumps into a boat and rows to save her family. Tom can barely believe his eyes when he sees his sister emerge out of the darkness. She presents "such an entirely new revelation to his spirit, of the depths in life, that had lain beyond his vision which he had fancied so keen and clear" (*MOF* 654). He guesses "a story of almost miraculous divinely-protected effort," and Maggie confirms, "God has taken care of me, to bring me to you" (*MOF* 654). Maggie's "story," of the intense reality of "spiritual conflict," impossible to imagine for nearly all the novel's stolid, conventional, or self-absorbed characters, triumphs at the end of the novel as its reality becomes *the* reality, apparent even to Tom (*MOF* 627). In a novel that asserts George Eliot's strongly held principle that "the responsibility of tolerance lies with those who have the wider vision," Maggie offers a glimpse of the wider vision to those who will live beyond her, as well as to Tom, who will die with her (*MOF* 630).[12]

When the narrator describes the moments of the flood in an ambiguous free, indirect discourse (is it the narrator's "factual" report of the events or Maggie's perspective?)—"it was the transition of death, without its agony – and she was alone in the darkness with God"—all Maggie's solitariness, throughout the novel, is answered in a unity that finally does not pose conflict or temptation (*MOF* 651). If in *Adam Bede* human fellowship and divine fellowship are pursued simultaneously— Dinah comes to Hetty and they pray together, Adam and Dinah's burdens are shouldered together, "till death" (*AB* 578)—Maggie's only companion in the darkness is God. Into that "aloneness with" enters Tom, allowing Maggie and Tom to return to the Edenic unity of childhood, unmediated by speech or thought, in which names correspond to essence (Tom calls out to her, "Magsie"), uttered in "a long deep sob of that mysterious wondrous happiness that is one with pain" (*MOF* 655). Here, Eliot describes a return to the primordial state of things, the moments before God created the world in speech, dividing undifferentiated matter into two categories.

At the time of the writing of *The Mill on the Floss*, Marian doubted whether she would ever be in touch with her own brother again. She completed the novel in March 1860 in a rush of writing and emotion, with her eyes getting "redder and *swollener* every morning as she lives through her tragic story," as Lewes put it in a letter to Blackwood (GEL 3: 269). Eliot would never return to such a deep, free representation of childhood. Nor would she represent again the solitary invention of a sufficient faith, made manifest in a life of prayer and meditation, guided by the imitation of Christ. Maggie would be Eliot's last "pilgrim on earth," learning her way through the cycle of temptation, sin, and return, to find herself finally "alone in the darkness with God," with a mission to bless.

"Spiritual conflict," however, would generate new novels. Difficult and costly choices would constitute their conditions and their climactic moments. George Eliot would affirm the truth that "the great problems of life are not so clear" (*MOF* 607). And in that uncertainty she would find enough material to concentrate her imagination fully in this world, a pilgrim no longer.

Notes

1. Davis reads *The Mill on the Floss* as "the autobiography of why and how George Eliot had had to come into being"; *Transferred*, p. 270.
2. Stefan Collini, *Public Moralists: Political Thought and Intellectual Life in Britain, 1850–1930* (Oxford: Clarendon Press, 1991), p. 63.
3. Collini, *Public*, pp. 65, 85.
4. à Kempis, *Imitation*, p. 28.
5. à Kempis, *Imitation*, p. 17.
6. à Kempis, *Imitation* pp. 14, 154, 73.
7. à Kempis, *Imitation*, pp. 29, 2.
8. See Nina Auerbach's revisionary, stylishly written 1975 account of the "demonic" nature of Maggie Tulliver, which may help us understand Marian's fear of unrestrained female selfhood: "The Power of Hunger: Demonism and Maggie Tulliver," in *George Eliot Scholars*, ed. Beverley Park Rilett, https://GeorgeEliotScholars.org (accessed April 20, 2023).
9. Auerbach is intent on Maggie's failure. Knoepflmacher, another brilliant reader, diminishes the *Imitation*: it is at best "a concealed kernel of truth" that cannot teach Maggie as only experience can (*Early*, p. 218). However, I suggest that Maggie meets experience through its prism.

10. Note the autobiographical dimension of the harsh double standard by which women were judged when they made autonomous, unconventional, or illegible sexual decisions. We might answer Auerbach's analysis by saying that it mattered more to Eliot to dramatize that harshness than to save Maggie.
11. Paul Yeoh's outstanding analysis in "Saints' Everlasting Rest: The Martyrdom of Maggie Tulliver," *Studies in the Novel* 41.1 (2009), pp. 1–21, suggests that Eliot represents "martyrdom as an ethical practice grounded in communicative action" (p. 16).
12. The ethically imaginative Philip comes to see that there is something stronger in Maggie than he has recognized—"I can measure your sacrifice by what I have known," he writes to her—and Lucy simply tells Maggie, "You are better than I am" (*MOF* 635, 643).

10
The "Soul's Own Warrant," 1860–1863

Within a few days of completing *The Mill on the Floss* in late March 1860, Marian and Lewes were on their way to Italy via Paris, to "absorb some new life and gather fresh ideas," as Marian wrote to Blackwood (GEL 3: 279). They spent three months in Italy before returning to London with Lewes's oldest son, seventeen-year-old Charles, who came to live with them. While Marian had corresponded warmly with Lewes's three sons, they now met in person for the first time and Marian became an active stepmother, especially to Charles, who would play a significant role in her daily life for the next two decades, even beyond his father's death. Meanwhile, the news from London was heartening, with Blackwood writing to tell them that *The Mill on the Floss* had sold a remarkable 6,000 copies within weeks of its publication; it had "found its way to the great public" (GEL 3: 307). From this point forward, Marian and Lewes would live with enough financial security that Marian would feel the freedom to write what she liked. By June 1860, on the eve of their return to England, she reported back to Blackwood that both she and Lewes felt "immensely enriched with new ideas and new veins of interest" (GEL 3: 307).

Their Italian journey had pointed Marian toward a novel of the Renaissance after Lewes had suggested to her that the impassioned Dominican preacher and reformer Girolamo Savonarola's "life and times afford fine material for an historical romance" (GEL 3: 295). *Romola* would merge an interior portrait of Savonarola's personal claim to prophecy, announcing Florence as the New Jerusalem, with a set of fictive characters living at the meeting point of Christian and classical inheritances. Marian was not alone in her interest in the

Italian Renaissance, as Victorian artists and scholars eagerly followed the Risorgimento that ended in Italian unification in 1861.[1]

Yet the project, whose stakes Marian raised by casting it from the outset as a great secret, was intensely ambitious for a writer with her intellectual and scholarly capacities. Rather than easing her path, Marian's lifelong capacity to read voraciously, to think historically— that is to say, to understand events, figures, and their contemporary report as fully shaped by a context that could be ignored only at the peril of ignorant misconstrual—established impossible standards for her writing of the novel. Time and place were a barrier: even the "translation" into English of events she imagined transpiring in the language and idioms of Renaissance Florence stood in her way. The contemporary art, the food, the dress, the political and religious jockeying for power, the intellectual exchanges: all these she attempted to capture, while writing a novel that dramatized miscarriages of justice in this world, the absence of the divine word or act, and the mismatch between outward law and inner feeling.

Romola narrates the marriage of the noble but cloistered and utterly unworldly Romola to the winning and beautiful scholarly stranger, Tito. Eliot traces Tito's descent into amorality and immorality as he betrays his promises and his faith to Romola with a second wife and children; he betrays Romola's aging father, who has pinned his hopes on the younger scholar helping him finish his life's work and preserve his collection of manuscripts and antiquities; he betrays his own adoptive father, who was abducted into slavery and has trusted his son to redeem him; and, as a double agent working for his own interests, he betrays multiple political parties in Florence. The novel charts Romola's education as she seeks to escape her poisonous marriage but is redirected by Savonarola to return to the city of Florence, where she can pay her "debt" as a fellow citizen among the poor and suffering, and be true to her own promises (*R* 431).

Romola, as some of its critics noted at the time, was deeply rooted in nineteenth-century concerns. As if to concretize the fears of those who imagined that no morality without divine authority could safeguard social life, *Romola* dramatized the terrible costs of Tito's choices, all made according to hedonistic and utilitarian calculi, rather than in relation to any claims beyond the self's comfort. Yet in tracing Romola's recoil from Tito and her search for a life that prizes more than personal pleasure, Eliot could no longer represent the Christian faith of a Janet Dempster, Dinah Morris, or Maggie Tulliver as a sufficient personal or social solution. *Romola* bridges Eliot's early and later novels by taking the plot line of the search for meaning and fellowship *past* finding Christian faith, to *losing* such faith and surviving its loss. In a sense, Eliot's novels caught up with Marian's autobiography only in the early 1860s.

Romola maintained continuity with Eliot's earlier works in its focus on the inescapable centrality of human suffering and the competing desire for joy.[2] As previously, Eliot represented joy as a dangerous temptation, allied to egoism and duplicity. Again, Eliot found herself tracing in *Romola* a solitary, bruised heroine's search for a clue to live by and to give meaning to suffering; the search is answered in the discovery of Christian teachings of renunciation and their Comtean analogue of living for others. These teachings come to Romola, as they came to the earlier heroines Janet and Maggie, via a powerful male voice with greater spiritual experience, which provides a model and even a motive for living, as well as a conduit to divine comfort. Faith, for them, as for Dinah, comforts tragedy.

Yet both Eliot's novels of the early 1860s—*Romola* and *Silas Marner*, the short novel she wrote in the midst of preparation for *Romola*—moved beyond faith's comforts to crisis: the loss of faith. *Romola*, in particular, allowed Eliot to explore the fallibility of religious authority and the potentially imperative demands of personal autonomy. Now Eliot wrested apart outward law (whether civic or religious) and inward conviction, setting them in extreme conflict, a conflict that was autobiographically resonant both in her apostasy and in her decision to live with Lewes. Submission, the hallmark of her understanding of religious life, could no longer be represented as a satisfying resolution, even within fictional structures.

Before Romola could emerge to embody sacred rebellion, the tale of *Silas Marner* "thrust itself between me and the other book I was meditating," as Marian wrote in her journal in January 1861 (*Journals* 87). She began to write in late September 1860 and six months later the novel was published. *Silas Marner* allowed Eliot to prepare in miniature for writing *Romola*'s lacerating betrayals and disappointment of faith. *Silas Marner* is often remembered as the simple tale of a miser whose golden coins are stolen; shortly thereafter, a golden-haired child appears in the very place from which the coins disappeared, and she teaches him that human connection is the true wealth. Because of the vivid visual substitution of the coins for the girl, and the explicit moral, it is easy to recall *Silas Marner* solely as fable and forget its realist and even sensationalist elements. Yet Eliot provides a backstory for Silas that is all-important to her purposes. Silas, an artisan from a small, fervent dissenting sect, has left his home in Lantern Yard as an exile sixteen years before the story's action begins, devastated at his abandonment by man and God.

Framed by his malevolent best friend, Silas is accused of stealing the community's small savings and is unable to defend himself since he suffers from epileptic seizures which render him unconscious, leaving him without memory of the robbery. When Silas realizes that William has committed the robbery, his faith in his fellow is terribly shaken, yet he does not expose William, and only repeats, "God will clear me" (*SM* 9). Eschewing any legal proceedings as non-Christian, the community decides to draw lots to determine Silas's guilt or innocence, a method Silas trusts as well. But the lots indicate that he is guilty. Crushed by disappointed faith, Silas blasphemes before the community: "there is no just God that governs the earth righteously, but a God of lies, that bears witness against the innocent" (*SM* 10). No one inquires further nor steps to Silas's defense; shortly thereafter, his fiancée breaks off her attachment and smoothly shifts her pledge to William, and Silas leaves Lantern Yard.

In this small vignette Eliot offered a portrait of fervent religiosity among those working people and artisans without broad experience or knowledge, in whose religious practice "the form and the feeling have never been severed by an act of reflection" (*SM* 10). Far from the "vague" sense of comfort or fear which Eliot depicted as religious feeling among the uneducated in *Adam Bede*, Silas's community represent those who believe in God's visible, intelligible intervention in daily life. Turning to her anthropological mode, Eliot describes the superstitious reliance on lots as commonplace, offering "a ground of surprise only to those who are unacquainted with that obscure religious life which has gone on in the alleys of our towns" (*SM* 10). The fact that Silas does not doubt the efficacy of the lots should also not surprise:

We are apt to think it inevitable that a man in Marner's position should have begun to question the validity of an appeal to the divine judgment by drawing lots; but to him this would have been an effort of independent thought such as he had never known; and he must have made the effort at a moment when all his energies were turned into the anguish of disappointed faith. (*SM* 10–11)

Eliot specifically identifies the unlikelihood of "independent thought," in a collective whose ordinary religious life not only does not require it but depends upon its absence for solidarity and coherence. William, the false friend, embodies the only "independent thought"; such thought, directed toward his own selfish interests, manifests in the breakdown of collective trust and good will.

In the above passage, Eliot brilliantly identifies the extreme difficulty of such independence and innovation precisely when it is most necessary—when previous paradigms have failed. In his shock and anguish, Silas does not abandon the forms of his religious life: he judges God from *within* those forms. Rather than denying God's existence, he denies God's goodness. He blasphemes—the sin of a believer—and declares God to be unjust, a "God of lies," who allows sin to triumph. It is difficult to imagine any greater despair than believing in a powerful and unjust God. (Blackwood, for his part, responded to the opening of the tale with the hope that the child's appearance would "restor[e] the unfortunate Silas to a more Christian frame of mind" [GEL 3: 379].)

Yet the narrator's summary of this episode expresses not horror at Silas's sinful speech but pity for the heavy costs of ignorance: "If there is an angel who records the sorrows of men as well as their sins, he knows how many and deep are the sorrows that spring from false ideas for which no man is culpable" (*SM* 11). *Silas Marner* offers a written record that examines the range of untested, often barely articulate, theologies that Eliot saw unlettered people fashioning, to make sense of what they could not make sense of. Their lives, as Eliot depicted them from the inside, often provided more grist for theological challenge than the lives of those cushioned by wealth and education, even as they came to the challenge with fewer tools. The composition of *Silas Marner* suggests that before Eliot could take herself and her readers to Renaissance Italy, she needed to complete the work she had begun in her earlier novels. In the slowly dawning relationship between Silas and Dolly Winthrop, the well-meaning villager who assists the inexperienced father after Eppie enters his life, we are made privy to the largely unspoken theology of Christians who cannot distinguish superstition or fetishism from doctrinal faith, who go to church or to chapel, say their prayers, memorize hymns and recite the catechism, take the sacrament, baptize children and name them from the Bible, maintain the family tradition of pricking the letters I.H.S. into breads and cakes, and see God's providential hand in life events, especially those they suffered under or struggled to understand.[3]

Yet Eliot's portrait of this folk religion grants it more dignity and theological seriousness than at first glance. Theodicy remains a central concern. And when we read it alongside *Romola*, we can see it as a text engaged in the problem of believing in a God who exists but no longer communicates directly, or even indirectly, with humanity. Faith has not a single practiced or learned spokesperson in *Silas Marner*, unlike Eliot's earlier novels, all of which feature a preacher or pastor or articulate, reflective hero. Eliot represents theological faith here as ignorant, sometimes comically, but she also idealizes it, as it comes to function primarily as the inherited form into which right feeling is poured.

A channel for simple "good" (a word that recurs in the story 127 times and harkens back to the scriptural refrain after each day of the world's creation, "And God saw that it was good"), the rituals of faith range from the personal to the communal, and comprise the musical, verbal, visual, and culinary. These rituals both make this world "better" and attest to another "better" world above. Repeatedly, Dolly seeks to persuade Silas to come to church by explaining the uplift of her religious experience:

> And you may judge what it is at church, Master Marner, with the bassoon and the voices, as you can't help thinking you've got to a better place a'ready—for I wouldn't speak ill o' this world, seeing as Them put us in it as knows best—but what wi' the drink, and the quarrelling, and the bad illnesses, and the hard dying, as I've seen times and times, one's thankful to hear of a better. (*SM* 85)

For Dolly, "this world" holds trials over which human beings exert some control, and also no control; whose causes and purposes are often impossible to understand; and which repeat eternally ("times and times"). Dolly sees very clearly that "there's trouble i' this world, and there's things as we can niver make out the rights on" (*SM* 144). These things can look "ill," but they precede a "better place," and they may look different to the Creator who "knows best" (good, better, best). Church rituals animate her knowledge, making it a feeling.

Dolly's theology is built on a pretty solid foundation once she must begin to describe it to Silas. God is a distant God (as the narrator puts it, Dolly's respectful plural nomenclature for the divine is "no heresy of Dolly's, but only her way of avoiding a presumptuous familiarity" [*SM* 83]), rather than a compassionate or interventionist one, but not capricious nor unjust. Dolly draws a straight line from human beings to "Them as are above us," and understands each limited, involuntary human lifespan in relation to divine eternity and omnipotence: "Them as was at the making on us"; "Them as put us in it [this world]"; "Them as we must all give ourselves up to at the last" (*SM* 144). God precedes and creates human beings, puts them in the world, and gathers them in at the last.

Dolly believes in fairness, in divine justice, and in reciprocity: "if we'n done our part, it isn't to be believed as Them as are above us 'ull be worse nor we are, and come short o' Their'n" (*SM* 83). Not only will God match human efforts, in just reciprocity, but God must be more compassionate than human beings, by the logic that the Creator cannot be less than the Created: "Them above has got a deal tenderer heart nor what I've got—for I can't be anyways better nor Them as made me" (*SM* 144).

The consequence of Dolly's beliefs is, first, a constant awareness of human limitation and, especially, limited understanding; and second, a commitment, nonetheless, to "doing our part." Dolly's ignorance, which Eliot renders comically for the benefit of her better-educated readers, instantiates a profound religious teaching on the relation of the human to the divine. Dolly is a walking exemplar of the insufficient knowledge, limited experience, and constrained perspective that characterize any human being in traditional theology. When she is confronted by what she cannot make sense of, she recognizes her limitations: "and if anything looks hard to me, it's because there's things

I don't know on"; "there was a rights in what happened to you, if one could but make it out" (*SM* 144). We can read this as apologetics or a humility with disturbing political quiescence for women and the laboring classes. But it also reflects honestly on the difficulties of theodicy for all believers in a God who is good. There are questions without answers. All the same, human beings must act and choose in this world.

Given the predominance of superstition in Eliot's portrait of folk religion, it is notable that while Dolly does believe that "there's good words and good things to keep us from harm," she does not imagine a God who actively intervenes by signs or otherwise in human life (*SM* 126). Trust is the ultimate consequence of all her convictions, but her trust in God is inseparable from her trust in herself. The unity of her religious experience, in which "form and feeling" have not been "separated by an act of reflection," allows her to experience her own selfhood in unity with the divine. Since one cannot make out causes or penetrate appearances, the only thing possible, for Dolly, is "to trusten...to do the right thing as fur as we know, and to trusten" (*SM* 144). The absence of an object—trust in whom? in what?—makes this intransitive trusting an active form that produces independent acts of goodness. In the end, Dolly comes back to human instinct and feeling: "do the right thing as fur as we know," with the ultimate clarity coming only from inside. Again, reasoning from little to great, from good to better/best in her unified world, Dolly asserts: "For if us as knows so little can see a bit o' good and rights, we may be sure as there's a good and a rights bigger nor what we can know—I feel it i' my own inside as it must be so" (*SM* 144–5). While she respects clerical authority and teaching, she is her own final arbiter. And the aim of her religion is immediate and tangible goodness: "if there's any good to be got, we've need of it i' this world," a phrase she repeats like her own private catechism (*SM* 81; cf. 82, 85).

Eliot's reliance on the language of goodness is charged with meaning for Silas's narrative. His restoration to life in the aftermath of his losses depends on his ability to see goodness, that quintessential and scriptural quality of created, animate being. As Silas comes to love Eppie, the growing child who has come to him "in place" of the gold coins, the narrator explores at length Silas's coming to understand the difference between what lives and forges links to the wider, living world, and what does not live and keeps his thought in an "ever-repeated circle, leading to nothing beyond itself" (*SM* 127). The fetishism of the coin-worship can be set aside once Silas finds again "the feeling that God was good to me" in Eppie's arrival (*SM* 166). Silas's restoration of faith is not a return to Calvinism, certainly, nor is it a new interest in the Anglican Church or any explicit belief in a heaven above or an afterlife. It is merely, and consequentially, the return of a belief in divine goodness: "'There's good i' this world— I've a feeling o' that now" (*SM* 145).

This felt experience of the world holding good, even as it also holds ill, allows Silas to set aside the demand for fuller knowledge. He seems now content to leave all the rest—from trouble to blessing—shrouded in mystery:

> and it makes a man feel as there's a good more nor he can see, i' spite o' the trouble and the wickedness. That drawing o' the lots is dark; but the child was sent to me: there's dealings with us—there's dealings. (*SM* 145)

The "more nor he can see" is what Eliot elsewhere refers to, in her letters as well as her fiction, as the "unseen": the Unseen Powers, Unseen Pity, Unseen Love, Unseen Justice, Unseen Purity, Unseen Goodness, Unseen Perfectness. In *Silas Marner*, all that is unseen by Dolly and Silas and all the other characters serves to emphasize limited human sight as much as the abstract divine ideals in whose existence they believe. Eliot's short "legendary tale," as she described it, encapsulates her respect for the best elements of folk religion (GEL 3: 382). Its simplicity reads as a necessary antidote to the complexities that Eliot anticipated in the erudition and psychological depth of *Romola*.

In April 1861, the month after Marian completed *Silas Marner*, the Leweses returned to Italy for further research into *Romola*. From this point forward, the historical novel was a painful, protracted process interrupted by depressions more intense than any which Marian could remember (she was in the habit of returning to her journal to check impressions and memories against evidence). She began to write in October 1861 but in early November was already wondering whether she should give it up, a doubt that would arise repeatedly. In December, she set out the full scheme for the novel but could not move past research to writing. By the end of February 1862, she had reached only the end of the fourth chapter of a novel that would extend to seventy-two chapters, plus Proem and Epilogue. The work ahead of her overwhelmed her.

Yet even as her own doubts could not be settled, the outside world was affirming its faith in her. The publisher George Smith began to inquire about publishing the new book and, in a remarkable show of confidence, offered her £10,000 for a novel she was not confident she could write (Lewes noted in his journal that it was the "most magnificent offer" ever made for a novel [GEL 4: 17]) as well as offering Lewes the editorship of the new *Cornhill Magazine*. In the end, after a complicated and bruising set of exchanges with the Blackwoods, she opted to publish with Smith at the price of £7,000 for a serialization plan that suited her better than what he had proposed for the higher sum. Publication began in July 1862, nearly a full year before she finished writing.

Romola was as different a canvas as possible from *Silas Marner*, particularly in its shift from a set of uneducated characters to a world of scholars, politicians, and a preacher of Savonarola's rhetorical force. Yet *Romola* shared with *Silas Marner* a focus on the problem of justice on earth and the appearance of sin's triumph. The latter had been very little preoccupied with theodicy as represented by problems of causeless suffering (the "bad illnesses and the hard dying") and very much preoccupied with human malevolence. At the very end of the story, a limited retributive justice prevails, but William's betrayal is never redressed (he gets away with the stolen money, the community, and the wife). Silas's life has been blessed with Eppie, surely, so perhaps the good are rewarded, but sin has triumphed, too. That triumph is left "dark," as Silas puts it.

Romola, for its part, is driven by figures intent on retributive justice; Eliot focuses on the degradation of justice when it turns into the drive for revenge or personal predomination. Tito appears to achieve his goal of doing evil without paying for it. Only at the very end of the novel does Tito pay for all his betrayals in one fell swoop, as he is pursued by a Florentine mob which he narrowly escapes, only to be delivered directly into his father's murderous hands. Justice for Tito comes in his early death. Yet his father dies alongside him, in a bitter end to his own tragic losses, without any witness to the truth of his claims against Tito. And since Tito's various sins are not fully brought to light, his reputation is left ambiguous, thus not tarnished according to strict justice. Eliot did—uncharacteristically—record in her journal having "killed Tito with great excitement," with no regret or compunction at his punishment (GEL 4: 84). Yet the consequences of Tito's actions—from the sale and dispersal of his father-in-law's singular library to the torture and execution of Savonarola—cannot be reversed or redressed. The novel does *not* confirm a faith that even if "the wages of men's sins often linger in their payment," eventually they will be paid (*R* 49). Indeed, Eliot chose to represent a history that was, of course, less flexible than fiction. Beyond her fictional plot, in which Eliot could kill off villains with glee even if she could not kill off their deeds, the historically faithful narrative of *Romola* traces serious miscarriages of justice (*R* 49).

Does Savonarola, the preacher excommunicated by the Pope, tried, tortured, and publicly executed, receive justice? In Eliot's account a great man, in whom ambition and the highest aims mixed, is brought low and finally to death by an immensely tangled set of circumstances that can barely be traced out. But one thing is clear: no misdeed, no "shadow of political crime," "not one stain...on his private conduct," is satisfied by his death (*R* 661). The narrator clarifies that, in terms of this world, justice is not served by Savonarola's death: his "distinction from the great mass of the clergy lay, not in any heretical belief, not in his superstitions, but in the energy with which he sought to make the Christian life a reality" (*R* 539). He is no worse than any other of the clergy; on the contrary, says the narrator, he dies because he is better. If we consider Eliot's severe critique of nominal religion, this assessment of Savonarola is high praise.

Eliot takes pains to dramatize the way that, in Renaissance Florence, the felt necessity to shore up political power ends in individuals paying unjust costs. Merging fiction with history, she depicts the execution in 1497 of the historical Bernardo del Nero, whom she identifies as Romola's beloved godfather, alongside four other Mediceans. This execution is meted out by highly questionable Florentine justice, with the tacit approval of Savonarola, who chooses not to intervene in their defense. His acquiescence causes Romola to look at Savonarola himself as a fallible individual, acting in his own party's interests, which he has become incapable of distinguishing from those of the kingdom of heaven. But when the kingdom of heaven can no longer distinguish between the virtue or guilt of individual persons, Romola can no longer subscribe to its truth.

Eliot's Savonarola so ardently pursues divine justice that he forgets he is an imperfect vessel for its satisfaction. Savonarola, driven by "his own burning indignation at the sight of wrong; in his fervent belief in an Unseen Justice that would put an end to the wrong, and in an Unseen Purity to which lying and uncleanness were an abomination," acts on the belief that justice in the Church and in the world is attainable and imminent (*R* 272); such justice is necessary to rebut the impossibility that "the world... [had] ceased to have a righteous Ruler" (*R* 271). Yet Savonarola's "ardent, power-loving soul, believing in great ends, and longing to achieve those ends by the exertion of its own strong will" ceases to see any distinction between God's party and his own (*R* 272). The imperious dictates of "Self" become "inseparable from a purpose which is not selfish" (*R* 666). Justice miscarries here. Perhaps it is not too whimsical to suggest that Savonarola's equation of his certainties with the divine will recalls Dolly Winthrop's trust in herself—"I feel it in my own inside"—and her conflation of trusting in God and doing "the right thing as fur as [she] know[s]." Unlike Dolly, however, Savonarola believes he is God's prophet, and his prophecy is uttered before a "vast multitude of warm, living faces, upturned in breathless silence towards the pulpit" (*R* 289).

Though Eliot immersed herself in all Savonarola's writings, her imaginative interest settled upon the places where his moral greatness yielded to what she judged superstition rather than religion. She regarded as superstition Savonarola's personal "claim to special inspiration," and especially his predictive prophecies and promises of miraculous intervention (*R* 663). Eliot's Savonarola is thus no Hebrew prophet, nor a false prophet, but a man of her own shared modernity, defined by his time and place and their "strange web of belief and unbelief," a web familiar, of course, to educated English mid-Victorians (*R* 49). Savonarola comes to grief when he prophesies in ways that demand a clear, public response from God to his claims that Florence enjoys a special providence; he escapes responsibility only because of political events—the visit of the French king, the long-awaited break from famine when corn arrives—that allow such an interpretation for those who so desire. General prophecies can be borne out by general results: Savonarola "consented to have his frock stripped off him if, when Florence persevered in fulfilling the duties of piety and citizenship, God did not come to her rescue" (*R* 445). And it is just possible for the Florentines to hear, in "the distant tread of foreign armies, coming to do the work of justice," "what the prophets of old had heard in Cyrus' coming" to return Israel from exile (*R* 273). Yet Savonarola's more specific prophecies and assurances of miracle catch him in his own web of belief and unbelief.

Eliot's Savonarola avows and disavows God's action in contemporary history. Near the end of the novel, his conviction in his own status as prophet leads to the proposal that he walk through fire as proof. When he examines his own convictions, Savonarola must own to himself that he does not believe God will intervene miraculously to protect him. He thus avoids the trial. Yet, in so doing, he loses the people's faith. As Eliot offers extended analysis of Savonarola's internal discord, she gives us a man who believes in his own prophecies and their proof by miracle... but not quite:

> Not that Savonarola had uttered... a falsity when he declared his belief in a future supernatural attestation of his work; but his mind was so constituted that while it was easy for him to believe in a miracle which, being distant and undefined, was screened behind the strong reasons he saw for its occurrence, and yet easier for him to have a belief in inward miracles such as his own prophetic inspiration and divinely-wrought intuitions; it was at the same time insurmountably difficult to him to believe in the probability of a miracle which, like this of being carried unhurt through the fire, pressed in all its details on his imagination and involved a demand not only for belief but for exceptional action. (*R* 611–12)

Eliot uses Savonarola's predicament and his prevailing unbelief in a clear divine miracle to bring her Renaissance Florence decisively towards religious modernity. In this recognizable modernity, animated by continuous human impulses and experiences, God exists. But even for the ardently faithful, God cannot be depended upon to intervene in specific, desired ways in human affairs.

In Eliot's portrait of a passionate man of God, a limit case if ever there was one, she makes him incapable of imagining a clear, intelligible divine message that opposes or reverses the laws of nature. Passionate faith in God and the moral life survives and outlives the faith in miracle. Eliot's more educated readers would have recognized this focus on miracle, a tenet of belief much debated by Victorian theologians and thinkers who confronted both empirical science and increasing textual sophistication as to the historical limitations of the witnesses to events they described as miracles. As in *Silas Marner*, where Eppie's appearance, experienced by Silas as miraculous, is explainable by natural events, in *Romola* Eliot rejects the belief in miracles; in the latter even more decisively, given that it is Savonarola himself who, try as he might, cannot bring himself to trust.

But it is not only miracles that Eliot assails. More broadly, she rejects the possibility of articulate divine–human communication and instead asserts what we might see as a hallmark of religious modernity: a recognition that the self is all human beings have with which to arbitrate divine will, as it has come down to them through text and tradition. This turn to individual interpretation arises more naturally from a generally Protestant orientation than from a Catholic orientation which invests the Pope with supreme authority and establishes religious intercessors. In Eliot's work, the claim to personal access to the divine will tends to serve as a warning sign. From the "Assurance of salvation," claimed by Silas Marner's treacherous associate William, to Savonarola's claim to prophecy, Eliot associates such assertions with human fallibility and culpability (*SM* 7). William's claim is made with knowing falsity, while Savonarola's claim is more mixed in its origins and aims but nonetheless tainted by pride and ambition. Moral-religious decisions are made, and must be made, in these novels in the absence of divine illumination.

Perhaps it is on this matter of self-determination that *Romola* seems to break forward in Eliot's oeuvre to a less "religious" orientation, in the particular sense of religion as submission that she introduced in *Scenes of Clerical Life* and frequently used in her early novels. We see this conflict between self and religious authority played out with perfect clarity in the dynamic relationship between Romola and Savonarola, a relationship that begins in Romola's "bend[ing] the knee and bow[ing] the head" but ends with Romola's fierce assertion of independence and, finally, her ability to honor Savonarola's memory without idealizing him or capitulating to his authority (*R* 454). Romola first encounters Savonarola on her own brother's deathbed at San Marco.

The "Soul's Own Warrant," 1860–1863

After being raised by their father with "a silent ignoring of any claims the Church could have to regulate the belief and action of beings with a cultivated reason," Dino had abandoned the classical teachings of his father for a cloistered Christianity (*R* 210). At the painful scene of her brother's death, Romola sets her eyes on the crucifix and becomes conscious of the limitations of her own upbringing: "if there were much more of such experience as his in the world, she would like to understand it – would even like to learn the thoughts of men who sank in ecstasy before the pictured agonies of martyrdom. There seemed to be something more than madness in that supreme fellowship with suffering" (*R* 396).

When Romola encounters her own first deep suffering, in the "double solitude" of her marriage (to be distinguished from Eliot's often-used phrase, "double life," to describe her own union with Lewes), it is Savonarola who stops her from escaping, literally turning her around on the road leaving Florence (*R* 312). He commands her, "My daughter, you must return to your place," and the narrator tells us that "Romola felt it impossible to question his authority to speak to her" (*R* 429). At the sound of his voice, she feels "the strength there might be in submission" if he had "some valid law to show her" (*R* 430). When he counsels her, "Conform your life to that image [of crucifixion], my daughter; make your sorrow an offering," she begins to see herself linked to suffering others, to whom she has an obligation of which her father took no notice (*R* 433).

Like Maggie Tulliver, Romola sets out to "thread life by a fresh clue," and the heart of her plot line is her entry into the city's common life, a lasting conversion that outlives her obedience to Savonarola's authority more generally (*R* 440). Romola consecrates herself to easing the suffering of her fellow Florentines according to Savonarola's teaching, yet his command that she remain bound to her marriage is far more problematic. The marriage has become an example of solely external form. As Romola struggles between "the demands of an outward law, which she recognized as a widely-ramifying obligation, and the demands of inner moral facts which were becoming more and more peremptory," she questions whether Savonarola has been correct to equate her desire to leave her marriage with Tito's own "light abandonment of ties," "whether inherited or voluntary, because they had ceased to be pleasant" (*R* 552).

In a critical passage that comes as a relief to any feminist reader, Eliot redefines the marriage outside Savonarola's terms, names it anew, and asserts her own truth: "the relation had become for her simply a degrading servitude. The law was sacred. Yes, but the rebellion might be sacred too" (*R* 552). Intervening here in contemporary Victorian debates over the woman question, the legal justifications for divorce, and more broadly, the circumstances of a mismatch between outward law and inner reality—all subjects immensely potent for Marian Lewes—Eliot drew together Romola's and Savonarola's plots:

> To her, as to him there had come one of those moments in life when the soul must dare to act on its own warrant, not only without external law to appeal to, but in the face of a law which is not unarmed with Divine lightnings – lightnings that may yet fall if the warrant has been false. (*R* 553)

Like Savonarola himself, Romola must finally judge for herself and must acknowledge that she is doing so: "Father, you yourself declare that there comes a moment when the soul must have no guide but the voice within it, to tell whether the consecrated thing has sacred virtue" (*R* 576). Whether the lightning that falls is divine or natural remains unanswered.

As Eliot described a hollow but legal form in delineating Romola's degrading marriage, she described the inverse of her own experience with Lewes and perhaps touched some aspect of Lewes's experience with his legal wife, Agnes, who bore children with another man. But both *Silas Marner* and *Romola*, the two novels of the early 1860s, featured another dimension of Marian's experience, too. Both novels included adoptions: voluntary, extra-legal ties of generosity in which human beings name and consecrate new relationships and experience them as fully binding. While *Romola* featured in Tito and his father an adoption that failed spectacularly (also allowing Eliot to ask whether adoptive parents might be selfishly seeking special love), at the same time, in depicting Romola's brother's abandonment of their father, the novel acknowledged that a natural, biological relation might prove no better. *Silas Marner*, likewise, offered the case of Eppie and her biological father, who selfishly denies her claims upon him in contrast to the mutual love and duty between Eppie and Silas. And as if to challenge its failed adoption story, *Romola* ends with the remarkable image of the heroine caring for the children of Tito and his extra-legal wife, Tessa, while never telling Tessa or the children the truth of her own identity.[4]

As Eliot wrote these two intertwined novels, Charles Lewes had come into her home and daily life, and her other stepsons became real, known, precious people to her. She became to them "Mutter," a category invented solely for her. In the Proem to *Romola*, Eliot described "the little children" as the enduring "symbol of the eternal marriage between love and duty" (*R* 50). In these novels that sought out a model for obligation fed by feeling, adoption became a relation in which "duty and love have united in one stream and made a common force" (*R* 169); under these conditions, Eliot saw a kind of redemption, a moment "when all outward law has become needless" (R 169).

Notes

1. See Hilary Fraser, *The Victorians and Renaissance Italy* (Cambridge, MA: Blackwell, 1992).
2. See Felicia Bonaparte, *The Triptych and the Cross: Central Myths of George Eliot's Poetic Imagination* (New York: New York University Press, 1979), for an extended analysis of the confrontation between classical and Christian inheritances.
3. For example, Nancy Lammeter's providential thinking bleeds into superstition: "To adopt a child, because children of your own had been denied you, was to try and choose your lot in spite of Providence.... When you saw a thing was not meant to be, said Nancy, it was a bounden duty to leave off so much as wishing for it.... She would have given up making a purchase at a particular place if, on three successive times, rain, or some other cause of Heaven's sending, had formed an obstacle; and she would have anticipated a broken limb or other heavy misfortune to any one who persisted in spite of such indications" (*SM* 156–7).
4. On Eliot's relation to her stepsons, see Bodenheimer, *Real Life*, pp. 189–231. I am not suggesting here an idyllic relation with the young men who required time and attention and occasioned other sacrifices as well. I suggest that adoption became a figure in which Eliot saw the merging of love and duty.

11
"A Heart without a Livery"?
1864–1869

About *Romola*, George Eliot famously said that she began it a young woman and finished it an old woman.[1] *Romola* was not the final novel in which Eliot represented a young woman finding or seeking a wider world view with greater moral demands. However, it was the final novel in which Eliot would pivot to that wider world view through the heroine's exposure to transformative Christian figures or ideas. Christianity as a set of particular doctrines, shaped by a theology of sin, suffering, salvation, organized by its claims upon eternity, receded in Eliot's works from this point forward, yielding its centrality to other ethnicities and religions, as well as their nationalist implications. Meanwhile, in Eliot's English landscapes, the higher yearnings of "religion" became more disconnected from initially doctrinal Christian expressions, as if processes of personal ethical development no longer needed to be routed through Christian conversion. Such religious convictions as Eliot represented in her Christian characters became more rapidly assimilated to political or social convictions and affiliations.

This significant alteration transpired on the heels of two uncertain years, 1864–5, in which Marian published a number of periodical articles and short poems, unsure what major projects would come next and in which genre they would find their form. From the historical romance of *Romola* she moved toward drama and toward poetry, the genre still most esteemed by Victorians. In the end, the mid-1860s came to be defined for Eliot by literary experiment that issued in two major works: a political novel, *Felix Holt, the Radical*, and a long poem, "The Spanish Gypsy."

These two works were written in alternation, much the way that *Silas Marner* interrupted *Romola*, enabling Eliot to return afterwards to her difficult historical romance. Likewise, *Felix Holt* relieved Eliot's despair at the labor of "The Spanish Gypsy," which she initially cast as a drama. Seeing her intense depression as she completed its fourth act, Lewes prevailed upon her to set it aside in February 1865. The end of March saw her begin work on *Felix Holt*, which returned her to the form of the three-volume novel and a familiar English context, as well as to her original publisher, Blackwood, with whom she remained securely for the rest of her career.

The challenges of *Felix Holt* were real, but manageable: a complex plot of inheritance for which Marian sought out legal advice, and a central political focus, the expansion of the franchise via the Reform Bill of 1832. Immersed as always in wide reading and rereading that supported her work directly and indirectly—a great deal of J. S. Mill (*Political Economy*, *On Liberty*, the series of *Westminster Review* essays on Comte), Comte's *Social Science*, the Bible, Aristotle's *Poetics*, Shakespeare's *King John*, Aeschylus's *Agamemnon*, William Blackstone's legal writings, *The Annual Register* for 1832, and Samuel Bamford's *Passages in the Life of a Radical*, among other things—Eliot completed the novel at the end of May 1866 and Blackwood brought it out in two weeks to appreciative reviews.

After a two-month trip with Lewes to Holland, Belgium, and Germany, Eliot returned to "The Spanish Gypsy." Deciding it was "impossible to abandon," she began to recast it as a tragic poem, exercising the freedom from monetary constraint that the success of her novels had granted her. Lewes supported her impulse and enjoyed the same freedom, "plung[ing] at his will into the least lucrative of studies," as she later described him (GEL 4: 465). Ensconced as of late 1863 in The Priory, a house that was to become synonymous with their famous "at-homes" on Sunday afternoons as Eliot's literary standing overshadowed her marital status, the two expressed appreciation for their good fortune. The only exceptions were their worry over Lewes's sons abroad and the near-constant concerns of ill health, increasingly requiring Lewes to break from his work and relocate for attempted cures and rest.

Perhaps because of such concerns, Marian notes in her letters the sense of impending mortality: "there is little time left me," she writes to Sara Hennell, for the studies she so enjoys.[2] Such preoccupations were not new, but they appear to have increased in this period. They likely contributed to her inventing a type new to her fiction: an aging woman, defined by her past. In *Felix Holt*, the young heroes—Felix, the earnest radical, and Esther Lyon, the daughter of a dissenting minister who will discover her high birth precisely when it has lost its allure for her—take second stage to the novel's compelling psychological center. Mrs. Transome is a woman "between fifty and sixty," whose life has become to her all bitterness and disappointment. Her early impulse to follow pleasure against law and religion dictates that her adult life will be lived in fear of consequences: the exposure of her infidelity and her son's illegitimacy (*FH* 86). An outlaw who rebels, but not in service of any higher law, Mrs. Transome undergoes no transformation, no religious or moral conversion. She is a figure solely of suffering, of a woman's small and narrow life, and as such she serves Esther as a warning of a life "where poetry was only literature"; that is to say, all noble things are only imaginary (*FH* 547).

Yet in *Felix Holt* the life of "poetry" is distinct from religious faith. Esther, the sole figure in the novel to undergo a conversion, has been raised by an adoptive father, Rufus Lyon, an Independent minister of deep feeling and fervent belief, as well as intellectual animation. But none of it has touched her. In fact, Rev. Lyon speaks a language that has no sharers in the novel. Convinced (like Savonarola in *Romola*) that genuine religion cannot be cordoned off from the workings of the world, Rev. Lyon holds that the pulpit, the courtroom, and the classroom must all engage religion and politics equally. From the pulpit, he seeks to instruct men in "their duties to the commonwealth": "Does God know less of men than He did in the days of Hezekiah and Moses? Is His arm shortened, and is the world become too wide for His providence?" (*FH* 146). Yet for all his engagement in the world, Rev. Lyon is repeatedly trivialized publicly when he addresses politics through a religious lens. Though the narrator credits him with nobility of character, with eyes that convey "enthusiastic thought and love," as his teachings pour out of him, Rev. Lyon's social impact is negligible (*FH* 243).

Even Esther, who comes to appreciate the depth of her father's character, cannot appreciate nor adopt his particular faith:

> Her father's desire for her conversion had never moved her....
> Unfitness for heaven (spoken of as 'Jerusalem' and 'glory'), the prayers of a good little father, whose thoughts and motives seemed to her like the *Life of Dr. Doddridge*, which she was content to leave unread, did not attack her self-respect and self-satisfaction. (*FH* 214)

Esther sees her father as belonging to that harmless, forgettable past which houses the likes of doddering Dr. Philip Doddridge (1702–51), to Esther only a dusty portrait and another biography. Her father's reverence for Doddridge—a Nonconformist minister, educator, and prolific hymn-writer, author of *The Rise and Progress of Religion in the Soul*, which was widely translated, reprinted, and described as responsible for prompting William Wilberforce's initial spiritual movements—is the sort of affiliation that lies outside the pages of this novel, outside the town of Treby Magna, where Rufus Lyon has no audience and prompts no conversions.

Until Esther meets Felix, no religious impulse has ever animated her. It takes Felix, who is not a believer, to translate Rev. Lyon's convictions in such a way that Esther is moved. "Ask...yourself," he challenges her, "whether life is not as solemn a thing as your father takes it to be – in which you may be either a blessing or a curse to many" (*FH* 211). Felix's desire for Esther "to change"—to convert her way of thinking and living—is a turning point in her experience: "For the first time in her life Esther felt herself seriously shaken in her self-contentment. She knew there was a mind to which she appeared trivial, narrow, selfish" (*FH* 213).

While Rev. Lyon identifies in Felix a form of "Christian unworldliness"— Felix chooses to forgo selling his father's quack medicines and to support his mother by cleaning clocks and watches, and teaching working-class boys—in fact, Felix's rejection of middle-class employment and relative luxuries lies aloof from any Christian asceticism (*FH* 145). His "conversion," he tells Rev. Lyon, comes from a few weeks' debauchery that teach him that "This world is not a very fine place for a good many of the people in it. But I've made up my mind it shan't be the worse for me, if I can help it" (*FH* 143). Felix's aim is to begin to educate the working-class men, preaching to them where he finds them, aiming to help ready them to execute the responsibilities of the franchise knowledgeably. (His "radical" plans are thus not particularly radical in the political short term, but closer to Marian Lewes's own convictions that gradual social change was far more desirable.)

Although Felix plans to forgo all kinds of personal pleasures, we are not looking here at the asceticism of Dinah Morris or Rev. Tryan or even the enthusiastic Maggie Tulliver. What Rev. Lyon classifies as possibly Christian unworldliness is Felix's visceral reaction to a world empirically riddled with pain: it's the "life of the miserable," Felix tells Esther, "that's got into my mind like a splinter...the spawning life of vice and hunger" (*FH* 363). No divine design inheres in his account. Felix's vision is divorced from any narrative of salvation or consolation whatsoever. Felix describes Rev. Lyon's beliefs as an "awful creed, which makes this world a vestibule with double doors to hell, and a narrow stair on one side whereby the thinner sort may mount to heaven" (*FH* 156). In spite of the narrator informing us clearly that Rev. Lyon's experience has prompted him to wider and less conventional views of salvation than Felix guesses, the division in orientation between the novel's two earnest, passionate men is profound, regardless of their political overlap. Felix's orientation—this world is a vestibule to nowhere and begs attention purely for its own ills—prevails in the novel, not least because Felix is young, at the outset of his life's action, and Rufus Lyon is old, ceding action to the next generation.

In Felix's description of the world's empirical misery we see something new and less faithful in George Eliot's thought and writing, perhaps linked to her own sense of aging. Felix insists on a world that is simply not a source of good for many (most?) of its inhabitants: "This world is not a very fine place for a good many of the people in it" (*FH* 143). To this Silas-Marner-like, dark intensity the novel positions no Dolly Winthrop to answer for the Creator's benevolence or intentionality, only Felix's own response: "But I've made up my mind it shan't be the worse for me, if I can help it"' (*FH* 143).

Marian shared this dark view. In March 1865, the same month she began writing *Felix Holt*, she wrote Cara Bray in the aftermath of her beloved daughter Nelly's early death. There could be no consolation for such loss, wrote Marian, yet she believed there was a truth in their "complex world," to the oft-spoken idea that "the gods loved those who died young" because they escaped the pain of existence:

> Life, though a good to men on the whole, is a doubtful good to many, and to some not a good at all. To my thought, it is a source of constant mental distortion to make the denial of this a part of religion—to go on pretending things are better than they are. To me early death takes the aspect of salvation; though I feel, too, that those who live and suffer may sometimes have the greater blessedness of *being* a salvation. (GEL 4: 183)

Marian here proposes that, for many human beings, salvation comes only when death relieves life's suffering. The proposition that life is a good to mankind as a species is presented here as an incidental truth, a subordinate phrase within commas, before the real matter of the sentence: that life "is a doubtful good to many, and to some not a good at all." Like Felix, Marian does not venture a guess as to whether *most* people experience life as a doubtful good; suffice it to say, "many" find themselves with a genuine question as to life's goodness. Benevolent design, a sense of God's creation as good, is absent.

The primacy of suffering pushes Felix to embrace a "harder discipline" (*FH* 363). He refuses personal ease: " 'I'll never be one of the sleek dogs. The old Catholics are right, with their higher rule and their lower. Some are called to subject themselves to a harder discipline, and renounce things voluntarily which are lawful for others. It is the old word – 'necessity is laid upon me" ' (*FH* 363). When Esther tells him, " 'It seems to me you are stricter than my father is," Felix disagrees, saying that he opposes no pleasures that are not "base or cruel," but that "one must sometimes accommodate one's self to a small share" (*FH* 363). Felix is no ascetic: he objects only to an unjust allocation of pleasures.

Religion comes to Esther through the shock of Felix's adamant refusal of all the things she has judged valuable. Felix's awareness of a wider world, and his sense of obligation to others and to the best version of himself (his intent not to enter the race for material success, knowing its self-propelling logic), surprise Esther, in spite of her upbringing: "Esther had been so long used to hear the formulas of her father's belief without feeling or understanding them, that they had lost all power to touch her. The first religious experience of her life – the first self-questioning, the first voluntary subjection, the first longing to acquire the strength of greater motives and obey the more strenuous rule – had come to her through Felix Holt" (*FH* 369).

Heroic impulse and action do not belong in this novel to avowed Christians as they did in Eliot's earlier novels. (When Rev. Lyon engineers what he hopes will be a historic public debate on the constitution of the true Church, his opponent fails to show, rendering his high drama nothing but farcical.) Heroic action belongs instead to the social and political reformer. The fact that Felix's scope is in the end possibly limited by marriage, like Dinah Morris's, does not alter the power of his moral role in the novel. If anything, the comparison between these two figures, Dinah and Felix, who first reject marriage as outside their assumed "harder discipline," reflects primarily Eliot's progression from locating moral-religious heroism first in an evangelical preacher and later in an unbelieving social and political reformer. Late in the novel, when Esther's father is asked if Felix is one of his flock, he answers regretfully that Felix's virtues would witness to the faith if only Felix were a believer: "Nay – would to God he were! I should then feel that the great virtues and the pure life I have beheld in him were a witness to the efficacy of the faith I believe in and the discipline of the church whereunto I belong" (*FH* 567). Felix's godless faith and discipline are exemplary but can do no credit to the Christian church, which Felix actively rejects. The religious problem that organizes the double plot line of *Romola*—when does rebellion become a sacred duty?—is likewise transposed in this novel into political and social terms. As Rev. Lyon puts it, "the right to rebellion is the right to seek a higher rule, and not to wander in mere lawlessness"; again, the exemplar of such seeking is Felix (*FH* 242).

Perhaps because its primary preoccupations were political and legal, *Felix Holt* may stand out as Eliot's only novel without a spiritual crisis in its unfolding action. Felix's future faces great risk, yet he confronts no great interior crisis. Esther must choose whether to accept wealth and title or to seek a simple, passionate life with Felix; yet the novel allows her time to grow into the knowledge of herself and the world in such a way that she can make the decision without suffering. Mrs. Transome faces the inescapable consequences of her remote past, yet her life's great choices—which she failed at the time to recognize as massively consequential—have been made before the novel's action begins. She misses the opportunity for spiritual crisis, attesting to her impoverished knowledge of self and world (she resembles Janet before Repentance: "God had no pity," Mrs. Transome judges from her own center of self, "else her son would not have been so hard"

[*FH* 595]). Notably, for an Eliot novel, Mrs. Transome's suffering is morally inefficacious, serving only as a warning for others. Only Rufus Lyon experiences a genuine spiritual crisis of the sort we recognize in Eliot's novels, yet his crisis—falling in love with a friendless French Catholic widow, resigning his ministry, marrying her, and adopting Esther—precedes the action of the novel. Rufus Lyon's intense, complicated battle with himself, his shadowy religious doubts and their confluence with his fiery passion, his various resignations, his sacrifices all exist as prehistory for a novel set adamantly in a modern England, peopled by a "pence-counting, parcel-tying generation such as mostly fill your chapels," as Felix puts it rather harshly to Rev. Lyon (*FH* 146). George Eliot found herself writing a novel without a genuine spiritual crisis but instead a developing social and moral conscience.

It is no surprise that the spiritual barrenness of this novel yielded to the high tragic poem, "The Spanish Gypsy," that Eliot recast between the autumn of 1866 and the spring of 1868. In a letter to François D'Albert-Durade after its completion, she noted the disjuncture between her tastes and those "of our noisy, hurrying, ostentatious times" (GEL 4: 466). Writing poetry in such times, however, brought her "added happiness": "I seem to have gained a new organ, a new medium that my nature had languished for" (GEL 4: 465).

It is worth noting that in the 1860s it was still the case that, of literary genres, poetry retained the highest cultural value. The need to defend the novel's potential from what Eliot saw as its trivial (female) instances reminds us that the genre was still in the process of making a claim to literary seriousness and that Eliot did not *inherit* a high literary form but served as a major force in its mid-century cultural elevation.[3] Poetry's exclusive patina of high literary value and lasting meaning emerged from the Bible's historical identification as *the* major instance of poetry, as Charles LaPorte has described: "the Bible epitomized poetic beauty."[4] It was natural that, as a young evangelical, Mary Ann Evans had begun her writing career by publishing religious poetry. Religious truth and poetry's value were mutually affirming.

LaPorte convincingly contends that because of the strong association between scripture and poetry, Victorian writers understood their own original poetry as best positioned to create a new religious culture.[5] In this period of the 1860s we can see Eliot defining the linked terms "religious" and "poetic" for her own purposes. "Religion" she had reclaimed as early as *Scenes* to mean something wider than dogma, as she reiterated in her 1863 letter to Sara Hennell: "The contemplation of whatever is great is itself religion and lifts us out of our egoism" (GEL 4: 104). And "poetic"—while linked to religion—indicated a quality of lived life consecrated by a higher enthusiasm, as when Eliot described the Church of England as generating a "portion" of her "most poetic memories" (GEL 4: 214).

Yet in spite of these revised definitions, in which one could achieve a life of poetry and religion without Christian belief, perhaps *Felix Holt* depressed Eliot. It was her first novel that did not charge Christian teaching with efficacy and she followed it by shifting into poetry—and over to other ethnic, religious, and national affiliations—to seek again something hallowed and hallowing. Perhaps at this transitional moment in the trajectory of her novels, prose seemed emptied out of its religious potential, out of that store of feeling she imagined as wrought from ancient, great forces. It probably helped that poetry was not a lucrative endeavor ("Of course...it is not a work to get money by," she wrote to Blackwood [GEL 4: 355]); this economic disincentive would have affirmed for Eliot its sacred value.[6]

In her "Notes," Eliot described "The Spanish Gypsy" as inspired by an image of the Annunciation, attributed to Titian, that she saw in Venice. The image suggested to Eliot a "new train of thought": a young woman on the cusp of marriage finds she cannot live the ordinary lot of women but must take on a historical destiny. "She is chosen," wrote Eliot, "not by any momentary arbitrariness, but as a result of foregoing hereditary conditions: she obeys. 'Behold the handmaid of the Lord.'"[7] Yet Eliot appropriated what might have been a celebratory image for her own tragic purposes, merging it with what she understood (likely inaccurately) to be the historical conditions of the Roma, whom she called gypsies. Eliot rewrote the promise of the Annunciation as the problem of a divided female will, a young woman unable to realize her personal and collective identity simultaneously. The Christian image of chosenness that results in a world-redemptive birth led, for Eliot, to death and dissolution.

Eliot's propensity for tragedy—one she herself acknowledged—prepared her to see even in the Annunciation the problem to which her fiction recurred: love and duty in tragic conflict (GEL 4: 301).

This problem organized *The Mill on the Floss*, where Maggie renounces her passion for Stephen Guest because it will hurt others; Maggie knows the love is ethically flawed precisely because it will shatter any continuity with her past affiliations. "The Spanish Gypsy" reprises the scenario of a passionate love affair that transpires between the foundling Fedalma, raised in the Spanish court, and Duke Silva, the Catholic Spanish knight. Unlike Maggie and Stephen, these two fall in love blamelessly, though betrayal threatens: in the suspicious times of the Inquisition, Silva's uncle, Father Isidor, doubts Fedalma's loyalty to the Church, given her uncertain lineage. Still, if Fedalma is beneath Silva by birth and likely only grafted onto the church, nonetheless their love does not usurp anyone else's rightful place nor harm early loyalties. What emerge to divide them are religious, racial, and national differences: the facts of birth and past that Fedalma carries unconsciously.

Soon enough, the poem's first crisis comes when Fedalma discovers that she is the daughter of the Zincali chief, Zarca, who is imprisoned by Silva's court. Zarca presents Fedalma with a choiceless choice—between culpable personal ease in marriage to Silva, on one hand, and on the other her inherited destiny as his daughter and future queen of the gypsy people. When Fedalma reasonably says, let me marry Silva and then he will aid your aims out of his love for me, Zarca refuses such a utilitarian plan, insisting on an everlasting enmity between the gypsies and the Christians, and demanding Fedalma's total fidelity. In this way, Eliot insists on tragedy rather than any sort of potential compromise.

As hereditary representatives of different nations and races, Fedalma and Silva are divided by obligation writ large. Fedalma bears the burden of a long-harbored hope to gather the gypsies into a unified body and build a nation in Africa under the leadership of Zarca; Silva bears the trust of Spanish Christendom to guard against Muslim incursion. Yet, out of love for Fedalma, Silva rebels against his own high birth, accommodating Zarca's law by electing to join the despised race of gypsies alongside Fedalma. In doing this, he elects precisely the act that Zarca forbids Fedalma, stripping himself of all hereditary identity and affiliation. At the same time, he reverses gendered expectations of hierarchy in marriage and kinship affiliations, perhaps lowering himself even further.

If the outcome seems likely to be tragic, Eliot nevertheless organizes her tragedy to test Silva's idea of a world beyond human particularity: can universal human fellowship carry the day? Can a human being shed all inherited markers of identity—including gender—and encounter the world as "a heart without a livery – naked manhood," as Silva puts it? (*Poems* 334). From the outset, this experiment in universalist identity is rejected by the Jewish sage, Sephardo, who knows of what he speaks when he replies to Silva, "there's no such thing/As naked manhood" (*Poems* 334). Those punished and suspected for their identities, like the Jews under the Inquisition, or the Roma, understand human life as absolutely a matter of particularity: "While my heart beats, it shall wear livery," Sephardo concludes (*Poems* 334). Indeed, to join Fedalma, Silva cannot be merely a heart without a livery. He must put on new livery, the badge of that group, "More outcast and despised than Moor or Jew," as Fedalma puts it, in chagrin, when she first acknowledges her own identity (*Poems* 299). This livery attests not to any belief but strictly to affiliation.

Eliot made a consequential choice to explore matters of particularity and universality through the Roma, rather than, say, turning immediately to the Jews, as she would do in a sustained way in her final novel, *Daniel Deronda*. While she described settling on the Roma because her plot demanded volition—the Jews and Muslims were expelled from Spain, rather than electing to leave—the choice served her purposes in other ways as well. Sebastian Lecourt has explored Eliot's interest in the Jews as a landless people defined by a powerful material textual culture; Eliot defines the Roma, by contrast, in terms of the single principle of group loyalty—"their only faith is faith to each other" (*Poems* 301).[8] While they do seek a national seat, they lack a god, a creed, and a religious narrative, whether history or prophecy. Zarca describes that lack as the basis for his adhesion: the gypsies are "wanderers whom no God took knowledge of / To give them laws, to fight for them, or blight / Another race to make them ampler room; / Who have no Whence or Whither in their souls, / No dimmest lore of glorious ancestors / To make a common heart for piety" (*Poems* 299). "No favorites of heaven or of men," he concludes, "Therefore I cling to them!" (*Poems* 300). The recurring "no" emphasizes all they lack, and the absence of all the divine and human actions—to give, to fight, to make—that other peoples enjoy.

Zarca's triumphant reversal of all the negatives—"Therefore I cling"—offers a stinging rejection of the content of religious and national pride that undergirds alternative identities.[9] Although Fedalma sees her father as a religious leader who will transform the gypsies, just as the Jews, Christians, and Muslims were transformed—"They, too / Were slaves, lost, wandering, sunk beneath a curse, / Till Moses, Christ, and Mahomet were born" (*Poems* 303)—Zarca himself does not imagine a founding religious narrative. His hope is to instill nothing so teleological, but "impulses / Of generous pride, exalting fellowship / Until it soars to magnanimity" (*Poems* 302); he aspires to "call our Holy Place / The hearth that binds us in one family" (*Poems* 303). Faith is simply faith to fellow wanderers: "the fidelity / Of fellow-wanderers in a desert place / Who share the same fire thirst, and therefore share / The scanty water: the fidelity / Of men whose pulses leap with kindred fire." The fidelity—even to tempo and word here—is self-justifying and elemental. It aspires mainly to survival, in pulses and impulses.

Eliot insists on this palpable absence of content—of any reason for pride—at the center of the gypsies' identity. David Kurnick has persuasively interpreted the erratic and interrupted poetic rhythms of "The Spanish Gypsy" as indicating Eliot's experiment in imagining "community formed around the interruption of community, a polity somehow centered on the fact of outsiderdom."[10] Kurnick argues that in advance of *Daniel Deronda*, where Eliot would consider the "comforts of national belonging" via Jewish statehood, in "The Spanish Gypsy" she recognized that not all vulnerable minorities could aspire to statehood: what protection, what justice, could they find outside national belonging, in ethnically defined states?[11]

However, another way to understand the absence of content at the center of the gypsy identity is as religious critique. Such a reading makes good sense biographically speaking, in this transitional period in which Eliot moved away from a Christian model of conversion. Indeed, Zarca's leadership is one concentrated rebuke of Christendom's violence. This rebuke recalls both Feuerbach's understanding that religious love necessarily entails religious hatred and Marian Evans's rejection of an evangelicalism founded on such hatred (as she argued in her essay on Cumming). As Zarca says, a God who loves his people will "blight / Another race to make them ampler room" (*Poems* 299).

Each nation's god declares, "Life and more life unto the chosen, death / To all things living that would stifle them!" (*Poems* 419). Religious faith turns any outsider into nothing but a living "thing," seen only in terms of its challenge to the supremacy of the chosen nation; their death becomes the only alternative. When Zarca tells Fedalma the two peoples can never be at peace, he describes the Christians as faithless and avaricious: they "wring out gold by oaths they mean to break; / Take pay for pity and are pitiless" (*Poems* 379). The gypsies' ethical standard "on earth" is more rigorous because they claim no allegedly higher purposes or modes of adjudication: "We have *no* altars for such healing gifts / As soothe the heavens for outrage done on earth. / We have *no* priesthood and *no* creed" (*Poems* 396, emphases mine). Again, the repeating "no" is a source of contentless but palpable pride. This pride depends on the rebuffing of Christian values.[12]

Eliot provides ample support for Zarca's ethical claims by making Father Isidor and his prosecution of the Inquisition exemplars of the way in which "love must needs make hatred. He who loves / God and his law must hate the foes of God" (*Poems* 292). By contrast, Zarca voices a humanitarian curb on superfluous violence, and on vengeance itself. When the gypsies have the opportunity to put Father Isidor to death by fire, Zarca commands a quicker, less painful death by hanging. If they sink to vengeance, they will mimic their oppressors: "Punishing cruel wrong by cruelty / We copy Christian crime" (*Poems* 423). "High vengeance," rather than low, "tortures not the torturer, nor gives / Iniquitous payment for iniquity"; this way, they show the Christians that they "obey / A better law than his" (*Poems* 424).

Zarca may at first suggest to us Eliot's particular brand of secularization. Certainly, he voices her move toward a human ethics. But he does not voice anything like Felix Holt's gospel of making people's lives on earth a bit better, also heard in Eliot's longstanding refrain of "we poor mortals." Zarca is no universalist and he is no reformer. He is a tyrant without a god. He does not need religious creed to enslave his own daughter: "You have no right to choose," he tells her, given that she is of her father's blood (*Poems* 308). About himself, he asserts: "I choose not – I *am* Zarca. Let him choose / Who halts and wavers" (*Poems* 302). Like God, whose essence is synonymous with existence, Zarca cannot imagine a conflicted or divided identity. Fedalma (a name that bears within it the root of fidelity as well as the Hebrew term for maiden, *alma*, which Christians understand as the Prophet Isaiah's reference to the Virgin Mary) briefly resists her father's claims upon her identity: "I only owe / A daughter's debt; I was not born a slave" (*Poems* 309). Yet she cannot prevail, with "the weakness of a self / That is not one; denies and yet believes" opposite Zarca, "the steadfast man / Whose life was one compacted whole" (*Poems* 322).

Wholeness and its alternative, self-division, are the predominating qualities that Eliot used to manage the limited characterization of figures in the poem. Zarca and Father Isidor exemplify men absolutely identified with their beliefs and aims (both die), whereas Fedalma and Silva suffer a romantic love that subjects them to compromise either their personal or collective affiliations. Fedalma resolves to be her father's daughter and is willing to die personally for that inherited destiny. Silva, by contrast, is willing to kill off his identity-by-destiny and embrace a vital personal life with Fedalma. Ironically, it is his high birth and education that have shaped the man who can proudly assert: "I will elect my deeds, and be the liege / Not of my birth, but of that good alone / I have discerned and chosen" (*Poems* 402). And the irony of his rebellion is only reinforced when he declares, "I have a right to choose my good or ill, / A right to damn myself!", alerting any practiced reader of Eliot to recall that of course he does *not* have such a right. Eliot's characters have debts and obligations (following Comte), and the very terminology of "rights" tends to embed its own critique (*Poems* 412). Fedalma explains to Silva that following one's own impulses is a kind of moral childhood: "I made my creed so, just to suit my mood / And smooth all hardship, till my father came / And taught my soul by ruling it" (*Poems* 405).

Under duress, Silva does come to see that he cannot deny the claims upon him. When Silva's close comrades are killed in conflict with the gypsies and his uncle is condemned to death, the narrator offers us this insight into Silva's experience: "Silva had but rebelled – he was not free; And all the subtle cords that bound his soul / Were tightened by the strain of one rash leap / Made in defiance" (*Poems* 429). The self-division of Silva and of Fedalma, the limits to what they know of themselves, may have been the elements that made it impossible for Eliot to write this material as pure drama; a narrator was required to step in to parse the complication.

But Silva's and Fedalma's internal conflict also make them moderns for Eliot. If Father Isidor and Zarca live without dissonance, but instead in wholeness, it is no coincidence that both die without realizing their visions; they signify a consciousness far more difficult to sustain in modernity. Charles Taylor has described the way that the age of secularism might be defined by the experience of seeing one's faith as a choice among others, which is to say, *seeing* one's faith at all, being capable of seeing it rather than simply living it; of having no choice but to recognize the reality of multiple orientations, diverse ways of believing and living.[13] In "The Spanish Gypsy" Eliot outlines a world that makes at least some of its inhabitants aware of alternatives and expels them from the comfort of oneness; yet this world does not yet afford freedom for genuine, active choices. They possess knowledge without freedom.

In Fedalma, Eliot registers the pull toward a unity of experience impossible to regain once consciousness has interrupted it. Early in the poem, she dances before the people in answer to an irresistible impulse: "The joy, the life / Around, within me, were one heaven: I longed / To blend them visibly: I longed to dance / Before the people – be as mounting flame / To all that burned within them! Nay, I danced; / There was no longing: I did but the deed / Being moved to do it" (*Poems* 265). Longing is subsumed in the action that consummates it before it can even be felt; being and doing are one. The divisions between persons; between what is around and what is within; between them, I, and it; are all blent. Any gap between "I longed / To blend" is cancelled. Dance embodies the fullness of such experience. Later, when Fedalma is bereft of such unity, she looks at a young gypsy girl who has never learned "sad difference / For her, good, right, and law are all summed up / In what is possible: life is one web / Where love, joy, kindred, and obedience / Lie fast and even, in one warp and woof / With thirst and drinking, hunger, food, and sleep" (*Poems* 387–8). Natural urges and needs are no different, and impossible to separate, from social norms (listen to the enclosure of "what," "one web," "where," "one warp and woof," "with"). She will never have to choose.

Yet Fedalma will. And even when she and Silva finally part, and she tells him to "think of me as one who sees / A light serene and strong on one sole path / Which she will tread till death…" (*Poems* 449), Fedalma still differs from any woman was has not faced a "double path"

(*Poems* 388). Silva himself sets off for Rome in order to make the only possible pardon, "In deeds of duteous service" to Spain; to "regain the only life / Where he is other than apostate" (*Poems* 449). "In the thick of action," like Fedalma in dance, he may possibly reconsecrate his life.

It is fitting that a poem so consumed by problems of unity and division ends as Silva pulls away from shore, and "the waters widen between them" (*Poems* 452). If the poem seems to end by dividing its lovers, confirming the supremacy of affiliation by birth, Fedalma nevertheless says something more challenging at farewell: "We rebelled– / The larger life subdued us. Yet we are wed," because each carries the pressure of the other's soul (*Poems* 451). They did not succeed in defining themselves against their births, she says, yet they did not fail.

In a conviction consistent through all of George Eliot's work, the impress of one human being upon another, even when short-lived, even when separated by distance and death, matters. While the world shrinks down at the parting moment to the love between the two protagonists, Eliot resists the frame of merely human experience, but zooms out to watch the waters widen and achieves a larger frame by which to judge.

Tragedy was not empty. It was history and even "religion."

Notes

1. Cross, *Life*, 2: 255.
2. Cross, *Life*, 2: 447.
3. See Leah Price, *The Anthology and the Rise of the Novel, From Richardson to George Eliot* (Cambridge: Cambridge University Press, 2000), esp. pp. 105–56, for her claim that the anthologizing of Eliot "canonized her novels by packaging her as a poet" (p. 10); "decontextualization...transpose[d] Eliot's words from the most secular of nineteenth-century genres to the most sacred" (p. 113). Price argues that the hierarchy of genres was transformed into a gendered hierarchy of readers by the late nineteenth century.
4. Charles LaPorte, *Victorian Poets and the Changing Bible* (Charlottesville and London: University of Virginia Press, 2011), pp. 188–230, p. 9.
5. LaPorte, *Victorian*, p. 232.
6. "The Spanish Gypsy" succeeded in quickly selling out its first two editions. Eliot was pleased that it eventually sold nearly 4,000 copies in England and won the esteem of American poets.

7. See Avrom Fleishman, *George Eliot's Intellectual Life* (Cambridge: Cambridge University Press, 2010), pp. 130–1, who notes that Eliot chose not to write the Annunciation "itself as tragedy but to take it as archetypal," and then to find a historically resonant moment.
8. See Sebastian Lecourt, *Cultivating Belief: Victorian Anthropology, Liberal Aesthetics, and the Secular Imagination* (Oxford: Oxford University Press, 2018), pp. 102–29.
9. See David Kurnick, "Unspeakable George Eliot," *Victorian Literature and Culture* 38.2 (2010), pp. 489–509. He argues that the Roma interest Eliot because they are "by definition resistant to the redemptive logics of racial and cultural dignity," thus allowing her to examine the "differential availability of nationalism's rhetoric and reality" (p. 492).
10. Kurnick, "Unspeakable," p. 494.
11. Kurnick, "Unspeakable," p. 492.
12. To get a sense of the contemporary stakes of the poem, its ability to offend, consider the response of the American feminist reformer and ardent admirer of Eliot, Melusina Fay Peirce: "And then you made all the people in the book faithful but the Christian! Is that indeed the shallowest of all human allegiances? Nay. By Him who hung on the Cross, if I could not die with joy at the foot of it if he called me, I would choose to die now. Life else would have no value equal to the burden.... And how many thousand felt and have felt the same in every age" (GEL 8: 463).
13. Taylor, *Secular*, p. 3.

12
"With Measured Wing," 1869–1872

Eliot's final two novels, *Middlemarch* and *Daniel Deronda*, followed the tumultuous events of the summer of 1869. Lewes's son Thornie returned from South Africa fatally ill and suffered terribly from spinal tuberculosis until his death in October at twenty-five years old, with Marian by his side. Exhausted and shattered, Lewes and Marian mourned Thornie in three weeks of seclusion in Surrey. At Christmas, they visited his grave after the service and anthems at Rosslyn Hill Unitarian Chapel. In her journal Marian wrote, "This death seems to me the beginning of our own" (*Journals* 139); a month later, she wrote to her dear friend Barbara Bodichon, who had been a visitor throughout Thornie's illness, "I have a deep sense of change within, and of a permanently closer relationship with death" (GEL 5:70); the following July, she attested, "for nearly a year death seems to me my most intimate daily companion" (GEL 5: 107). In spite of the other significant deaths Marian had survived, her father's and her sister Chrissey's chief among them, she would never outlive one of the main problems faced by freethinkers of her generation: a post-theological relation to death.

In earlier writings, and in her own experience too, Marian had moved rapidly from death scenes to the afterlife of moral influence. She had responded to her father's death by asking what could now restrain her, as if his existence, and perhaps his tie to traditional belief, had held her intact. But memory quickly became for her a sacred trust. She inclined to end her early works with funerals and gravesite scenes in which the living visited the tombs of those who had acted powerfully on them in life, as in the Conclusions to two of the *Scenes of Clerical Life* and *The Mill on the Floss*.

Yet in the period of writing immediately before and after Thornie's death, Marian chose not to sentimentalize or redeem death by imagining a moral afterlife of personal influence. She put to the test even her precious hope that, through art or moral excellence, human lives could achieve a kind of immortality. While *Middlemarch* would allow her to dramatize a set of three difficult, non-exemplary deaths, Eliot first reconsidered death in a long poem inspired by the earliest chapters of Genesis, those that relate human history before the encounter with monotheism or the birth of any particular religion.

She focused on Cain, the first human being to murder and thus to witness death, but also the father of Jubal, Tubal-Cain, and Jabal, the hereditary lines from which all invention and culture originate in the scriptural account. In expanding a terse, interpretively challenging section of Scripture, Marian showed herself still very much interested in religious narratives as sources of meaning. Cannily, in calling her poem a "legend," she both commented on the non-historicity of Scripture, as she saw it, and also protected herself from the presumption of which any modern interpreter might be accused in taking on the authority of Scripture.

In terms of her own needs, the poem provided Marian with the chance to write death as a personal tiding—"our own"—by imagining a world in which death was as yet unknown and required conceptualizing and naming. In "The Legend of Jubal," begun in the summer and completed in January 1870, Eliot took human mortality to be a generative consciousness and represented death as a human fate inescapable, intensely lonely, and individuating. Eliot's poem opens with a backstory not found in Scripture in which Cain, banished as a wanderer, seeks to escape the land in which Jehovah reigns, and to find instead a "far strand / Ruled by kind gods who asked no offerings / Save pure field-fruits"; "Wild, joyous gods, who winked at faults and folly" (*Poems* 91). Just as Eliot had described in *Silas Marner* the primitive belief in territorial gods bound by land, here she evoked the amorality of such gods and linked Cain's belief in them to what he knew of himself: "He looked within, and saw them mirrored there" (*Poems* 91). This Feuerbachian gesture to the back-and-forth projection of human and divine qualities is rendered here as pre-existing any sort of monotheistic or Christian belief, suggesting a continuity from the earliest human history.

Yet the limitless nature of time and space in this world does differ fundamentally from the modernity Eliot represented in her novels. In the scriptural account, deep time includes humanity. Nature and humanity extend, repeat, expand: "Man's life was spacious in the early world," it "grew from strength to strength through centuries; / Saw infant trees fill out their giant limbs, / And heard a thousand times the sweet birds' marriage hymns" (*Poems* 91). Eliot's Cain, alone of humans, knows of the ending that is death, but believes he has left it behind. He sees no signs of illness or bodily degeneration, no sign of physical vulnerability to time or force, until his descendant Lamech strikes and kills his fairest boy in play (the scriptural account does not specify that the victim is his son or that the death occurs in play). All try to wake him, until Cain intercedes, with explanation: "He will not wake; / This is the endless sleep, and we must make / A bed deep down for him beneath the sod" (*Poems* 93). Cain lays death at Jehovah's angry will, telling his sons that not one of them will escape death because Jehovah has found him.

With death, time is invented. The consequences of time materialize in eagerness, anxiety, haste, the pressure of an ending. Now, "Time, vague as air before / New terrors stirred, / With measured wing now audibly arose / . . . Work grew eager, and Device was born" (*Poems* 93). (Of course, poetry too, Eliot's chosen form for this exploration of the emergence of art from death, depends on the divisions of time, arising "audibly" "with measured wing.") From a timeless present, past and future emerge as goads to activity. Individual identity, too, is born in the recognition that memory and imagination differentiate and perpetuate the image of each person: "Come, let us fashion acts that are to be, / When we shall lie in darkness silently, / As our young brother doth, whom yet we see / Fallen and slain, but reigning in our will / By that one image of him pale and still" (*Poems* 94).

But Eliot softens the knowledge of future loss by asserting that love is refined when its temporal limits are recognized: "No form, no shadow, but new dearness took / From the one thought that life must have an end; / And the last parting now began to send / Diffusive dread through love and wedded bliss, / Thrilling them into finer tenderness" (*Poems* 94). "No" form, "no" shadow turn to "new," as the knowledge includes *all* things seen fresh. "Now" the bond of marriage, too, shifts from sheer bliss to tenderness from the knowledge that it will not last forever. Morality itself seems born from the knowledge of death; human relations take a new tenderness in this world where Jehovah's capacity to end life introduces into being something beyond joy and wildness, beyond the easily given gifts that Cain had preferred to painful sacrifice. The world of Eliot's poem begins to look more like the world her readers know.

With mortality and then morality come the inventions of art and technology. We might imagine that art and technology would be preservers of human memory, given the way this poem is going, yet they are not. Expanding dramatically on the single scriptural verse that details Lamech's three sons each founding a category of culture (the nomadic cattle-herding life, metalwork, and music), Eliot describes Jubal building the lyre and bringing forth song and harmony. From here forward the poem frees itself of all scriptural basis, as Eliot offers a tale of quest and attempted return. Jubal's gifts spread so rapidly that he wishes to take himself to distant lands to learn new songs. He travels an ever-extending world until he finally seeks home, with weakened capacities. He imagines reuniting with his brethren. Yet at this point he is unrecognizable: "in ignorant eyes / No sign remained of Jubal, Lamech's son, / That mortal frame wherein was first begun / The immortal life of song" (*Poems* 107). Hope grows when music reaches his ear and he hears the refrain of his own name, Jubal: "The longing grew that they should hold him dear / Him, Lamech's son, whom all their fathers knew, / The breathing Jubal –him, to whom their love was due" (*Poems* 110). "Him," repeated three times to clarify beyond a doubt the identity of the sign, "Jubal," with its referent. Lamech's son, the breathing Jubal, enclosed between the two "hims" is meant to be held dear, with love due. Yet Jubal is not welcomed and he suffers from his very human longing "to claim the deed / That lived away from him, and grew apart, / While he as from a tomb, with lonely heart, / Warmed by no meeting glance, no hand that pressed / Lay chill amid the life his life had blessed" (*Poems* 110).

For someone of Eliot's stated beliefs, this should be the moment in which Jubal's own impending death is assimilated into the vibrant "life his life had blessed." Yet the assimilation fails. For the living, mortal man there is no warmth, no value to this immortality through abstraction and separation (the deed that lives on, away from him), through memory that is defined by the one who remembers rather than the one remembered. As if he has come back from the dead to see a world without himself, Jubal suffers what seems almost a usurped identity. When he cannot help himself but cries out "I am Jubal," he is met with derisive laughter, which soon flares into anger against the felt desecration, paradoxical as it may be, of his own name: "Jubal was but a name in each man's faith / For glorious power untouched by...slow death" (*Poems* 111). Two believers violently cast him out (two being the operative number of division) to his death. In these climactic sections of the poem, Eliot insists on the pain of a double, divided identity, witnessing to the tragic end of a single mortal life: "The immortal name of Jubal filled the sky / While Jubal lonely laid him down to die" (*Poems* 112).

Yet in the last stanzas Eliot tries to repair tragedy and to reglorify the immortal gift Jubal has given to humanity, that "nought but Earth's destruction can destroy" (*Poems* 114).[1] Jubal sees a face of love which gazes on him and speaks to him, mystically reunifying himself and Song; his present, past, and even future. Further, Jubal is told that his death is an atonement for the greatness of his gift, a way to "atone / For too much wealth amid their poverty" (*Poems* 114). His death is thus marked by no tomb, no cemetery, nor gravesite scene, the poem's final line affirming instead "The All-creating Presence for his grave" (*Poems* 114). While this vague description leaves more questions than it answers, it suggests some kind of subsuming into the divine presence, the dissolution of personal ego in universal space and time.

By the time she wrote this poem, Eliot had achieved her standing among England's premier novelists. It would only be strengthened after the death of Dickens (felt as a personal loss by Marian and Lewes) in June 1870. Yet "The Legend of Jubal" was of a piece with other poetry that Eliot included in her 1874 collection of poems, none of which, Fionnuala Dillane notes, easily affirmed the bromide that an individual could achieve immortality, whether through art or any other sort of legacy. In Eliot's works "personal erasure," Dillane demonstrates, is not represented as a "generous act of will" but as an "uncontrollable outcome" of the vicissitudes of memory and historical change, and the unpredictable nature of artistic reception and circulation.[2] *Middlemarch* would afford Eliot a grand stage on which to consider these problems.

She had begun writing *Middlemarch* the summer before Thornie's death in 1869, composing a few chapters detailing the old miser, Featherstone; the middle-class Vincy family; and the ambitious doctor-scientist, Lydgate, in a plot line that would turn out to be only one strand of the novel's web. After finishing "Jubal" and a second long poem, "Armgart," Marian resumed prose writing in November with a distinct narrative that she called "Miss Brooke." This narrative ultimately became the commanding opening of her novel. With Dorothea Brooke's entrance into *Middlemarch*, a change became evident: much of the anxiety that had characterized her novel-writing until that point in life seemed to fall away. For a long stretch, neither Marian's journal nor her letters convey desperation or extreme lack of confidence.[3] Even her remark to Blackwood in March 1870, "My novel, I suppose, will be finished some day: it creeps on," rings lightly ironic and is immediately left for other subjects (GEL 5: 81).

The quiet in her journal and letters attests to intensive work, clarity of purpose, and gathered powers. The feminist educator and founder of Girton College, Emily Davies, met her around this time and wrote to a third party, "She thinks she has done very little, in quantity.... It is still amazing to me, though she seemed only to feel how *little* she had done, how she has managed to get through so much work, actual hard labour, in the time. A great deal of it must have been very rapidly done" (GEL 8: 466).

One striking feature of the letters penned during Eliot's writing of *Middlemarch* is the very strong continuity between the tone of the historical woman, Marian Lewes, and her narrator, as well as a number of near-identical overlaps in content. Perhaps she felt an unprecedented ease occasioned by leaving poetry and returning to the novel, its generic claims less closely associated by readers and by herself with sacred texts; its shorter history, leaving her field wide open; and its flexible multivocality, uniquely inviting for a writer capable of everything from humorous dialogue to ironic commentary, to scientific analogy, to informed moral philosophy. Now, too, she was writing without any burden of disguise at a time when her partnership with Lewes had outlived the social recoil, and she had returned "home" from the experiments of her middle period—historical romance, poetry, and condition-of-England novel—to a provincial English novel set in the remembered past. She had also returned to the beloved, familiar landscape and mindscape of the Midlands, a reference her title suggested as well.[4]

Middlemarch is a huge novel: huge in the place it occupies in the English canon and the history of the development of the novel, and huge as a readerly challenge. Yet when we consider it biographically, it stands out as Eliot's most comprehensive novel about marriage and about death. In scrutinizing marriage and death, *Middlemarch* became the novel that most closely broached deeply personal religious matters that Marian never chose to write as autobiography nor to dramatize as George Eliot in a directly transposed fiction. In *Middlemarch*, contemporary marriage and its demands for the transformation of interpersonal relations became the lens through which Eliot considered religious faith and its necessary transformations. Yet the consequence of this overlap between marriage and religious faith was finally a far more secularized version of religion.

Focalized through her young heroine Dorothea's first marriage to the desiccated scholar Edward Casaubon, Eliot depicted, first, the childlike relations of simple faith and the blind worship of a powerful deity; and second, the painful evolution of such worship into far less hierarchical adult relations. In these relations, human beings pity and love (rather than worship) imperfect others, in a state of knowledge and a recognition of personal freedom always tempered by the rightful claims of dependent others. In this complex schema, death took a very particular role—a limiting function—rather than a theological meaning. Death served to clarify the extent to which any one human being could make claims on another's life. Rather than serving as a force for positive moral influence or a legacy of good, as Eliot seemed to preach in other works, in *Middlemarch* death repeatedly features as a bar to undue influence; it seems to issue anew the verdict of human mortality on people who seek power beyond the grave, a power we might think of as godlike.

In tracing Dorothea's path to and then through her ill-matched marriage, Eliot offers us the anatomy of a relation "awful in the nearness it brings," in which secrets of personality and past actions will eventually out (*MM* 729). Yet first Eliot shows us the phases of illusion, which she describes as faith. When a hopeful Dorothea listens to Casaubon, she does not note what is missing from his words or what opposes or offers counter-evidence to her own hopes: "She filled up all blanks with unmanifested perfections, interpreting him as she interpreted the works of Providence, and accounting for seeming discords by her own deafness to the higher harmonies" (*MM* 66).

Eliot comments on the gendered inequalities of such projections—and their costs—across the novel. In Dorothea, Eliot depicts what an ardent young girl might think of a highly educated man when she lacks or denies empirical information. In her depiction of the failed marriage between the ambitious doctor-scientist Lydgate and the provincial beauty Rosamond Vincy, Eliot notes that Lydgate's scientific curiosity never extended to the range of female psychologies, suggesting that he bears culpability for his poor choice. Dorothea's culpability is less pronounced because, as a young woman without any helpful guardian, she has had a badly limited education.

Yet Eliot is interested as well in a type of personality that has a great capacity for worship and belief, in an era without a religious framework sufficient to such instincts. As a relation between two human beings, marriage cannot but collapse under the inequality of worship. Dorothea's affectionate belief seeks an outlet, like "every sweet woman, who has begun by showering kisses on the hard pate of her bald doll, creating a happy soul within that woodenness from the wealth of her own love" (*MM* 181). Such imaginative play is a version of the Feuerbachian dialectic in which a human being misrecognizes her own resources in a being she herself has animated. But Dorothea remains childlike into her young adulthood, possessing

> a nature which was entirely without hidden calculations either for immediate effects or for remoter ends. It was this which made Dorothea so childlike, and, according to some judges, so stupid, with all her reputed cleverness; as, for example, in the present case of throwing herself, metaphorically speaking, at Mr. Casaubon's feet, and kissing his unfashionable shoe-ties as if he were a Protestant Pope. She was not in the least teaching Mr. Casaubon to ask if he were good enough for her, but merely asking herself anxiously how she could be good enough for Mr. Casaubon. (*MM* 44)

Dorothea's "ador[ation] without criticism," "her worship...[of] him with perfect trust," ultimately harms her, in setting up an unsustainable basis for the close, daily living-together of marriage (*MM* 382). When she receives Casaubon's stilted proposal of marriage, she trembles, falls on her knees, buries her face, and sobs. She cannot even pray: "she could but cast herself, with a childlike sense of reclining, in the lap of a divine consciousness which sustained her own" (*MM* 37–8). That reclining extends beyond the divine to the object of her adoration.

Later, when her eyes are opened to her husband's fallibility, the narrator tells us that it had been "easier...to imagine how she would devote herself" to Casaubon, easier to hope to "become wise and strong in his strength and wisdom," than to see him as human, one among the "we poor mortals," and "to conceive with that distinctness which is no longer reflection but feeling —an idea wrought back to the directness of sense, like the solidity of objects— that he had an equivalent centre of self" (*MM* 193). It is much more difficult to know how to proceed, to know what is required of her, when she learns—with the same fullness in which she had previously reclined—that he is imperfect, bearing his own private hurts and desires. Then she cannot rest on his wisdom but must continuously supply her own wisdom to determine how to act.

Casaubon's death highlights this dilemma even more than his life because it is only from his will that Dorothea learns he has secretly suspected her of an affiliation with his cousin Will Ladislaw. Casaubon's will asks of her two things: not to marry Will, on pain of giving up her inheritance, and to devote herself to finishing his own fruitless scholarly work, the "Key to All Mythologies." But Casaubon goes too far in death: the insult of suspecting Dorothea of anything ignoble results in her feeling free from all further obligation. Casaubon claimed her pity in life, but it ends with his death. Like all mortals, Casaubon has had his chance while alive. Yet while Casaubon's death does allow for Dorothea to find more happiness in love, it does not solve the novel's problem of faith, of what to believe in, of how to believe, of the discrepancy between faith in those "higher harmonies" of Providence and the empirical evidence of our own senses.

For Eliot, the "how-tos" of faith were framed less as an existential problem than as a historical problem. *Middlemarch* poses at the outset the difficult mismatch between a "passionate, ideal nature" that seeks to shape "thought and deed in noble agreement" and the "meanness of opportunity" in a historical moment shaped by no "coherent social faith and order" (*MM* 1). Emily Davies remembered Marian telling her that the "want of education" made a "theoretic or dogmatic religion impossible for the mass of the English people," and that since the Reformation there had been no possibility of an "imaginative religion" (GEL 8: 465). In Dorothea Eliot created a heroine who, in another time, might have elected a life that would see her later canonized as a saint.[5] Yet in the 1830s, in provincial England as a young woman of birth and fortune, she has only the path of marriage lying obviously before her.

While "the hereditary strain of Puritan energy" "glow[s] alike through [her] faults and virtues," Dorothea's own religion is doctrinally vague, especially if we compare her to earlier Eliot heroines who are at least exposed to powerful doctrine, even if they are not fully articulate nor educated believers (*MM* 5). Impulsive, curious, and utterly unselfconscious, Dorothea understands the Christian keystones of sacrifice and renunciation to be obvious parts of her religion, yet until her marriage there is nothing of moment that she is called upon to sacrifice or renounce. Her "religion" seems largely self-invented, as she later tells Will Ladislaw: "I have always been finding out my religion since I was a little girl" (*MM* 357). In a reflection of the novelist's dislike for sectarian divides, Dorothea confidently believes "ecclesiastical forms and articles of belief" to be less important than "that spiritual religion, that submergence of self in communion with Divine perfection," yet the narrator's tone in this description leans more to irony than affirmation (*MM* 19–20). The irony perhaps comes from the difficulty of taking such an abstract belief as a life program. What specific deeds nobly agree with such lofty thoughts?

Yet Dorothea's religion, abstract as it is, does motivate her action in the novel and, equally important, it organizes her capacities of thought. Her "communion with Divine perfection" is paradoxically— and characteristically for Eliot—rooted in the here and now. There may as well be no world to come for all the difference it makes to Dorothea's faith. Like Felix Holt, Dorothea desires to make *this* world better, to make people's lives easier. Her "generous schemes" (mostly condescended to or ignored by those around her) are appropriately nineteenth-century: to build improved cottages for those on her uncle's estate and to encourage nearby gentry and nobility to do the same; and when she comes into her own fortune, to set up an industrial village, where workers can be employed and educated on-site (*MM* 5).

But Dorothea's influential actions in the novel originate in her special propensity for self-evacuating thought and affirming belief. She recognizes and responds to others' needs even when they preempt her own, and she believes in figures whom others suspect or judge wrongly (she also writes philanthropic checks at the right moment).[6] Worldly-wise she is not. She is ardent. Her faith in others creates new realities in Middlemarch; as David Carroll puts it, this sort of act "brings into being what it believes to be true."[7] Across the novel we find examples that suggest this sort of faith does not go to waste.

Yet Eliot knew that it *would* be possible to read this provincial *Middlemarch* as a story of waste, of the meanness of opportunity triumphing over an ardent, intelligent woman and limiting her to the round of wife and mother, eventually the helpmeet of a public man, her second husband, Will Ladislaw. The novel holds that possible interpretation within its pages from first to last. Yet the "Finale" tries to cut that sense of disillusionment and waste by affirming the effects of Dorothea's goodness, her active adherence to what had become for Eliot the main article of faith: the duty not to stand apart self-protectively but to ease any of the shared human suffering one witnesses nearby. "Her finely-touched spirit had still its fine issues, though they were not widely visible. Her full nature...spent itself in channels which had no great name on the earth. But the effect of her being on those around her was incalculably diffusive: for the growing good of the world is partly dependent on unhistoric acts" (*MM* 766). Legacy here becomes thoroughly impersonal ("no great name") and absorbed into a general meliorism. The intensity of Dorothea's defining "fine spirit," and "full nature," come in the end to something that is no longer hers, an "effect" which is "diffusive," the adjective and noun diffused themselves by what comes in between: "those around her." Such a schema addresses and perhaps consoles the painful finality of a human death (always individual).

Feminist critics, most of all, have rightfully questioned the restraints Eliot imposed on her heroines while living a more realized life herself. In terms of vocation, they are correct. Yet in a novel so preoccupied with marriage, it is worth noting that the second marriage to Will Ladislaw—a marriage misunderstood, rejected, and maligned by good society—allowed Dorothea to prevail where "The Spanish Gypsy"'s Fedalma had not: the "larger life" did not "subdue" Dorothea. Personal happiness needs to be recognized in the work of George Eliot, and in the context of mid-Victorian dominant moral culture, as itself "rebellion," just as Fedalma says. Fedalma's end had prompted the feminist reformer Melusina Fay Peirce (who would soon after leave her own marriage) to write to Eliot, "Darling, The Spanish

Gypsy made me sad, it was so noble...but must noble women always fail? Is there no sumptuous flower of happiness for us?" (GEL 8: 463).

Middlemarch offers us another biographical insight as well: at this moment in her career, Marian Evans Lewes said much the same sort in her letters as George Eliot said in her novels.[8] To the young educator Oscar Browning she wrote on January 31, 1870, that he was correct in being grateful for "unquestionable duties," which were better than "vague ambitions": "One must care for small immediate results as well as for great and distant ones—and in my own mind nothing takes greater emphasis than the possibility of being certain that our own character and deeds make a few lives near to us better than they would have been without our presence in the world. Scepticism has less chance of creeping in here than in relation to larger results" (GEL 5: 76). In writing to another close friend six weeks later, Marian thanked her for being among friends "who make an English life dear .... One lives by faith in human goodness, the only guarantee that there can be any other sort of goodness in the universe. See how diffusive your one little life may be. I say that àpropos of your longing for a wider existence" (GEL 5: 82–3). To Emily Davies she had written the year before, with regard to the opening of Girton College with five female students: "I care so much about individual happiness, that I think it a great thing to work for, only to make half a dozen lives rather better than they might otherwise be" (GEL 8: 468).

The language of the novel's driving questions and her own experience had coalesced. If earlier in her writing life her novels often trailed her own lived convictions and re-examined faith positions she had inhabited in her past, the panoply that is *Middlemarch*—the novel that Virginia Woolf so famously named a novel for grown-up people—brought Marian Evans Lewes and George Eliot in step.

Notes

1. I read this quite differently than Dillane, who suggests that Eliot is emphasizing the precariousness of human legacy in a post-human world. This phrase, "nought but," suggests to me the opposite: an extreme and unlikely limit. See Fionnuala Dillane, "George Eliot's Precarious Afterlives," *19: Interdisciplinary Studies in the Long Nineteenth Century* 29 (2020), pp. 1–26, https://doi.org/10.16995/ntn.1981.
2. Dillane, "Precarious," p. 3.

3. Harris and Johnston note that Eliot abandoned her diary as she entered more fully into *Middlemarch*: "the months of silence are a provocative contrast to the almost daily record of despair in the painful writing of *Romola*" (*Journals* 91–2).
4. Ruth Livesey notes that the provincial novel also allowed Eliot to represent class in the paradoxical way that characterized her politics (cf. *Felix Holt*), both radically attentive to representing the underrepresented and unwilling to countenance class opposition or upset: "George Eliot's pattern of setting her fiction in the just-historical period of her own, or her parents' youth, back into a rural landscape is a means to stage relations between the classes impossible in modern city life, where workers and employers lived increasingly divided and differentiated lives. Contemporary class relations are, in this sense, ever present in her fiction in the narrative mode that invokes them to set them aside" (Livesey, "Class," p. 101).
5. See David Carroll, *George Eliot and the Conflict of Interpretations* (Cambridge: Cambridge University Press, 1992), pp. 234–72. In a virtuoso chapter on the novel, Carroll sees *Middlemarch* as asking, via Dorothea: "Can the life of a saint with its hagiographic sequence of renunciation, testing, and martyrdom, provide a hermeneutic for the heroine's career in the decentered world of Middlemarch?" (pp. 242–3). Carroll reads Bulstrode, too, in terms of "radically redefined martyrdom," arguing that he becomes a "justified sinner" through a "natural supernaturalism" (p. 263).
6. I am grateful to Nina Auerbach, who pointed out Dorothea's heroic check-writing to me.
7. Carroll, *Conflict*, p. 271.
8. Bodenheimer has definitively clarified that the letters were another stage upon which successive personae were crafted, yet the overlap here is still notable.

13
"In Heaven or On Earth," 1873–1881

Middlemarch was acknowledged by Victorian readers and reviewers as a masterpiece. By the time of its publication, "George Eliot" was not only an unrivalled literary great but also a sacred celebrity, having survived the years of scandal and exclusion to become a sought-after London address. She received letters and gifts from readers and attracted young and ardent admirers, as well as major figures of the British establishment, from the Queen, Crown Prince, and Princess Royal downward. She met with Charles Darwin, John Ruskin, and Matthew Arnold, and frequently with Alfred Lord Tennyson, Anthony Trollope, and the Burne-Jones family; outside England, she maintained ties with Franz Liszt and met Ivan Turgenev, maintained a warm correspondence with Harriet Beecher Stowe and commanded the awe of Emily Dickinson. In 1871, she granted permission for her works to be excerpted and anthologized in a volume entitled "Wise, Witty and Tender Sayings," as the novels and the poetry continued to sell, bringing her significant income in royalties (by 1879, *Middlemarch* had sold nearly 30,000 copies worldwide). She and Lewes made semi-regular trips in the late 1860s and 1870s to Oxford and to Cambridge, visiting with such major intellectual and cultural forces as the liberal theologian and translator Benjamin Jowett, Master of Balliol College from 1870, who became a highly trusted friend, and the moral philosopher Henry Sidgwick, among others. While Marian chose not to resume relations with Fanny Houghton, her half-sister, it seemed that only her brother, Isaac, still maintained his harsh ban.

If Isaac read *Middlemarch*, he likely would have been strengthened in his position. *Middlemarch* was the novel in which Eliot came closest to a love song to Lewes. Against a backdrop of failed legal marriages,

Middlemarch granted an ardent heroine freedom to make the controversial, widely decried choice of a man to whom she was intensely attracted, with whom she fell in love, by whom she was fully appreciated and passionately loved. The novel offers us no view of that intimacy from its inside, focusing instead on the point of view of its detractors and its skeptics. But in everything Marian Evans Lewes wrote about her own longstanding union with Lewes—who was as sunny as Will Ladislaw, as witty and responsive to suggestion; who was, like Will, more principled and loyal than others took him for; and who was far more intellectually wide-ranging and brilliant than Will—the joys of their life together never abated, in spite of early scandal, familial demands and difficulties, hard work at their chosen careers, financial pressure (that abated over time), the deaths of Lewes's sons Thornie and Bertie (in 1875), and all along much ill health for both.

After *Middlemarch*, Eliot would write one more novel, *Daniel Deronda*, and one genre-bending set of essays, *Impressions of Theophrastus Such*, before Lewes's cataclysmic death on November 30, 1878. After and as part of the intense mourning of his death, she would immerse herself in bringing out a final volume of his *Problems of Life and Mind* before she again defied all expectation and married the young banker, her financial advisor and intimate family friend, John Cross. Rehabilitating herself in the eyes of her brother (not incidentally returning to her childhood name, Mary Ann, at the same time that she added her first legally married surname), she lived with Cross less than a year before her own death in December 1880.

The great Eliot scholar Gillian Beer has written that Eliot's final novel, *Daniel Deronda*, is, of all her works, most focused upon the future.[1] We complete the novel as its English hero, Deronda, newly aware that he is a Jew, newly married to a fellow Jew, sets off for the East with largely undefined national aspirations. Meanwhile, we leave the novel's other main character, Gwendolen, still young, recently widowed, without children, newly aware of an immense world beyond herself in which she can choose to be a moral agent. These are very open-ended conditions, ones which, in other Eliot novels, often mark the middle of the action. Here, not only does the novel end on such conditions, but Eliot offers us none of the postscripts that she and other Victorian novelists adopted to delimit the future of novels whose endings in marriage and conversion lay open to question or doubt. The "idea of a future," which had preoccupied Marian for decades in the wake of unorthodoxy, was perhaps finally coming into sight.[2] The future now connoted an unknown that was visibly rooted in this world, in history, and in a combination of feeling, thought, and activity that would shape it. Eliot's imagination was not drawn, however, to the idea of a Christian future.[3] The dynamic future in Eliot's final novel is Jewish, Hebraic, and proto-Zionist.

Daniel Deronda has been read in recent years as Eliot's argument for the limits of cosmopolitan identity, given that Daniel, raised as a Christian but always unsure of his birth, finds purpose in discovering his particular history. Only when he learns what is not his to will, that he was born to a Jewish mother, can he imagine and dedicate himself to a future. He embraces the close family relations, the demands of a new education and language, and the pioneering national action that his identity now offers him. In affirming his Jewish identity, one that other figures in the novel imagine would naturally inspire shame, rejection, or benign neglect, Daniel affirms one of Eliot's most beloved beliefs: that all morality, and thus (for Eliot) all religious feeling, blossom best from affective ties to particular, early experiences of places and people. In Daniel's case, Eliot expands this principle dramatically, to even those attachments that are inherited rather than personally lived: a chest of documents that had been his grandfather's; writings and teachings bequeathed to him by his spiritual mentor, Mordecai; synagogue melodies that stir him, in spite of not having been raised with them. Daniel welcomes these kind of strong connections as claims upon him and accepts them as directives for the future.

A mystical cast characterizes these powerful transgenerational and interpersonal exchanges; they challenge purely rational explanation or prediction.[4] Daniel appears out of the fading daylight to Mordecai, just as Mordecai has imagined he will; before Daniel meets his mother and discovers his Jewish roots, he has already been well predisposed to, even hopeful for, such an outcome, by having chanced to save the young Jew, Mirah, and then encountered the dying Jew, Mordecai, who will turn out to be her brother. While predominantly realist Victorian novels trade regularly in such unlikely revelations of kinship and descent, Eliot's novels tend not to. And here, in the most "modern" of her novels, one set unusually close (for Eliot) to the time of its composition, concerned with the relationship between modernity, autonomy, and inherited religious identity, these coincidences and revelations cannot simply be explained as stock generic elements. Repeatedly, they pose the question of the world's working: are events prepared? Are they guided by spiritual or suprarational forces? Are individuals defined by souls they carry, without their own knowledge or will?

The novel opens famously with a tricky epigraph, radical in its implication, that Eliot quoted from no source but her own imagination: "Men can do nothing without the make-believe of a beginning" (*DD* 35). She goes on to argue that not only Poetry, which we might expect, but Science, too, can begin to measure time only "*in medias res.*" The epigraph ends: "No retrospect will take us to the true beginning; and whether our prologue be in heaven or on earth, it is but a fraction of that all-presupposing fact with which our story sets out" (*DD* 35). Though the novel is a search for beginnings—both Daniel's and Christianity's—the true beginning, says Eliot, is inaccessible. Not Scripture, nor science, nor any narrative can grasp its fullness.

Deronda is paradoxically Eliot's most searching novel with respect to the problem of the spiritual and the empirical, but at the same time the most explicitly agnostic in its answer.[5] The phrase "in heaven or on earth" inscribes the question of whether human life originates with (and perhaps is directed by) the supernatural, returning readers to a problem that, since "Janet's Repentance," Eliot delimited to the province of individual characters' experiences and convictions. But at this much later moment in her oeuvre and in her life, Eliot suggests that the answer to the question matters less than an acknowledgment of the limits of human knowledge, whatever one believes. "Whether the prologue is in heaven or on earth," the outcome is the same with respect to human beings, who can grasp but a fraction of the "all-presupposing fact" of a beginning; human beings write a "story" enmeshed in a world of fact, spiritual or empirical, to which we have but the most partial access.

Eliot is unwilling to "superciliously prejudge," as she has Deronda put it, any sort of faith, whether in Science or in Providence (*DD* 553).[6] This is nineteenth-century agnosticism laid out before us: no direct contradiction of "whether...in heaven," but a ready admission of insufficient knowledge. And in this agnostic key the novel unfolds. The novel repeats the coupled phrasing, "heaven and earth," "heaven or earth," five times (in *Middlemarch*, it does not appear at all), over and over pulling together the divine and the human realms that Christian theology so regularly divides as a way for Eliot to indicate totality.

At the same time, this unification never renders a judgment on heaven or its workings.

We can see the agnostic disposition in Eliot's refusal to represent spiritual or suprarational phenomena as superstitious. (Like many educated Victorians, including Charles and Erasmus Darwin, George Eliot and Lewes had been open and interested enough to attend a seance in January, 1874, but left before it was over, unimpressed. In June 1872, Eliot had written tactfully in response to Harriet Beecher Stowe's report of communication with the spirit of Charlotte Brontë that she found it "(whether rightly or not) so enormously improbable," and had "but a feeble interest in these doings, feeling my life very short for the supreme and awful revelations of a more orderly and intelligible kind which I shall die with an imperfect knowledge of" [GEL 5: 280–1]). While Eliot represents gambling as running on primitive superstition, by contrast, she represents spiritual phenomena as credible when ethical agents such as Mordecai experience them in tandem with sacred obligation, untainted by personal ambition.[7] At times such agents can be elevated by rational others to the level of spiritual visionary. For the visionary, the personal and collective past carry affective force with powerful influence on the future; meanwhile, the idea of the future works as so powerful a lever for present action that they see and feel somewhere across time.

Mordecai describes this state in wholly spiritual, but also historical, terms, as carrying a recreated soul through exilic time and space toward national redemption:

> It was the soul fully born within me.... It brought its own world—a mediaeval world, where there are men who made the ancient language live again in new psalms of exile. They had absorbed the philosophy of the Gentile into the faith of the Jew, and they still yearned toward a center for our race. One of their souls was born again within me, and awakened amid the memories of their world. It traveled into Spain and Provence; it debated with Aben-Ezra; it took ship with Jehuda ha-Levi; it heard the roar of the Crusaders and the shrieks of tortured Israel. And when its dumb tongue was loosed, it spoke the speech they had made alive with the new blood of their ardor, their sorrow, and their martyred trust: it sang with the cadence of their strain. (*DD* 555–6)

Mordecai understands his soul as inherited from the greatest medieval poets and scholars who traveled among the nations, taking from what is best (the philosophy of the Gentiles) and mixing it with their national impulse, expressing it in Hebrew prose and poetry for the ages. Eliot describes this "soul" as characterizing a time traveler so shaped by awareness of a human history of collective, national faith that all his personal purpose coalesces in seeing and awaiting a future redemption with complete faith and patience.

By insisting on a Jewish future as well as a storied Jewish past, Eliot distinguished her novel against prevailing social and literary norms. In her early story "The Lifted Veil," Eliot seemed to suggest that Judaism was a dead religion, but by the time she wrote *Daniel Deronda* she was concerned by the general English ignorance of Judaism on its own terms and as the roots of their own national religion. The novel traces Daniel's dawning awareness as he awakens from the misperceptions that Judaism is an "eccentric, fossilised form" that an "accomplished man" need not know anything about (*DD* 411); that all "learned and accomplished Jews" "had dropped their religion, and wished to be merged in the people of their native lands" (*DD* 246). As the novel's events unfold, Daniel and others close to him are confronted by the "hitherto neglected reality that Judaism was something still throbbing in human lives" (*DD* 411). The novel's ending in a marriage between two Jews, Daniel and Mirah, rather than in the conversion of a Jewish heroine and the "erasure" of her identity in marriage to a non-Jew (a plot line raised and dismissed out of hand in the novel) or the exile of Jewish elements, was Eliot's repudiation of English ignorance.[8]

The Jewish medium of *Daniel Deronda* was informed by Eliot's voluminous reading of Jewish history and her entry into the foundational texts of the religion. Her notebooks from this study are replete with detailed tables and information about the Jewish calendar; the Hebrew names for the months and sacred days; long quotations from the liturgy of the High Holidays; descriptions of daily and weekly Sabbath practices; analysis of the distinct weave of the Talmud into its component parts of law and story (with Hebrew terms *halakha* and *aggada*), as well as external quoted sources (*b'raita*); stories of the ancient rabbis and the eventual composition of the oral law as written; major medieval poets and philosophers; the history of English Jewry from their expulsion under Edward I to their gradual return around the time of

Cromwell, their persecution and their protection under Charles II, and their path to acceptance as official subjects over the eighteenth century; the relation between Catholic emancipation and Jewish enfranchisement; the observation that the seven Jews in Parliament represented the Jewish minority of 60,000 in England more fully than any other minority; and descriptions of synagogues of note, distinction of leadership roles within the synagogue, sketches of communities, neighborhoods, and schools.[9]

Emanuel Deutsch (1829–73), Eliot's learned Jewish friend from 1867 until his death, was a significant influence at this time. Though he served only as an assistant in the library of the British Museum from 1855, he was a well-published and accomplished German-trained scholar of classical Jewish texts, ancient cultures, and languages, Near Eastern archaeology and antiquities, and Islam. Deutsch introduced her to the Talmud in a major article for *The Quarterly Review* that she read in proof in late 1867. The article went into an unprecedented seven reprints, thus countering the ignorance of the British public, as well as the equally ignorant embarrassment English Jews felt about the "much maligned Talmud," as *The Jewish Chronicle* put it in a grateful review.[10]

Bringing the Talmud to a broad audience was a challenging but critical task, given its centrality to Jewish culture. Almost exactly as Marian herself had written about Spinoza years earlier, Deutsch cautioned against a "translation" of the non-legal sections of the Talmud, suggesting that it would be more profitable to render an account that attempted to focus on Talmudical metaphysics and ethics (his essay was but an introduction to the larger work he planned but did not survive to write).[11] In the essay, Deutsch reoriented his readers by centering his approach to Jewish textuality from *within* Jewish culture (as if to say, "But why always Christian hermeneutics?"). The Talmud was understood by traditional Jews to be a divine revelation of the Oral Law, transmitted down the generations from Moses, just as the Torah was the divinely revealed Written Law. As Deutsch clarified the centrality of the Talmud to Jewish culture, he implicitly contested Christian ideas of the New Testament as the culmination of the Hebrew Bible. This shift posed a threat, particularly to missionizing Christians, who responded vehemently in writings of their own arguing for the priority, supremacy, and "divine authenticity" of the

New Testament.[12] Yet Deutsch's essay also suggested the Talmud as a vital repository of knowledge for Christians open to considering the origins of some elements of their own faith.

Deutsch's evocation of the Talmud was exactly suited to arouse Eliot's fascination and arguably influenced key words and preoccupations of *Daniel Deronda*. Contesting the inherited prejudice that Jews were bound by the letter and Christians by the spirit, Deutsch wrote:

> But the Talmud is more than a book of laws. It is a microcosm, embracing, even as does the Bible, *heaven and earth*. It is as if all the prose and *the poetry, the science*, the faith and speculation of the Old World were, though only in faint reflections, bound up in it *in nuce*.[13] (first two emphases mine)

Such a quintessentially Victorian description of the Talmud—uniting heaven and earth; prose and poetry; science, faith, and speculation; and at the same time reflecting a developmental historical reality ("Old World")—could not have been more aptly formulated for Eliot. If, as we have seen, English Victorians tended to identify their own poetry with the Bible and the Bible with poetry, Deutsch described a microcosmic second Jewish "book" (actually, many books, impossible to define generically) that unified prose and poetry, as Eliot did over the course of her career and often within single works. Similarly, Deutsch refused a simple division between poetry and science—a call that Eliot elaborated repeatedly and at length throughout *Daniel Deronda*.

But most of all, Deutsch very possibly prompted Eliot to consider the imaginative staging of a meeting between the unthinking Christian "universalist" appropriation of Jewish scripture and living Jews, who interpreted those poetic and prophetic texts toward particularist ends. Cynthia Scheinberg suggests that in *Daniel Deronda* Eliot developed "something we might call appropriation with acknowledgment, which claims that non-Jews can have access to the power of Hebrew texts and ideas only through a genuine engagement with and acknowledgment of the Jewishness that underlies them."[14] We might see this move as Eliot's signature decentering of the ego now writ large, writ national and religious.

If the move toward considering how Jews might interpret and live by their own scriptures was outward-facing, Eliot was still, as always, considering the world of her nurture. Islam, Hinduism, and Buddhism were not in her purview, in spite of the fact that they commanded contemporary interest as imperial concerns, and also as elements in the sociological, comparative approach to religion, in what J. Barton Scott has called the late Victorian "tactical alliance" between empire and comparative religion.[15] Marian and Lewes had met Max Müller and read aloud his *History of Religions*, yet the broader perspective did not impact Marian's fiction (GEL 8: 461).[16] Likewise, Eliot's lack of interest in Palestine as a colonial site seems tied to her project of representing Christian–Jewish relations primarily in terms of historical inheritance. It is as if the dramas of Deronda, Mirah, Mordecai, Gwendolen, and Grandcourt are all played out in service of a hermeneutic debate that Eliot could not but engage at this late stage of her career. In her retrospective judgment, her Anglican nurture, her evangelical young adulthood, and perhaps even her early freethinking, in which she had been immersed in biblical studies and translation, had missed the mark in their assumed superiority over all things Jewish (apart from Hebrew poetry, which she had always given its due). This last novel redressed the meeting between non-Jews and the origins of their faith.

Indeed, in *Daniel Deronda* she judged English Christianity more harshly than she ever had, by contrasting it with the vivid—if vague and fantastical—future of the Jews, animate with relation to a living past. *Daniel Deronda* represented a world without a single Christian figure that could rescue suffering or what doubles for and precedes suffering in the novel: purposelessness and lack of meaning.[17] Once, there were the earnest, faithful voices of Rev. Tryan, Dinah Morris, and Thomas à Kempis; then there were the unorthodox but ardent strivers including Felix Holt, Romola, and Dorothea. Yet by the time Eliot wrote *Daniel Deronda*, she could not embody English religious enthusiasm. Compassion still circulates in England: we meet a kindly, thoughtful rector, yet he is even less interventionist than *Adam Bede*'s Rev. Irwine, and a Dutch mother and girls whose St. Teresa-like tendencies are granted a medium that extends to exactly one Jewess, who, they must learn, does not want to be converted. The English world of the novel is bereft of moral vision or will: at best, it is governed by chance, unschooled impulse, and distant investment. At worst, in the malevolence of Gwendolen's sadistic husband, it is a picture of terror and hell that no longer has a theological language, as Philip Davis astutely observes, but is perhaps more terrifying for its absence.[18]

Though Eliot was anxious about the public reception of the Jewish elements of the novel, she was highly gratified when representatives of the Jewish community thanked her effusively. After she completed the novel, Marian and Lewes spent two and a half months in France and Switzerland in the summer of 1876, buoyed by the knowledge that early sales of the novel exceeded those of *Middlemarch*. In December, John Cross assisted their purchase of the country home they had long desired, The Heights at Witley.

In the final of Eliot's amazing shifts in literary form, she succeeded *Daniel Deronda* with a challenging work largely unread today, *Impressions of Theophrastus Such*. Ten days before his death, Lewes sent her manuscript to Blackwood; she would edit the proofs deep in mourning, under the duress of feeling Lewes would have wanted her to finish the work. From the fully realized novel that was *Daniel Deronda*, Eliot had created *Impressions* as a set of eighteen short essays sketching different types of character written by "Theophrastus Such," a character invented by Eliot, described as "a writer nobody is likely to have read," and a bachelor who will leave the world with no children (*Imp* 7). From the title to the reference-laden and at times autobiographically shaded essays, Eliot's last work was a provocation to readers, unceasingly demanding the labor of interpretation; perhaps it was intended primarily for other authors.[19] Though we do not know for whom she wrote, Eliot did not hold back in this work—not in its challenging conception nor in its execution. Her wide and deep reading, her critical intelligence, her cutting, subtle irony are all on display here, without almost any aid of plot to hold a reader's attention. What we get is character as it emerges through *voice*. Theophrastus Such lives only by virtue of his observation of other characters and the consideration of himself in relation to them.

Thus, the experience of reading *Impressions* is most like reading Eliot's novels only when we consider Theophrastus Such as worthy of the sympathetic interest we might give Dorothea Brooke. Yet the difference here is not only that we have no plot within which to come to care about our character (imagine a volume of Impressions written by Dorothea!) but that this difficult volume gives us no Eliotic narrator to ease our access to the range of characters observed and analyzed.

We have learned to read Eliot with all the invaluable assistance of the guide that is the narrator. In this final volume, that narrator has disappeared, forcing us to ask at every point whether we should trust this all-too-human narrator, Theophrastus Such: is his wisdom good? Are his ethics our ethics? And who is he anyway?

As Nancy Henry has very helpfully laid out, the historical Theophrastus was a student of Aristotle and was identified only by the name given him by his teacher, rather than his father, identifying a cultural lineage rather than a biological one. As author of a set of character sketches, each of which opened, "Such a type," Theophrastus inaugurated a genre that gave rise to adaptations over the centuries, a tradition Eliot reinvents in her time. In giving her Theophrastus the surname "Such," Eliot plays upon the genre: "What he has is a linguistic connection in 'Such' to the literary tradition of character writing."[20] "Such" is thus not analogous to "Brooke" (we recall here Ian Watt's argument that the emergence of surnames in eighteenth-century novels was one crucial marker of the generic beginnings of realism, as surnames indicated the fictional imitation of the historical) but instead a surname that announces—to those in the know—non-referentiality.[21] It tells us that our "author" is hidden from us; the text represents no private man with a literal patronym. In that spirit, the name Theophrastus, Greek for "Spoken by God," becomes a greater irony. In Eliot's time, only an anonymous author, who sets up a narrator to mediate reality for readers, can claim—perhaps mirthfully—omniscience, to speak in a godly fashion.

In moments across her fictions, for example, in *The Mill on the Floss* and *Adam Bede*, Eliot's narrators speak in the first person and appear sketchily embodied—we know where they sit or stand as they engage in retrospective telling.[22] Yet that recourse to explicitly first-person narration is extremely limited over the course of the ensuing fiction; so much so that readers can easily forget that a "character" is narrating. Instead, many readers imagine the Eliotic narrator as quintessentially not human but "omniscient." Because not only is the Eliotic narrator capable of seeing into the hearts of all its characters, it (always a question, the Eliotic narrator—he? she? it? they?) also impresses us as being so full of wisdom, so full of ethical depth, that omniscience becomes a moral even more than an epistemological quality. That Eliot chose to give so little heft, so few appearances, so little description, to her first-person narrators further suggests her ambivalence over their epistemological limitations.

In this final work Eliot did an extraordinary thing, then, by writing a fully, continuously, adamantly first-person fiction.[23] After all her work, her immense career spent justifying through each of her novels the sure authority she claimed as narrator, she pivoted to require readers to question the narrator's reliability. She resituated wisdom in the frail body of a single, fallible human being, with particular biological forbears and, in this case, no biological descendants—full of the learning of ages, but always and necessarily limited by his own scope of vision and imagination. We might read this shift as the reinvention of her voice as human. As if to say, the novels were never a new scripture.[24] They were a scripture only if scripture is as limited as any aspiring human self. As Theophrastus writes in the essay "Looking Inward," "in noting the weakness of my acquaintances I am conscious of my fellowship with them...the only recognized superiority is that of the ideal self, the God within, holding the mirror and the scourge for our own pettiness as well as our neighbors" (*Imp* 13).

In this return to Feuerbach, "Theophrastus Such" offers an anthropology of Eliot's lifework. In a first person that ranges between rooting itself in the singular and adopting the plural, Eliot left behind the exclusively plural, her grand and sweeping "we," that functioned, yes, to breed empathy but also always to assert the extraordinariness of the Eliotic narrator, her unique capacity to create a far wiser, far more deeply self-aware "we" than any collective encountered off the page. In creating Theophrastus Such, Eliot stepped down. Her series of superhuman narrators were quietly, brilliantly revealed as the human projections they always were.

When Marian Lewes lost her partner, she secluded herself in grief. In the months after Lewes's death, she saw no one and turned to the intellectual labor of completing the fourth volume of *Problems of Life and Mind*, a final testament to the deep, exclusive mutual understanding between two extraordinarily creative, analytical minds that had developed in tandem for two and a half decades.

Ailing and having lost a great deal of weight, she admitted to her company first "Johnnie" Cross, who had recently lost his own mother, and then some of her closest friends. With Cross, she returned to playing the piano and reading aloud. When she married Cross at St. George's

Church on May 6, 1880, with the blessing and presence of Lewes's son Charles, who called her Mutter and whose children were grandchildren to her, many were surprised. Her closest friends were informed only the day before her wedding, by letter. Her late return to the norms of church and state disappointed some observers and delighted others. Her lifelong friend Barbara Bodichon had sufficient imagination to make perfect sense of it, remarking that "all love is so different that I do not see it unnatural to love in new ways—not to be unfaithful to any memory" (GEL 7: 273).

Yet the short life of the couple left no literary traces other than Cross's highly curated version of her life and letters. She died on December 22, 1880. Cross came quickly to understand that she was too controversial a candidate to be buried in Westminster Abbey without a public struggle, and so she was buried beside Lewes, in Highgate Cemetery. The Unitarian minister Dr. Thomas Sadler of Rosslyn Hill Chapel, who had married Charles Lewes and his wife Gertrude Hill, had christened their children, and had conducted the memorial service for Lewes, now memorialized her in the overflowing Nonconformist chapel, stating to the crowds who had arrived: "a nature might be profoundly devout and yet not accept a great deal of what is usually held to be religious belief."[25] She was memorialized as both "Mary Ann Cross" and "George Eliot" on her tombstone.

She had traveled as far from the parish of her birth as any poor mortal could.

Notes

1. Gillian Beer, *Darwin's Plots: Evolutionary Narrative in Darwin, George Eliot and Nineteenth-Century Fiction* (Cambridge: Cambridge University Press, 1983), p. 169.
2. See Orr, *Religious*, p. 41, for the claim that Eliot explores the problem of "appearing to die in vain and the equally heroic but more quotidian problem of appearing to live in vain," a problem exacerbated without the belief in an afterlife.
3. Any Christian future depended on a deeper and truer understanding of its relation to its Jewish prehistory. I am indebted here to Cynthia Scheinberg, "'The Beloved Ideas Made Flesh': *Daniel Deronda* and Jewish Poetics," *ELH* 77.3 (2010), pp. 813–39.
4. See Irene Tucker's narratological-historical reading of *DD*'s position at the intersection of late nineteenth-century nationalism and the decline of realism, concerned with innovating modes of community formation,

particularly those which Jewishness made visible, in *A Probable State: The Novel, the Contract, and the Jews* (Chicago: University of Chicago Press, 2000).
5. See Adela Pinch, *Thinking about Other People in Nineteenth-Century British Writing* (Cambridge: Cambridge University Press, 2010), pp. 139–69, for a brilliant discussion of the limits of knowing. Pinch is not addressing matters of agnosticism but her claims about the novel's treatment of cause and effect, and the haziness with which characters can determine the effects of their thoughts on others, is linked to the agnostic quality I identify in the novel.
6. In a rich, complicated account, Levine argues that Eliot's late novels (*MM* and *DD*) reflect a new stage in her developing conception of reality. Levine reads both *DD* and Lewes's *Problems of Life and Mind* as attempts to work toward knowledge through a science characterized by empiricism inspired by idealism (that is, a guiding or hypothetically sound "idea about reality" [p. 43]). Levine, who is widely associated with the claim for the Victorian novel as fundamentally a secular form, points sensitively to the religious valence of this enterprise, noting the religiously inflected rhythms and language of Lewes's search for a systemic whole, albeit one that science, coupled with imagination, itself a moral function, might be able to identify (pp. 34–5). The biographical dimension of Levine's chapter is also illuminating for this late period of Eliot's life.
7. See Susan Meyer, "'Safely to Their Own Borders': Proto-Zionism, Feminism and Nationalism in *Daniel Deronda*," *ELH* 60.3 (1993), pp. 733–58, who argues that the novel is anti-feminist in allowing only Deronda, and not his artist mother, to find a pursuit that can merge collective and private purposes, and satisfy both duty and passion.
8. Michael Ragussis, *Figures of Conversion: "The Jewish Question" and English National Identity* (Durham: Duke University Press, 1995), p. 86. He acknowledges that it could be argued that Eliot excises the Jewish elements from England by transporting them to the East. See Fleishman, *Intellectual*, p. 216, who argues that "Zionism is a metaphor for the pursuit of a higher culture and that by the lack of some such ideal the culture of England is judged and found wanting." I do not see Zionism as a metaphor here. See also Todd M. Endelman, *The Jews of Britain, 1656 to 2000* (Berkeley: University of California Press, 2002).
9. I am grateful to the New York Public Library for access to the Berg Notebook in the Henry W. and Albert A. Berg Collection. See also *George Eliot's "Daniel Deronda" Notebooks*, ed. Jane Irwin (Cambridge: Cambridge University Press, 1996).
10. Beth-Zion Lask Abrahams, "Emanuel Deutsch of 'The Talmud' Fame," *Transactions & Miscellanies* 23 (1969–70), pp. 53–63, 56–7.
11. Emanuel Deutsch, "The Talmud," in *Literary Remains of the Late Emanuel Deutsch* (London: John Murray, 1874), *Google Books*, pp. 1–58, p. 49.
12. Abrahams, "Deutsch," p. 58.
13. Deutsch, "Talmud," p. 12.
14. Scheinberg, "Beloved," p. 832.

15. J. Barton Scott, "A Commonwealth of Affection: Modern Hinduism and the Cultural History of the Study of Religion," in *Constructing Nineteenth-Century Religion*, ed. Joshua King and Winter Jade Werner (Columbus: Ohio State University Press, 2019), pp. 46–64, p. 46. See also J. Jeffrey Franklin, *Spirit Matters: Occult Beliefs, Alternative Religions, and the Crisis of Faith in Victorian Britain* (Ithaca: Cornell University Press, 2018).
16. For more on Muller and Victorians' exposure to world religions, see William R. Mckelvy, "The Importance of Being Ezra: Canons and Conversions in *The Moonstone*," *ELH* 86.2 (2019): 495–523. Given the context that Mckelvy offers, and Eliot's own wide reading on the origins of religion, her inattention to religions besides Judaism and Christianity should not be seen as an oversight but as intentional. Her priority was to represent the tradition from which she came.
17. See Emily Walker Heady, *Victorian Conversion Narratives and Reading Communities* (Burlington, VT: Ashgate, 2013), pp. 75–104, who argues that conversion in late Eliot does not gauge character but is a form of risk-taking that indicates "that belief is still possible" (p. 76).
18. Davis, *Transferred*, p. 362.
19. Nancy Henry, "Introduction," *Impressions*, pp. vii-xli, p. xvii.
20. Henry, "Introduction," p. xix.
21. Ian Watt, *The Rise of the Novel: Studies in Defoe, Richardson and Fielding* (Berkeley: University of California Press, 1957).
22. It took me until I was rereading Eliot's novels in graduate school to recognize or care about the fact that some had first-person, supposedly embodied narrators. I say this to underscore the way their only very intermittent first-person traces can easily fail to register upon enthusiastic, non-professional readers.
23. She had done this in "The Lifted Veil" (1859), but that story preceded the emergence and widespread recognition of her narratorial voice in the novels.
24. A version of this argument is Norman Vance, *Bible and Novel: Narrative Authority and the Death of God* (Oxford: Oxford University Press, 2013), pp. 92–113: "Christianity could still be seen and reconfigured as a religion of humanity. Its partly outmoded scriptures... could be replaced by her own narratives" (p. 113).
25. "Funeral of George Eliot," *Times*, Dec. 30, 1880. George Eliot Archive, https://georgeeliotarchive.org/files/show/2117. On the contested afterlives of Eliot, and especially the debate over her piety, see the fascinating study by K. K. Collins, *Identifying the Remains: George Eliot's Death in the London Religious Press* (Victoria, CA: ELS Editions, 2006). Eliot's obituaries reflected the paradox of how "since a non-believer cannot be a great moral teacher," and she was a great moral teacher, "either she must have been a believer after all or (what amounts to the same thingh) we need to reexamine what counts as belief" (p. 6). See also the fascinating essay, Helen Anne O'Neill and Ruth Livesey, "The Rival Afterlives of George Eliot in Textual and Visual Culture: A Bicentenary Reflection," *George Eliot–George Henry Lewes Studies* 73.1 (2021), pp. 1–28.

Works Cited

Works by George Eliot

Novels etc.

Eliot, George. *Scenes of Clerical Life*. 1857. Ed. David Lodge. London and New York: Penguin Classics, 1985.

Eliot, George. *Adam Bede*. 1859. Ed. Stephen Gill. London: Penguin Classics, 1980.

Eliot, George. *The Mill on the Floss*. 1860. Ed. A. S. Byatt. New York and London: Penguin Classics, 1985.

Eliot, George. *Silas Marner*. 1861. Bantam Classics. New York: Bantam Books, 1981.

Eliot, George. *Romola*. 1863. Ed. Andrew Sanders. New York and London: Penguin Classics, 1980.

Eliot, George. *Felix Holt*. 1866. Ed. Peter Coveney. New York and London: Penguin Classics, 1972.

Eliot, George. *Middlemarch*. 1871–2. New York: Bantam Classics, 1985.

Eliot, George. *Daniel Deronda*. 1876. Ed. Barbara Hardy. New York and London: Penguin Classics, 1986.

Eliot, George. *Collected Poems*. Ed. Lucien Jenkins. London: Skoob Books, 1989.

Eliot, George. *Impressions of Theophrastus Such*. 1879. Ed. Nancy Henry. Iowa City: University of Iowa Press, 1994.

Eliot, George. *Selected Essays, Poems and Other Writings*. Ed. A. S. Byatt and Nicholas Warren. New York and London: Penguin Classics, 1990.

Journalism Published Anonymously

"Rachel Gray." *The Leader*. Vol. 7 (January 5, 1856), p. 19. *George Eliot Archive*, https://georgeeliotarchive.org/items/show/125.

"Three Months in Weimar." *Fraser's Magazine*. Vol. LI (1855), 699–706. *George Eliot Archive*, https://georgeeliotarchive.org/items/show/85.

Journals, Notebooks, Letters

George Eliot's "Daniel Deronda" Notebooks. Ed. Jane Irwin. Cambridge: Cambridge University Press, 1996.

Journals of George Eliot. Ed. Margaret Harris and Judith Johnston. Cambridge: Cambridge University Press, 1998.

The George Eliot Letters. Ed. Gordon S. Haight. 9 vols. New Haven: Yale University Press, 1954–78.

Other Works Cited

Abrahams, Beth-Zion Lask. "Emanuel Deutsch of 'The Talmud' Fame." *Transactions & Miscellanies* 23 (1969–70): 53–63.

à Kempis, Thomas. *The Imitation of Christ*. London and Glasgow: Blackie & Son Limited, n.d.

Anderson, Amanda, and Harry E. Shaw, eds. *Companion to George Eliot*. Malden, MA: Wiley-Blackwell, 2016.

Anon. "Funeral of George Eliot." *Times*. Dec. 30, 1880. *George Eliot Archive*, https://georgeeliotarchive.org/files/show/2117.

Armstrong, Isobel. "George Eliot, Spinoza, and the Emotions." In Anderson and Shaw, 2016, 294–308.

Arnold, Matthew. *Culture and Anarchy*. Ed. Samuel Lipman. New Haven and London: Yale University Press, 1994.

Ashton, Rosemary. *George Eliot: A Life*. New York: Viking, 1997.

Auerbach, Erich. *Mimesis: The Representation of Reality in Western Literature*. Trans. Willard R. Trask. Princeton: Princeton University Press, 1953.

Auerbach, Nina. "The Power of Hunger: Demonism and Maggie Tulliver." In *George Eliot Scholars*. Ed. Beverley Park Rilett, https://GeorgeEliotScholars.org.

Beer, Gillian. *Darwin's Plots: Evolutionary Narrative in Darwin, George Eliot and Nineteenth-Century Fiction*. Cambridge: Cambridge University Press, 1983.

Blumberg, Ilana M. "Reading George Eliot in Jerusalem," *Lilith*, Spring 2013. https://lilith.org/articles/reading-george-eliot-in-jerusalem/.

Blumberg, Ilana M. *Victorian Sacrifice: Ethics and Economics in Mid-Century Novels*. Columbus: Ohio State University Press, 2013.

Blumberg, Ilana M. "Sympathy or Religion?: George Eliot and Christian Conversion." *Nineteenth-Century Literature* 74.3 (2019): 360–87.

Bodenheimer, Rosemarie. *The Real Life of Mary Ann Evans: Her Letters and Fiction*. Ithaca: Cornell University Press, 1994.

Bonaparte, Felicia. *The Triptych and the Cross: Central Myths of George Eliot's Poetic Imagination*. New York: New York University Press, 1979.

Branch, Lori, and Mark Knight. "Why the Postsecular Matters: Literary Studies and the Rise of the Novel." *Christianity & Literature* 67.3 (2018): 493–510. https://muse-jhu-edu.eu1.proxy.openathens.net/pub/1/article/735877/pdf.

Burstein, Miriam Elizabeth. "Hybridous Monsters: Constructing 'Religion' and the 'the Novel' in the Early Nineteenth Century." In King and Werner, 2019, 171–89.

Butler, Joseph. *Analogy of Religion to the Course and Constitution of Nature*. Philadelphia: J.B. Lippincott, 1873, 218. Project Gutenberg, https://www.gutenberg.org/ebooks/53346.

Carlisle, Clare. "George Eliot's Spinoza: An Introduction." In *Spinoza's Ethics*. Trans. George Eliot. Ed. Clare Carlisle. Princeton: Princeton University Press, 2020, 1–60.

Carlisle, Clare. *The Marriage Question: George Eliot's Double Life*. New York: Farrar, Straus and Giroux, 2023.

Carroll, David. *George Eliot and the Conflict of Interpretations*. Cambridge: Cambridge University Press, 1992.

Collini, Stefan. *Public Moralists: Political Thought and Intellectual Life in Britain, 1850–1930.* Oxford: Clarendon Press, 1991.

Collins, K. K. *Identifying the Remains: George Eliot's Death in the London Religious Press.* Victoria, CA: ELS Editions, 2006.

Cross, John Walter. *George Eliot's Life as Related in Her Letters and Journals.* Boston and New York: Jefferson Press, n.d. Orig. pub. 1888.

Davis, Philip. *The Transferred Life of George Eliot.* Oxford: Oxford University Press, 2017.

Deutsch, Emanuel. "The Talmud." In *Literary Remains of the Late Emanuel Deutsch.* London: John Murray, 1874, 1–58. Google Books.

Dillane, Fionnuala. *Before George Eliot: Marian Evans and the Periodical Press.* Cambridge: Cambridge University Press, 2013.

Dillane, Fionnuala. "George Eliot's Precarious Afterlives." *19: Interdisciplinary Studies in the Long Nineteenth Century* 29 (2020): 1–26. https://doi.org/10.16995/ntn.1981.

During, Simon. "George Eliot and Secularism." In Anderson and Shaw, 2016, 428–42.

Endelman, Todd M. *The Jews of Britain, 1656 to 2000.* Berkeley: University of California Press, 2002.

Erdozain, Dominic. *The Soul of Doubt: The Religious Roots of Unbelief from Luther to Marx.* Oxford: Oxford University Press, 2016.

Federico, Annette R., ed. *My Victorian Novel: Critical Essays in the Personal Voice.* Columbia: University of Missouri Press, 2020.

Feuerbach, Ludwig. *The Essence of Christianity.* Trans. George Eliot. Amherst: Prometheus Books, 1989.

Fleishman, Avrom. *George Eliot's Intellectual Life.* Cambridge: Cambridge University Press, 2010.

Franklin, J. Jeffrey. *Spirit Matters: Occult Beliefs, Alternative Religions, and the Crisis of Faith in Victorian Britain.* Ithaca: Cornell University Press, 2018.

Fraser, Hilary. *The Victorians and Renaissance Italy.* Cambridge, MA: Blackwell, 1992.

Gaston, Sean. "George Eliot and the Anglican Reader." *Literature and Theology* 31.3 (2017): 318–37. doi:10.1093/litthe/frw026.

Gordon, Mary. "George Eliot, Dorothea and Me: Reading (and Rereading) *Middlemarch. New York Times.* May 8, 1994. https://www.nytimes.com/1994/05/08/books/george-eliot-dorothea-and-me-rereading-and-rereading-middlemarch.html.

Haight, Gordon S. *George Eliot: A Biography.* New York: Oxford University Press, 1968.

Hardy, Barbara. *The Novels of George Eliot: A Study in Form.* London: Athlone Press, 1963.

Hardy, Barbara. *George Eliot: A Critic's Biography*, London and New York: Bloomsbury Academic Press, 2006.

Harris, Margaret, ed. *George Eliot in Context.* Cambridge: Cambridge University Press, 2013. *Cambridge Core.* https://doi.org/10.1017/CBO9781139019491.

Heady, Emily Walker. *Victorian Conversion Narratives and Reading Communities.* Burlington, VT: Ashgate, 2013.

Hennell, Charles. *Inquiry Concerning the Origin of Christianity*. London: Smallfield, 1838. HathiTrust, https://catalog.hathitrust.org/Record/005767369.

Henry, Nancy. *The Life of George Eliot: A Critical Biography*. Malden, MA: Wiley-Blackwell, 2012.

Herbert, Christopher. *Evangelical Gothic: the English Novel and the Religious War on Virtue from Wesley to Dracula*. Charlottesville: University of Virginia Press, 2019.

Hughes, Kathryn. *George Eliot: The Last Victorian*. London: Fourth Estate, 2000.

Jay, Elisabeth. *Religion of the Heart: Anglican Evangelicalism and the Nineteenth-Century Novel*. Oxford: Oxford University Press, 1979.

Karl, Frederick. *George Eliot: Voice of a Century: A Biography*. New York: W.W. Norton, 1995.

King, Amy M. *The Divine in the Commonplace: Reverent Natural History and the Novel in Britain*. Cambridge: Cambridge University Press, 2019.

King, Joshua, and Winter Jade Werner, eds. *Constructing Nineteenth-Century Religion*. Columbus: Ohio State University Press, 2019.

Knight, Mark. *Good Words: Evangelicalism and the Victorian Novel*. Columbus: Ohio State University Press, 2019.

Knoepflmacher, U. C. *George Eliot's Early Novels, The Limits of Realism*. Berkeley and Los Angeles: University of California Press, 1968.

Kreuger, Christine L. *The Reader's Repentance: Women Preachers, Women Writers, and Nineteenth-Century Social Discourse*. Chicago and London: University of Chicago Press, 1992.

Kurnick, David. "Unspeakable George Eliot." *Victorian Literature and Culture* 38.2 (2010): 489–509.

LaPorte, Charles. *Victorian Poets and the Changing Bible*. Charlottesville and London: University of Virginia Press, 2011.

Larsen, Timothy. "Biblical Criticism and the Crisis of Belief: D. F. Strauss's *Leben Jesu* in Britain." In *Contested Christianity: The Political and Social Contexts of Victorian Theology*. Waco, TX: Baylor University Press, 2004, 43–58.

Larsen, Timothy. *Crisis of Doubt: Honest Faith in Nineteenth-Century England*. Oxford: Oxford University Press, 2006.

Larsen, Timothy. *John Stuart Mill: A Secular Life*. Oxford: Oxford University Press, 2018.

Lecourt, Sebastian. *Cultivating Belief: Victorian Anthropology, Liberal Aesthetics, and the Secular Imagination*. Oxford: Oxford University Press, 2018.

Levine, George. *Realism, Ethics and Secularism: Essays on Victorian Literature and Science*. Cambridge: Cambridge University Press, 2008.

Lewes, George Henry. *Sea-Side Studies at Ilfracombe, Tenby, The Scilly Isles, and Jersey*. Edinburgh and London: Blackwood, 1858.

Lewes, George Henry. *Letters of George Henry Lewes*. Vol 3. Ed William Baker. Victoria, CA: ELS Editions, 1999.

Livesey, Ruth. "Class." In Harris, 2013, 95–103.

Mckelvy, William R. "The Importance of Being Ezra: Canons and Conversions in *The Moonstone*." *ELH* 86.2 (2019): 495–523.

Mead, Rebecca. *The Road to Middlemarch: My Life with George Eliot*. London: Granta, 2014.

Works Cited

Meyer, Susan. "'Safely to Their Own Borders': Proto-Zionism, Feminism and Nationalism in *Daniel Deronda*." *ELH* 60.3 (1993): 733–58.

O'Neill, Helen Anne, and Ruth Livesey, "The Rival Afterlives of George Eliot in Textual and Visual Culture: A Bicentenary Reflection." *George Eliot–George Henry Lewes Studies* 73.1 (2021): 1–28.

Orr, Marilyn. *George Eliot's Religious Imagination: A Theopoetics of Evolution.* Evanston, IL: Northwestern University Press, 2018.

Pinch, Adela. *Thinking about Other People in Nineteenth-Century British Writing.* Cambridge: Cambridge University Press, 2010, 139–69.

Price, Leah. *The Anthology and the Rise of the Novel, From Richardson to George Eliot.* Cambridge: Cambridge University Press, 2000.

Ragussis, Michael. *Figures of Conversion: "The Jewish Question" and English National Identity.* Durham: Duke University Press, 1995.

Rectenwald, Michael. "Secularism." In Harris, 2013, 271–8.

Redinger, Ruby. *George Eliot: The Emergent Self.* New York: Knopf, 1975.

Scheinberg, Cynthia. "'The Beloved Ideas Made Flesh': *Daniel Deronda* and Jewish Poetics." *ELH* 77.3 (2010): 813–39.

Schramm, Jan-Melissa. *Atonement and Self-Sacrifice in Nineteenth-Century Narrative.* Cambridge: Cambridge University Press, 2012.

Scott, J. Barton. "A Commonwealth of Affection: Modern Hinduism and the Cultural History of the Study of Religion." In King and Werner, 2019, 46–64.

Sharp, Hasana. "The Force of Ideas in Spinoza." *Political Theory* 35.6 (2007): 732–55.

Snell, K. D. M. *Parish and Belonging: Community, Identity and Welfare in England and Wales, 1700–1950,* Cambridge: Cambridge University Press, 2006.

Snell, K. D. M., and Paul S. Ell. *Rival Jerusalems: The Geography of Victorian Religion.* Cambridge: Cambridge University Press, 2000.

Spencer, Herbert. *The Principles of Ethics.* Indianapolis: Liberty Fund, 1978.

Spinoza, Benedict de. *A* Theologico-Political Treatise. Trans. R. H. M. Elwes. New York: Dover, 1951.

Strauss, David Friedrich. *The Life of Jesus, Critically Examined.* London: Chapman, 1846. *HathiTrust.* http://hdl.handle.net/2027/hvd.rslfjs.

Taylor, Charles. *A Secular Age.* Cambridge and London: Belknap Press, 2007.

Tucker, Irene. *A Probable State: The Novel, the Contract, and the Jews.* Chicago: University of Chicago Press, 2000.

Turner, Frank M. *Contesting Cultural Authority: Essays in Victorian Intellectual Life.* Cambridge: Cambridge University Press, 1993.

Vance, Norman. *Bible and Novel: Narrative Authority and the Death of God.* Oxford: Oxford University Press, 2013.

Watt, Ian. *The Rise of the Novel: Studies in Defoe, Richardson and Fielding.* Berkeley: University of California Press, 1957.

Yeoh, Paul. "Saints' Everlasting Rest: The Martyrdom of Maggie Tulliver." *Studies in the Novel* 41.1 (2009): 1–21.

Index

Note: References to Notes are depicted by the Note number relating to the individual paragraph.

For the benefit of digital users, indexed terms that span two pages (e.g., 52–53) may, on occasion, appear on only one of those pages.

Adam Bede (*AB*) (GE) 108, 110, 126–7, 134–5
  challenging of orthodoxies 126
  characters
    Adam 117–19, 121–6, 142–3
    Arthur Donnithorne 115–22, 124–5
    Hetty 115–17, 119–25, 142–3
    Mr. Irwine 115–16, 119–21, 123–5, 200–1
    Dinah Morris (Methodist preacher) 122–7, 140–3, 146–7, 166, 168, 200–1
    Poyser family 115–16
  compared with *The Mill on the Floss* 129
  confession in 121
  on conscience 112
  first-person narration 202–3
  harvest-time metaphor 111, 115–16
  Hayslope, fictional village 120, 124
  human and divine fellowship, pursuing simultaneously 142–3
  on inequality 132
  infanticide 116–17
  natural and moral law 117
  Nemesis set up in 117
  on pain of death without reward 112
  pastoral background 111
  plots 116–17
  realism 117
  religion/Christianity 126, 129, 140–1, 148
  representation of a working and agrarian England 129
  suffering in 112–13, 115–16, 118, 125
  time of writing 113, 118, 129
  tragedy in 121
Adam (biblical figure) 113–14
adultery 65

agnosticism x
  in *Daniel Deronda* 195–6
  of Harriet Martineau 50–1
  nineteenth-century 195–6
à Kempis, Thomas 12–13, 200–1
  The Imitation of Christ 136
    in *The Mill on the Floss* 133–4, 138–40
  precious to GE 8, 46, 67, 133
allegory 36–7, 59–60
amorality 146, 180
"Amos Barton" see under *Scenes of Clerical Life* (*Scenes*) (GE)
Anglican Church *see* Church of England
apostasy of GE 26, 29, 45, 57, 66, 73–4, 113–14, 147
  see also questioning of religious doctrine and GE's loss of faith
  early 133
  public 24, 27
Arbury Hall estate, Nuneaton, Warwickshire (birth place of GE) 2
  library, access to GE to 5, 130
Arnold, Matthew 59–60, 192
art
  amplifying experience 83
  contemporary 81–2, 146
  GE creating own 86–7
  "idyllic" style of portraits on peasantry 84
  immortality through 180, 182–3
  interest of GE in 6–7, 9–10, 81–4, 86–7
  moving of audience 86–7
  and poetry 137
  realism, GE's focus on 81–2
  as sacred 84
  shared humanity, recognizing 83
  and technology 182

Ashbourne Church, Derbyshire 4–5
Astley Church, Warwickshire 2
atheism 16, 38, 50–1, 78–9
atonement, Christian 25, 112, 119
Attleborough Church, Nuneaton 10
Auerbach, Erich 84–6
Austen, Jane 91, 92 n.5
authorship
   friendships with authors 87
   reading of authors, vs. books 22
   "rigid secrecy as to" 111

barbarism 37–8
Barton Scott, J. 199–200
Beecher Stowe, Harriet 49, 192, 196
Bible
   see also Christianity; religion and religious faith
   biblical history 36
   Genesis 45, 98, 180
   Gospels *see* Gospels
   Hebrew Bible 84–6, 198–9
   language of 43
   liberal views of biblical criticism 37–8
   Luke 18:35 133
   Matthew 13 18–19, 67
   New Testament 18–19, 28, 85, 198–9
   Noah and the Flood 43
   Old Testament 28, 36–7
   parables 18–19
   Psalms 2:11 72
   Psalms 126:5 111
   St. Paul 27
bigamy 65
Blackwood, John 94–5, 108, 110–11, 116, 127, 141–2, 145, 170
   Blackwood's Magazine 91
   GE's letters to 100–1
   publication of first edition of *Scenes of Clerical Life* 110
   Romola only GE novel not published by 108 n.1
Bodenheimer, Rosemarie 24, 191 n.8
   The Real Life of Mary Ann Evans 30 nn.4,6, 31 n.13
Bodichon, Barbara 49, 63 n.1, 110–11, 179, 203–4
Bohn, Henry George 78

Brabant, R. H. 33–4
Bray, Cara (Caroline), née Hennell 20–2, 26, 32–3
   GE's friendship with 62, 65–7
   GE's letters to 61, 68–9, 112–13
Bray, Charles 19–20, 32, 59, 111, 127
   Coventry Herald owned by 34
   GE's letters to 43–4, 57, 68–9, 78, 112–13, 127
Bray family 20–1, 32–3, 40, 49, 95, 110
   see also Bray, Cara (Caroline), née Hennell; Bray, Charles
   discussion of GE's marriage prospects 32–3
   GE's friendship with 17, 65–6
   and open marriage 32
Broad Church movement 28–9
Brontë, Charlotte 196
   Jane Eyre 57
Browning, Robert 72, 190
Buddhism 199–200
Bulwer-Lytton, Edward George Earle Lytton
   Devereux 16
Burne-Jones family 192
Burstein, Miriam Elizabeth 15 n.15
Butler, Bishop Joseph 25
   The Analogy of Religion 31 n.9

Cain (biblical figure) 180–1
Calvinism 7–8, 20, 25, 47, 106, 130
Carlisle, Clare 72–3
Carlyle, Thomas 20, 64–5, 73
Carroll, David 188–9
Catholicism 77, 158, 167–9, 197–8
   see also Calvinism; Christianity; Protestantism
   Anglo-Catholicism 67
   Renaissance 104–5
   Roman Catholicism 158
Chambers, Robert 34
Chapman, John 33–4, 51, 55, 110
   GE's friendship with 56–8, 65–6
   GE's letters to 68–9
   Quarterly Series 58–9
Chilvers Coton, Warwickshire
   burial of Roger Evans at 47
   parish church 1–2, 131

Index

Christianity
   see also Church of England; Jesus Christ; Judaism; parish life; questioning of religious doctrine and GE's loss of faith; redemption; religion and religious faith; salvation; Scriptures
   Book of Common Prayer 7
   Calvinism 7–8, 20, 25, 47
   Catholicism 77, 158, 167–9, 197–8
      Anglo-Catholicism 67
      Renaissance 104–5
      Roman Catholicism 6, 158
   in *Daniel Deronda* 200–1
   and the Deity 25
   dogma and essence 71
   English Christianity, portrayal of 200–1
   ethics 52–3
   evangelicalism *see* evangelicalism
   Gospels *see* Gospels
   on immortality 97–8
   institutional 87
   nominal Christians 71, 120, 132
   piety 11, 16, 29, 46, 72–4, 77–8, 81, 100–2, 156–7, 172
   professing of belief without living up to it 70–1
   Protestantism 10, 26, 85–6, 131, 158
   as "religion of the Empire" 10–11
   revelation 17, 25, 38
   theology 98–9, 149–50, 162, 195–6
      Calvinism 25
      doctrine 102–3
      ignorance of 104
The Christian Observer 5, 9–10
Church of England 1–2, 169–70
   see also Ashbourne Church, Derbyshire; Astley Church, Warwickshire; Chilvers Coton parish church, Warwickshire; Christianity; Cow Lane Particular Baptist Chapel, Coventry; Dissent; questioning of religious doctrine and GE's loss of faith; religion and religious faith; secularism
   dominance and breadth of 4–5
   parish *see* parish life
   superior authority of 2–3, 6
   Thirty-nine Articles of Faith of Anglican Church 28–9
Coleridge, Samuel 25, 73
Collected Poems (Poems) (GE) 26, 172–7, 179–83
   "The Legend of Jubal" 180, 182–3
Collini, Stefan 134
Combe, George 66
Comte, Auguste 67, 108
Congreve, Maria and Richard 67
Coventry, England 17, 22
   see also *Coventry Herald*; Foleshill, nr. Coventry; Rosehill, nr. Coventry
   Cow Lane Particular Baptist Chapel 3–4
   Mary and Rebecca Franklin's boarding school 2–4
   Mechanics' Institute of Coventry 33
Coventry Herald 34, 40, 46
Cow Lane Particular Baptist Chapel, Coventry 3–4
Cross, John Walter (GE's husband) 2–3, 23, 57, 133, 193, 201
   George Eliot's Life as Related in Her Letters and Journals 14 n.9, 30 n.2
   marriage at St. George's Church (1880) 203–4
Cumming, John 76–8, 81–2

Daniel Deronda (DD) (GE) 179, 193
   agnosticism in 195–6
   characters
      Daniel Deronda 193–4, 199–200
      Grandcourt 199–200
      Gwendolen 193–4, 199–200
      Mordecai (spiritual mentor) 194–7, 199–200
   and cosmopolitan identity 194
   English Christianity, portrayal of 200–1
   future, focus on 193–4
   GE's final novel, as 172, 179, 193–4
   and *Impressions of Theophrastus Such* 201–2
   Judaism in 172, 193–4, 197–9, 201
   national belonging in 173
   opening of 195

Daniel Deronda (DD) (GE) (*cont.*)
  problem of the spiritual and the empirical 195
  religious faith 172–3, 195–6
  time of writing 200–1
Darwin, Charles 192, 196
Darwin, Erasmus 196
David, biblical figure 84–5
Davies, Emily 184, 187–8, 190
de Cervantes, Miguel
  Don Quixote 9–10
Defoe, Daniel
  Robinson Crusoe 9–10
Delaroche, Paul
  engraving of painting 40, 42
del Nero, Bernardo 155–6
Deutsch, Emanuel 198–9
Dickens, Charles 110, 132, 183
Dickinson, Emily 192
Dillane, Fionnuala 52, 63 n.4, 92 n.3, 183, 190 n.1
Dissent, religious 2–5, 55, 104–5
  see also Dissent, religious
Doddridge, Philip
  The Rise and Progress of Religion in the Soul 165
Durade, D'Albert 49, 169
During, Simon
  "George Eliot and Secularism" 108 n.2

Ebdell, Bernard Gilpin 1–2
ecclesiastical chart 11–12, 16
educated classes 34, 134
education of GE and Evans family 3–4
  see also school life
  formal, end of 5
  learning by GE 12–13
  scriptural 82
egoism 8–9, 12–13, 86, 127
  dangers of 133
  fight against 134
  and joy 147
  love as 125
  in novels 86–7, 124–5
  and religion 86–8
  and selfishness 88
Eliot, George (Mary Ann (Marian) Evans), early life and education 1–13, 131

  see also education; school life
  adolescence 4–5
  agriculture/farmland, growing up with 2–3
  baptism 1
  birth in Nuneaton (1819) 1–3
  early experiences of writing 6–7
  evangelicalism and self-scrutiny 8–9, 44, 47, 81
  family, importance of 2–3
  housekeeper to father Robert 5
  literature, love of 9–10
  move to Coventry 2–4, 17, 22
  music, love of 9–10
Eliot, George (Mary Ann (Marian) Evans), adult and personal life
  see also Eliot, George (Mary Ann (Marian) Evans), career
  art, interest in 6–7, 9–10, 81–4, 86–7
  as carer/nurse for father 40, 46, 50, 57
  common-law marriage to George Lewes *see under* Lewes, George Henry
  courage of x
  death and burial at Highgate Cemetery (1880) 193–4, 204
  depression of 43–4
  difference of opinion with brother Isaac 3–4, 192–3
  division of life into epochs 112–13
  "double life" (1854–1856) 64
  evangelical period *see* evangelicalism
  female identity 50–1
  as a freethinker ix, 38, 41
  friends *see* friendships and relationships
  in Geneva 49
  gradualism of GE 54
  health conditions 113
  intellect 6–7, 10, 16, 29, 42–3, 72–3
  journal, writing in 111–12, 127 n.1, 147–8, 153–5, 179, 184
  letters by see *The George Eliot Letters* (GEL) (ed. G Haight); letters by GE
  loss of faith *see* apostasy of GE; questioning of religious doctrine and GE's loss of faith
  love and duty, values of x, 7–8
  love of reading 5–6

marriage to John Cross 23
memorialization of in Poet's Corner, Highgate Cemetery ix
as mistress of the house/Roger Evans' housekeeper 5, 32
mourning Lewes's death 193
move to London (1851) 32
name changes 14 n.8
physical appearance 56
proficiency with languages 5, 33–5, 38–9, 41
remembering the past ix–x
response to death 45
travel 23, 40, 49–51, 64, 72–3, 145, 163
view of marriage 70–1
in Weimar 64–5, 69, 72, 75–6
young adult, as 32–47
Eliot, George (Mary Ann (Marian) Evans), career
see also Eliot, George (Mary Ann (Marian) Evans), works of; *under* fiction
autobiography 146–7
as editor 33–5, 52, 61, 64
egoism, fight against 134
feminist critics of GE's writing 189–90
fiction writer under an assumed name 23
financial success, impact on writing x
first publication 9–11
independence of mind/using own words x, 18–19, 28, 34–5, 37
instructive commentary 23
as journalist 34–5, 64, 81, 95
narratorial omniscience 23
overall impact ix
pronouns, use of 47
review of Mackay's *The Progress of the Intellect* (1851) 37
themes in writing
agnosticism 195–6
challenging of orthodoxies 126
conflict of love and duty 130, 170–1
death 106–7, 109 n.6, 112, 180, 184–5, 187
disenchantment 43
fallibility of religious authority 147
industrial and commercial relations, portrayal of 132

inequality 132, 185–186
making the world better 174–5, 188
marriage 159, 160–1, 184–6
miscarriage of justice 146, 154–6
political power 155–6
poverty 136
psychology 153
religion and loss of faith ix–x, 129, 146–59, 164–5, 168, 172–3, 184–5, 187–90, 195–6
retributive justice 154–5
search for meaning 146–7
sense of duty 7–8
suffering 67, 112–13, 115–16, 118
temptation 136
translations *see* translations by GE
Eliot, George (Mary Ann (Marian) Evans), works of
see also *Adam Bede* (*AB*) (GE); *Daniel Deronda* (*DD*) (GE); *Felix Holt* (*FH*) (GE); fiction; *Middlemarch* (*MM*) (GE); *The Mill on the Floss* (*MOF*) (GE); *Romola* (*R*) (GE); *Silas Marner* (*SM*) (GE)
Collected Poems (*Poems*) 26, 172–7, 179–83
"The Legend of Jubal" 180, 182–3
The Idea of a Future Life 59
Impressions of Theophrastus Such (*Imp*) 193, 201–3
"The Lifted Veil" 197
Scenes of Clerical Life (*Scenes*) see *Scenes of Clerical Life* (*Scenes*) (GE)
Selected Essays, Poems and Other Writings (*Essays*) 37–9, 46, 52, 54, 76–8, 81–4, 86–90
elitism 39, 53–4, 83
Ell, Paul S.
Rival Jerusalems 14 n.5
Erdozain, Dominic 31 n.12, 38
The Soul of Doubt 30 n.6
Essence of Christianity (*Essence*) (Feuerbach) 59–61, 68
translation by GE 17, 34, 59, 73, 78–9
ethics
Christian 52–3
and poetry 119–20
and science 76

Ethics (Spinoza)
  publication of 78
  translation by GE 17, 64, 72–9, 81
evangelicalism 3–5, 7–8, 20, 26
  see also Christianity; Church of England; questioning of religious doctrine and GE's loss of faith
  The Christian Observer 5, 9–10
  defined by Calvinism 106
  faith in 130
  GE's evangelical period 6–7
  human imperfection and sin, highlighting 9
  self-scrutiny, focus on 8–9, 44
  of younger GE 7–9, 44, 47, 81, 130
Evans, Christiana (Chrissey) (GE's sister) 3, 32, 93 n.14, 95–6, 108, 179
Evans, Christiana (*née* Pearson) (GE's mother) 1
  death of (1836) 3, 5
  loss of twins 3
Evans, Elizabeth (wife to Samuel) 4–5
Evans family
  see also Eliot, George (Mary Ann (Marian) Evans), early life and education; Eliot, George (Mary Ann (Marian) Evans), adult and personal life; Eliot, George (Mary Ann (Marian) Evans), career; Eliot, George (Mary Ann (Marian) Evans), works of; Evans, Christiana (Chrissey) (GE's sister); Evans, Christiana (*née* Pearson) (GE's mother); Evans, Isaac (GE's brother); Evans, Robert (GE's father); Evans, Robert (GE's stepbrother)
  education 3
  and local families 2
  religious diversity, exposure to 3–5
Evans, Harriet (first wife of GE's father Robert) (née Poynton) 2
Evans Houghton, Frances ("Fanny," GE's stepsister) 31 n.11, 32–3, 44, 65, 192
  GE's letters to 45, 95–6
Evans, Isaac (GE's brother) 17, 32, 66–7, 95–6
  burial of 120
  difference of opinion with sister GE 3–4, 192–3
  education 3–4
  GE's letters to 95
  on GE's marriage prospects 32
  Griff House left to 17, 51
Evans, Mary Ann (Marian) *see* Eliot, George (Mary Ann (Marian) Evans)
Evans, Robert (GE's father) 1–2
  burial of 47, 120
  church attendance 19
  death of (1849) 32, 42–3, 45–7, 179
  education, attitude to 3–4
  extended family 4–5
  GE as carer/nurse for 40, 46, 50, 57
  GE's decision not to accompany to church 17, 19, 23, 65–6, 94
  GE's letters to 28–9
  health issues 40
  move to Coventry with GE 2–4, 17, 22
  sacrificial thinking 70–1
Evans, Samuel (GE's uncle) 4–5, 19
Evans, Sarah (née Rawlins) (wife of Isaac) 17
experience
  art amplifying 83
  articulating 120–1
  categorizing 82–3
  divided 67
  of feeling 90
  felt 153
  framing of 85
  GE's, with Lewes 160–1
  human 43, 69–70, 113–14, 125–6, 177
  internal 132
  intimate 28
  and knowledge 1–2
  of Lewes, with legal wife Agnes 160–1
  life 99–100, 167
  limited 1–2, 151–2
  of living 123
  of need 141
  novelty of 50
  personal relationships 62
  portraying in novels 165–6, 176
  reading 46, 201–2
  religious 42–3, 105–6, 150, 152, 167, 179
  rural 103–4

socioeconomic 129
spiritual 147
of suffering 67, 126–7
Victorian x, 30 n.1, 115
of writing 110

Felix Holt (FH) (GE) 166–7, 174–5, 200–1
  beginning work on 163
  challenges 163
  characters
    Dr. Philip Doddridge 165
    Felix 163–8
    Esther Lyon 163–7
    Rufus (Rev) Lyon 164–6, 168–9
    Mrs. Transome 163–4, 168–9
  compared with *Middlemarch* 188
  on making the world better 174–5, 188
  novel without a spiritual crisis, as 168–9
  poetry in 164
  politics of 162
  psychology in 163–4
  religious faith 164–5, 168, 170
fellow feeling *see* sympathy
Feuerbach, Ludwig x, 59–60, 108, 173–4, 180
  Essence of Christianity (Essence) 17, 34, 59–61, 68, 73, 78–9
  Lewes on 61
  and theology 59–61
fiction 5, 34–5
  see also Eliot, George (Mary Ann (Marian) Evans), career; Eliot, George (Mary Ann (Marian) Evans), works of
  egoism in 86–7
  feminist critics of GE's writing 189–90
  first-person narration 85, 89, 202–3
  by GE
    on causality 75
    giving something back 111–12
    initial novels 81
    intellectuals in 87–8
    narratives of revelation and change 84
    realist novels 85–6
    social classes, representation of 87
    syntax 90
    types of novels written 39

uncertainties regarding 95
as writer under an assumed name 23
see also *Adam Bede (AB)* (GE); *Daniel Deronda (DD)* (GE); *Felix Holt (FH)* (GE); *Middlemarch (MM)* (GE); *The Mill on the Floss (MOF)* (GE); *Romola (R)* (GE); *Silas Marner (SM)* (GE)
loss-of-faith novels 39, 46
moral 39
objections by GE to novels advancing a religious affiliation 86–7
objections by GE to perfect heroines 86
realism in religious novels 15 n.15
social problem novels 39
Strauss on 36–7
unrealistic portraits of the working classes 84
Victorian novel 85
fidelity 171, 173–5
Finney, Charles Grandison
  Lectures on Revival 5–6
Foleshill, nr. Coventry 2–4, 17, 22, 41, 53
folk religion 150, 152–3
Franklin, Francis 3–4
Franklin, Mary 3–5
Franklin, Rebecca 3–5, 23, 32–3
Fraser's Magazine 72, 75–6
freethinkers 54, 78–9, 179, 199–200
  Bray family 17
  English 36
  GE as ix, 38, 41
  Hennell family 17
    Charles Hennell 35
  David Friedrich Strauss as 35–6
free will 24–5
friendships and relationships 6–7, 23–4, 45–6, 59, 90–1, 113–14, 190
  see also Cross, John Walter (GE's husband); Lewes, George Henry
  authors, with 87
    Harriet Beacher Stowe 49, 192
    Barbara Bodichon 49, 63 n.1, 110, 179, 203–4
    Bray family 17, 65–6
      Cara Bray 62, 65–7
      Charles Bray 65–6
    John Chapman 56–8, 65–6
    Maria and Richard Congreve 67

friendships and relationships (*cont.*)
   Emanuel Deutsch 198
   Rebecca Franklin 32
   Hennell family 17, 66–7, 69–70
     Sara Hennell 33, 65–7
   Martha Jackson 5, 131
   Benjamin Jowett 192
   Barbara Leigh Smith 65–6
   George Henry Lewes *see* Lewes, George Henry
   Martha Lewis 3–4, 17, 22, 32
   Bessie Parker 65–6
   at Rosehill 17, 22
   John Sibree 41
   Mary Sibree 20, 71–2
   Herbert Spencer 55–8
   David Friedrich Strauss 33–4
Froude, J. A. 45–6, 73, 110
   The Nemesis of Faith 46

Gaston, Sean 112–13
Genesis 45, 98, 180
The George Eliot Letters (GEL) (ed. G Haight) 1–12, 16–22, 25–7, 39, 42–4, 47, 49, 52–4, 56–7, 64–5, 69, 71, 91–2, 95–6, 110–12, 190
   see also letters by GE
   critical edition 78
German language, learning by GE 5, 34–5, 41
God
   see also Jesus Christ
   action in contemporary history 157
   being dishonourable to 28
   breath of 46
   commandments of 136–7
   decree and ordinance of 74–5
   exaltation of 60–1
   existence of 28–9, 149
   GE's view of 115
   glory of 77–8
   goodness of 60–1, 149, 151–2
   knowledge of 74–5
   mercy of 123–4
   message of 22
   passionate faith in 157–8
   power of 45–6, 74–5
   providence of 74–5
   recognition of 97–8
   sublime influence of 85–6
   voice of 135
   will of 75, 136–7
   word of 36
Goethe, Johann Wolfgang 72
Goldsmith, Oliver
   The Vicar of Wakefield 91
Gospels 17, 20–2, 35, 38–9, 113–14, 119–20, 123
   accounts of 17
   eternal facts of 44
   moral teachings 119, 122
   reconciling 36
   seen as eternal truth 122–3
   writers of 36–7
Great Exhibition (1851) 55
Greg, W. R. 55
   The Creed of Christendom 54
Gresley, W. 16
   Portrait of an English Churchman 16
Griff House, Warwickshire 2–3, 17, 22, 32, 50–1, 53

Habakkuk 2.5 13
Haight, Gordon
   The George Eliot Letters (GEL) *see The George Eliot Letters* (GEL) (ed. G Haight)
Hallam, Kirk 2
Hardy, Barbara 43
   George Eliot: A Critic's Biography xi n.3
Harper family, Chilvers Coton 1–2
Harper, Henry Richard 16
Harris, Margaret
   Journals of George Eliot (*Journals*) 147–8, 179, 183–4, 191 n.3
Harrison, Frederic 67
Hebrew Bible 85–6, 198–9
   see also Old Testament
   multilayeredness of human beings in 84–5
   representation style 85–6
Hegel, Georg Wilhelm Friedrich
   Lectures on the Philosophy of History 41
Hennell, Charles 21–2, 26, 33–4
   Inquiry Concerning the Origin of Christianity 30 n.3, 54
   as a Unitarian 35

Index

Hennell family 20–1, 32, 95
  see also Hennell, Charles; Hennell, Rufa (née Brabant); Hennell, Sara
  GE's friendship with 17, 66–7, 69–70
Hennell, Rufa (née Brabant) 21–2, 33–4, 78–9
Hennell, Sara 21–2, 26, 32–3, 78–9, 110
  Essay on the Sceptical Tendency of Butler's Analogy 24–5
  GE's friendship with 33, 65–7
  GE's letters to 27, 33–4, 40, 45–6, 51, 53–4, 61, 69–70, 90–1, 169–70
Henry, Nancy 65, 202
  Life 80 n.1
Herbert, Christopher 77
  Evangelical Gothic 14 n.12
heretics 22
Hinduism 199–200
historicity 36
  non-historicity of Scripture 180
Hoppus, John 5–6
Hughes, Kathryn 51
  George Eliot: The Last Victorian 14 n.3
Hunt, Thornton 54, 64
Huxley, Thomas 34

The Idea of a Future Life (GE) 59
immortality 25–6, 88–9
  absence of 89
  art, through 180, 182–3
  Christian teaching 97–8
  common 89
  hope of 180
  lack of belief in 89–90, 107
  and mortality 90–1
imperfection, human 9, 44
Impressions of Theophrastus Such (*Imp*), GE 193, 201–3
Incarnation doctrine 97–8
infidelity 53–4, 163–4
inquiry 20–1, 38
  conscience 112
  critical 22
  egoism 133
  freedom of 52
  philosophical 39
  professional 55–6
  and religion 38
intellectuals, English x, 17, 87–8, 131–2, 134

Islam 173, 199–200
Italian language, learning by GE 5

Jackson, Martha 5, 10
  GE's friendship with 5, 131
  GE's letters to 12, 17
Jacob, biblical figure 84–5, 98
Jay, Elisabeth
  Religion of the Heart 14 n.11
Jesus Christ 12, 18–19, 21–2, 28, 30, 67
  see also Calvinism; Christianity; God; Gospels; *The Life of Jesus* (*Das Leben Jesu*) (Strauss); questioning of religious doctrine and GE's loss of faith; religion and religious faith; Scriptures
  birth of 35
  child's vision of 124–5
  death of 17
  figure of 125
  miracles of 35, 133
  as repository of myth 59–60
  sacrifice of 9
  seen as the messiah 36–7
  as Son of God 123
  suffering of 123
  Thorvaldsen statute of risen Christ 40
The Jewish Chronicle 198
Johnston, Judith
  Journals of George Eliot (*Journals*) 147–8, 179, 183–4
Joseph, biblical figure 84–5
Journals of George Eliot (*Journals*) (ed. M. Harris and J. Johnston) 147–8, 179, 183–4, 191 n.3
Jowett, Benjamin 192
joy 125, 147
Judaism 10–11, 197
  and Catholic emancipation 197–8
  in *Daniel Deronda* 172, 193–4, 197–9, 201
  English ignorance of 197
  and faith 196, 199
  Hebrew Bible 84–6
  High Holidays 197–8
  history of English Jewry 197–8
  nationalist 104–5
  Oral Law 198–9
  religious doctrine, GE's views on origin of 28–9

Judaism (*cont.*)
　Sabbath practices 197–8
　Spinoza, Jewish background 73
　synagogues 197–8
　Talmud 197–9
　Torah 198–9
　Written Law 198–9

Keble, John
　The Christian Year 5–6, 134–5
King, Amy M.
　The Divine in the Commonplace 93 n.21
Knight, Mark
　Good Words 15 n.17
Knoepflmacher, U. C. 98–9
　George Eliot's Early Novels 93 n.15, 109 n.3
knowledge 8–9, 18, 75–6, 83–4, 103, 108, 126–7, 137, 141–2, 153, 172
　accumulated 130
　basic 9–10
　collective 129
　concrete 82
　deep 89
　of evil 117
　exceptional 38–9
　and experience 1–2
　of future loss 181–2
　of GE 38–9
　of God 74–5
　imperfect 196
　impoverished 168–9
　insufficient 151–2, 195–6
　limited 35
　new 98, 117
　newly felt 97–8
　of others 107
　and policy 55–6
　and reverence 92
　of Scripture 17–19
　self-knowledge 168–9
　of sinner 124
　Talmud as a repository of 198–9
　unlocking 55–6
　without freedom 176
Kreuger, Christine L.
　The Reader's Repentance 15 n.16
Kurnick, David 173

laboring classes *see* working classes
LaPorte, Charles 169–70
Larsen, Timothy 35
　Crisis of Doubt 30 n.1
　John Stuart Mill: A Secular Life 31 n.7
Lathom, Miss (boarding school, Attleborough) 3
Law of Progress 52
The Leader (radical weekly) 54, 69, 72
　"Rachel Gray" 81–2
Lecourt, Sebastian 172
letters by GE 6, 9–10, 16, 24–5, 28, 49, 51, 53–4, 203–4
　see also *The George Eliot Letters* (GEL) (ed. G Haight)
　to John Blackwood 100–1
　Bodenheimer's study of 24
　to Bray family 41–3
　　Cara 68–9, 112–13, 166
　　Charles 43–4, 57, 68–9, 78, 112–13, 127
　burning of 41–2
　to John Chapman 68–9
　Cross's curated version of 204
　to Isaac Evans 95
　to Robert Evans (father) 28–9
　forming a reading journal 5–6
　freedom to right 41–2
　to Hennell family 41–3
　　Sara 27, 33–4, 40, 45–6, 51, 53–4, 61, 69–70, 90–1, 169–70
　to Fanny Houghton Evans 45, 95–6
　to Martha Jackson 12, 17
　lack of confidence, portraying 183–4
　on Lewes 61–2
　to Maria Lewis 6–7, 10–11, 16–21
　on mental conflict and suffering 113–14
　to Elizabeth Pears 19–21
　private 56–7
　and religious faith 9–10, 19, 24, 85, 136–7
　　see also questioning of religious doctrine and GE's loss of faith
　Scriptures, incorporating into letters 72
　and sectarianism 20
　sense of impending mortality 163–4
　to John Sibree 41–2, 45, 50
　to Mary Sibree Cash 75–6
　signing of personal letters 95

Index

to Herbert Spencer 55
Francis Watts, correspondence with
    24–9, 42
on work completed 184
written in adolescence 3–4, 113–14
written in early twenties 118, 126–7
written during composition of
    Middlemarch 184, 190
Lewes, Agnes Jervis (George Lewes's first
    wife) 64, 69, 76, 95, 160–1
Lewes, Bertie (son of George) 192–3
Lewes, Charles (George Lewes's son)
    145, 204
Lewes, George Henry 54, 108
    anxiety of GE prior to meeting 113
    death (1878) 193
    exclusivity of GE's relationship with
        110
    on Feuerbach 61
    GE adopting surname 65
    GE as common-law wife to 2–3,
        64–79, 95
    GE getting to know 61–2
    GE traveling abroad with 23, 64–5,
        69, 145, 163
    interest in Spinoza 72–3
    interviews with 82–3
    letter to John Blackwood 91–2
    life with 125–6
    loving relationship with GE 57–8, 62
        compared with GE's relationship
            with Spencer 62
    meeting with GE (1851) 55
    non-legal marriage to GE 65, 71–2
    on science 92
    sons of 145, 179–80, 192–3, 204
    in Weimar 64–5, 69, 72, 75–6
    works by
        Comte's Philosophy of the Sciences 67
        Life and Works of Goethe 64
        Problems of Life and Mind 193, 203
        Sea-Side Studies 91–2
        The System of Positive Polity 67
    zoological expeditions 91–2
Lewes, Gertrude (née Hill) 204
Lewes, Thornie (son of George)
    179–80, 192–3
Lewis, Maria (governess to GE) 3–5, 9,
    19, 33, 113–14, 131
    death of 23

GE's friendship with 3–4, 17,
    22, 32
GE's letters to 6–7, 10–11, 16–21
Lichfield Cathedral, Staffordshire 4–5
The Life of Jesus (Das Leben Jesu) (Strauss)
    earlier translations 33–4
    GE's concerns with backing for 33
    translation by GE 17, 20–2, 33–4,
        38–40, 42, 59, 73
"The Lifted Veil" (GE) 197
Liggins, Joseph 110
Liszt, Franz 72, 192
Livesey, Ruth 191 n.4
loss of faith by GE *see* questioning of
    religious doctrine and GE's loss
    of faith
loss-of-faith novels 39, 46
Luke 18:35 133

Mackay, Robert William 38, 51, 59–60
    The Progress of the Intellect 37
marriage
    discussion of GE's marriage prospects
        32–3
    GE's common law marriage to
        George Lews *see under* Lewes,
        George Henry
    GE's marriage to John Cross 23
    GE's view of 70–1
    laws 71
    in *Middlemarch* 184–6, 192–3
    nominal 71
    poetry of 43
    and religious faith 184–5
    in *Romola* 146, 159–61
    sacrifice of mind in 32–3
Martineau, Harriet 33–4
    agnosticism of 50–1
Martineau, James 50–3
Matrimonial Causes Act 1857 80 n.1
Matthew 13 18–19, 67
Mechanics' Institute of Coventry 33
messianic era 36–7
middle classes 81, 87
Middle England 1–2
Middlemarch (MM) (GE) 120–1, 179
    characters
        Dorothea Brooke 183–90
        Edward Casaubon 184–7
        Will Ladislaw 187–90, 192–3

Middlemarch (MM) (GE) (*cont.*)
    Lydgate 185–6
    Rosamond Vincy 185–6
  childlike nature of Dorothea 186, 188–9
  compared with *Felix Holt* 188
  continuity between GE and narrator 184
  death portrayed in 180, 184–5, 187
  disenchantment in 43
  as a final novel 179
  and GE's portrayal of grandiose theories 55–6
  grandiose theories to provide "Key to all Mythologies" 55–6
  illusion 185
  inequality 185–6
  on making the world better 188
  marriage in 184–6
    failed legal marriage 192–3
  as a masterpiece 184–5, 192
  numbers of copies sold 192
  passionate ideals vs. meanness of opportunity 187–9
  publication of 192
  "rayless" figures 86
  religious faith 187–9
    loss of faith, examining 184–5, 187–90
  self-scrutiny, focus on 8–9
  size of novel 184–5
  time of writing 183–4
Midlands, England
  see also Middle England; provincialism/ parochialism of parish life
  local communities 2–3
  religious diversity 4–5
Mill, John Stuart 34, 163
The Mill on the Floss (MOF) (GE) 20
  agrarian background 129
  autobiographical novel 129, 131
  characters 134–6
    Stephen Guest 139, 140, 170–1
    Bob Jakin 133–4
    Dr. Kenn 132–3
    Lucy 139
    Maggie Tulliver 130, 131, 133–43, 144 n.12, 146–7, 166
    Philip 136–40, 142–3, 144 n.12
    Tom Tulliver 130, 141–3
  choice, dangers of 136–7
  compared with *Adam Bede* 129
  compared with *Romola* 159
  Conclusion 179
  conflict of love and duty 130, 170–1
  disenchantment in 43
  existential need 132
  fictional town of St Ogg's 132–3, 139
  first-person narration 202–3
  gender inequality 130, 136
  industrial and commercial relations, portrayal of 132
  life-struggles 135–6
  metaphors 135–6
  plots 130
  poverty in 136
  quotation from à Kempis 134
  references to *The Imitation of Christ* (à Kempis) 133–6, 138–40
  religious faith 129
  social conditions 132, 136
  temptation in 136
  time of writing 143, 145
Milner, Joseph
  History of the Church of Christ 5–6
Milton, John 9, 12, 39
miracles 35–6, 74–5, 156–8
morality 77, 107, 146–7, 181–2, 194
  creed stunting 88–9
  and dogma 76–7
  and religion 26, 38, 78–9
  secular x
mortality 89–91, 97–8, 180, 182, 185
  see also immortality
  GE's sense of 163–4
Müller, Max 199–200
myth 35, 59–60
  distinguished from allegory 36–7
  grandiose theories to provide "Key to all Mythologies" 55–6

natural law 24–5, 74–5, 112, 117
Newdigate family 2–3, 5
Newman, Francis 45–6
  The Soul 46
Newman, John Henry 6
New Testament 18–19, 28, 85, 198–9
novels *see* fiction; *specific works by GE*
Nuneaton, Warwickshire
  Arbury Hall estate 2, 5

Index

Old Testament 28
  prophecies 36–7
Oxford Movement tract writers 5–6, 9

Pantheism 25
parables 18–19
parish life 1
  see also Chilvers Coton parish church, Warwickshire
  'closed' nature of 2
  and identity 2
  provincialism/parochialism of 1–5
Parker, Bessie Rayner 65–6, 110
Parker-Newdigate, Francis 2
parody 13
Pears, Elizabeth 22, 33
  GE's letters to 19–21
Pearson family 2
  see also Evans, Christiana (*née* Pearson) (GE's mother)
Peirce, Melusina Fay 189–90
Pentecosts 45
piety 11, 16, 29, 46, 72–4, 77–8, 81, 100–2, 156–7, 172
poetry ix–x, 5–7, 12, 39
  see also *Collected Poems* (*Poems*) (GE); *Selected Essays, Poems and Other Writings* (*Essays*) (GE)
  and art 137
  and the Bible 169, 199
  Christian belief, without 170
  cultural value 169
  and *Daniel Deronda* 195
  and ethics 119–20
  in *Felix Holt* 164
  GE turning from/to 162, 184
  Hebrew 48 n.16, 197, 199–200
  'The Legend of Jubal" 180, 182–3
  literary value 169
  as literature 163–4
  long poems 162
  of love and marriage 43
  of maternity 43
  and prose 199
  and religion 43, 164, 169–70
  and science 199
  and scripture 169–70
  short poems 162
  "The Spanish Gypsy" 162–3, 169–71, 176–7, 189–90
  of the Talmud 199

  Victorian era 169–70
  written by GE 12, 162, 169, 181, 183–4, 192
    first poem 9–10, 11
poverty
  in *The Mill on the Floss* 136
  relative 131
  and religious faith 131
  romanticizing 84
prophetic teaching 18–19
Protestantism 10, 26, 85–6, 131, 158
provincialism/parochialism of parish life 1–5
Psalms 2:11 72
Psalms 126:5 111

questioning of religious doctrine and GE's loss of faith ix, 3–4, 113
  see also under religion and religious faith
  breaking with the Church 126–7
  creed stunting morality 88–9
  critique of faith from within the faith 38
  decision not to accompany father to church 17, 19, 23, 65–6, 94
  "holy war" 38–9, 66–7
  hypocrisy exposed 28–9, 62, 86–7
  independence of mind/using own words x, 18–19, 28–9, 34–5, 37
  Jewish origins of religion doctrine, GE's views on 28–9
  leaving Christian orthodoxy as a woman 50–1
  objections by GE to novels advancing a religious affiliation 86–7
  perceived harm to individuals and society 28–9
  renunciation of orthodox dogma 17, 19, 28–9, 37–8, 66, 76–7
  response to death 45
  spiritual loneliness 1–2
  view of God 115

rationalists 36
reading
  see also education of GE and Evans family; Eliot, George (Mary Ann (Marian) Evans), adult and personal life; Eliot, George (Mary Ann (Marian) Evans), career; publications; school life
  of authors, vs. books 22

reading (*cont.*)
  books allowable to Christian readers 12–13
  GE's love of 5–6, 17
  letters forming a reading journal 5–6
  omnivorous or voracious reading by GE 13, 146
  Scriptures, supernaturalist reading of 36
  skim reading 5–6
realism
  in art 81–2
  domestic 85–6
  of GE, compared with her idealism 98–9
  GE's objections to unrealistic portraits 84
  Homeric vs. biblical narrative 84–6
  and morality 88–9
  realist novels by GE 85–6
  Adam Bede (*AB*) 117
  and religious novels 15 n.15
  Victorian novels 84, 194–5
  Western modes of realist representation 84–5
redemption 161, 196–7
Reformation 10–11
religion and religious faith 105–6, 129
  see also Calvinism; Christianity; Church of England; evangelicalism; Jesus Christ; Judaism; parish life; Protestantism; questioning of religious doctrine and GE's loss of faith; religion and religious faith; Roman Catholicism; Scriptures; secularism
  adapting x
  Buddhism 199–200
  challenge of boundaries 12–13
  challenging x, 13, 19
  crisis of 30 n.1, 147
  critique of faith from within the faith 38
  defense of Christian faith, in Victorian times 24–5
  definition by GE ix
  disappointment 148–9
  Dissent 2–5, 55
  doctrinal 149–50
  of early Christians 52–3
  of Robert Evans 29
  and fiction 36–7, 101
  forms of 100
  fruits of 27, 53–4
  fundamental 76–7
  of GE
    active 6–7, 7
    in *Collected Poems* 182–3
    evangelicalism (in youth) 7–9, 44, 47, 81
    loss of ix, x, 25–6, 43, 143, 146–7
    in novels *see below*
    in "The Spanish Gypsy" 162, 172–4, 176, 189–90
    tolerance for xi n.3
    trials of 42–3
  GE's loss of faith *see* questioning of religious doctrine and GE's loss of faith
  in GE's novels
    Adam Bede (*AB*) 129, 140–1, 148
    Daniel Deronda (*DD*) 172–3, 195–6
    Felix Holt (*FH*) 164–5, 168
    Middlemarch (*MM*) 184–5, 187–90
    The Mill on the Floss (*MOF*) 129
    Romola (*R*) 146–8, 150, 154–9, 162
    Silas Marner (*SM*) 147–53
  Hinduism 199–200
  "how-tos" of 187–8
  Islam 199–200
  in Judaism 196, 199
  language of religious freedom 57
  loss of 147
  loss-of-faith novels 39, 46
  and marriage 184–5
  materials of x
  in miracle 157–8
  and morality 26
  new sort of 34–5
  passionate faith in God 157–8
  and philosophy 73–4
  in poem "The Legend of Jubal" 180, 182–3
  and poetry 43, 164, 169–70
  and poverty 131
  prayer meetings 3–4
  protests against 54
  publications, in England x, 5
  questioning *see* questioning of religious doctrine and GE's loss of faith

redemption 161, 196–7
religious diversity, exposure of Evans family to 3–5
religious vs. secular thought x
restoration of 152–3
rituals of 121, 150
in *Scenes of Clerical Life*
  "Janet's Repentance" 99–100, 102–6
  "The Sad Fortunes of Amos Barton" 97–100
and science 38
seeing as a choice among others 176
settling 16
simple 104
Sunday schools 3
theological 150
in uses of suffering 113–14
in Victorian England x, 26
repentance 98
revelation 17, 25, 38
Riehl, Wilhelm Friedrich 82–3, 89
  The Natural History of German Life 82
Roman Catholicism 6
Romanticism 73
Romola (R) (GE) 145–6, 160–1
  betrayal in 146–8
  characters
    Romola 146–8, 155–6, 158–60, 200–1
    Girolamo Savonarola 145–6, 154–60, 164
    Tito 146–7, 154–5, 159
  compared with *The Mill on the Floss* 159
  compared with *Silas Marner* 154, 157–8, 160–1
  on consequences of choices 146–7
  crisis of lack of faith 147, 162
  on disastrous marriage 146, 159–61
  disenchantment in 43
  double plot line 168
  on fallibility of religious authority 147
  miracles in 157–8
  on miscarriage of justice 146, 154–6
  nineteenth-century concerns 146–7
  preparation for 147
  psychology in 153
  religious faith 146–8, 150, 154–9, 162
  Renaissance Florence, setting of 145–6, 155–6
  researching 153–4
  on retributive justice 154–5
  search for meaning 146–7
  suffering in 147, 159
  theodicy, concern of 150
Rosehill, nr. Coventry 32, 51, 73, 78
  friends of GE at 17, 22, 59, 66
  "radical" circle at 32
Rousseau, Jean-Jacques 45–6
Ruskin, John 110, 192
  Modern Painters 81–2

sacrifice 12, 25, 30, 34, 56–7, 65–6, 68–70, 75–6, 119, 168–9
  of Christ 9
  Christian ideal 57, 67, 188
  divine 60–1
  efficacious 68
  and love 68
  of mind, in marriage 32–3
  as mode of thinking for GE 69–70
  painful 181–2
  personal 70
  proof of 69
  self-sacrifice 57, 68, 70
  and utterance 45–6
  worthiness 32–3
Sadler, Thomas 204
salvation 7–8, 17, 36, 76–7, 106, 112–14, 166–7
  and Christian atonement 112, 119
  predestined 20
  in *Silas Marner* 158
  from sin 9
Sand, George 45–6
Saul, biblical figure 84–5
Scenes of Clerical Life (Scenes) (GE) 106, 110–12, 158–9, 169–70, 179
  completion of (1857) 112–13
  Conclusion 179
  deaths in 106–7
  first edition 110
  "Janet's Repentance" 94–5, 104–6, 108, 140–1, 195
    Mr. Dempster 100–1, 106–7
    evangelical conversion 99–100
    evangelicalism 105, 106
    human and divine sympathy theme 100
    Janet Dempster 146–7

Scenes of Clerical Life (*Scenes*) (GE) (*cont.*)
    Mr. Jerome 100–2
    kindness 100
    Mrs Raynor 103–4
    religion vs. irreligion 100–1
    religious faith 99–100, 102–6
    sectarianism in 100–2
    submission to Blackwood 108
    Mr. Tryan (curate) character
        99–101, 105–7, 140–1, 166,
        200–1
    "Mr Gilfil's Love Story" 94–5, 99–100,
        103, 106–7
    "The Sad Fortunes of Amos
        Barton" 87–8, 90–1, 94–100,
        106–7, 109 n.6
    Mr. Cleves 99–100
    Mr. Hackit 98–9
    heathenism 98–9
    Milly 96–8, 106–7
    Mrs Patten 98–9
    religious faith 97–100
    Shepperton, villagers of 98–9
    unlikability of Amos 97
Scheinberg, Cynthia 199
Schleiermacher, Friedrich 36
school life
    see also education of GE and Evans
        family
    dame school 3
    Mary and Rebecca Franklin's
        boarding school, Coventry 2–4
    Miss Lathom's boarding school
        (Attleborough, Warwickshire) 3
    Mrs Wallington's school (The Elms,
        Nuneaton) 3–4
science 38–9, 59, 76–7, 195–6, 199
    empirical 157–8
    and ethics 76
    in the mid-nineteenth-century 92
    natural science 39
    and poetry 199
    and religion 38
Scott, Walter 9–10
Scripture 7, 10, 17–18, 35
    see also Bible; Christianity; New
        Testament; Old Testament
    challenge to authority of 36
    divine inspiration, GE's assessment
        of 28–9

    "heaven" mythology with 22
    incorporating into letters 72
    infallibility doctrine 36
    non-historicity of 180
    supernaturalist reading of 36
    writings 36
sectarianism 20, 73–4, 97
    in "Janet's Repentance" 100–2
secularism ix–x
    see also religion and religious faith
Seeley and Burnside (religious
    publishers) 11
Selected Essays, Poems and Other Writings
    (*Essays*) (GE) 37–9, 46, 52, 54,
    76–8, 81–4, 86–90
self-understanding 8–10
sermons ix–x, 20, 49, 63 n.1, 70–1, 83,
    102–3
    orthodox 49
    preaching 99–100
sexual freedom 32, 64–6
Shakespeare, William 9–10
Sharp, Hasana 75, 83–4
Sibree Cash, Mary 20, 75–6
Sibree, John 41–2, 45, 50
Sibree, Mary 20, 41, 71–2
Sidgwick, Henry 192
Silas Marner (*SM*) (GE) 166
    adoption in 160–1
    backstory 147–8
    belief in territorial gods 180
    characters 153, 158
        Eppie (child) 152–4, 157–8
        Silas 148, 160–1
        William 154, 158
        Dolly Winthrop 149–52, 156, 166
    compared with *Romola* 154, 157–8,
        160–1
    completion of 153–4
    composition of 149–50
    crisis of lack of faith 147
    defining what is unseen 153
    disenchantment in 43
    divine justice 151
    fairness 151
    ignorance, costs of 149–52
    independent thought 149
    interruption of *Romola* 163
    Lantern Yard 147–8
    publication of 147–8

Index

realist/sensationalist elements 147–8
religious faith 147–53
representation of theological
    faith 149–50
seen as a fable 147–8
simplicity 153
territorial gods, primitive belief in 180
theology 151
time of writing 147
the unseen theme 153
Smith, Barbara Leigh 65–6
Smith, George (publisher) 154
Snell, K. D. M.
    Parish and Belonging 13 n.1
    Rival Jerusalems 14 n.5
social class
    artisan classes 81
    educated classes 34, 134
    in GE's realist novels 85–6
    higher classes 83
    lesser educated classes 103
    middle classes 81, 87
    representation of 82
    working classes 41–2, 82–4, 87–8, 101, 131, 151–2
social problem novels 39
sophistry 117
soul 8–10, 12–13, 20, 27, 100, 104, 115, 123–5, 135–6, 140–1, 156, 160, 175, 177, 186, 197
    divine-human 46
    immoral 89–90
    individual 46
    inner 44
    living 46
    recreated 196
    sacred human soul 98
    whole soul 1–2, 19, 34, 139
"The Spanish Gypsy" 162–3, 169–71, 176–7, 189–90
    Annunciation, image of 170–1
    Father Isidor 170–1, 174–6
    Fedalma 170–7, 189–90
    Silva (Duke) 170–2, 175–7
    Zarca 171–6
Spencer, Herbert 34, 55–6, 110
    arts critic for *The Economist* 55
    casting in the wrong role by GE 57–9
    on evolution 55
    fields of interest 55

friendship with GE 55–8
GE's letters to 55
Social Statics 55
theories of 55–6
Spinoza, Benedict de 36, 72, 76–7, 83–4
    atheism of 78–9
    Ethics 17, 64, 72–9, 81
        see also translations by GE
    Froude's essay on 73
    Jewish background 73
    Lewes's interest in 72–3
    readership 79
    Theologico-Political Treatise (*TTC*) 50, 72–5
St. Paul 27, 141
Strauss, David Friedrich 22, 26, 33–6
    contrasted with English
        theologians 36
    as a freethinker 35–6
    GE's friendship with 33–4
    The Life of Jesus (*Das Leben Jesu*) 17, 20–2, 33–4, 38–40, 42, 59, 73
        see also translations by GE
    and Scripture 36–7
suffering
    in *Adam Bede* 112–13, 115–16, 118
    in "Amos Barton" 96–7
    "baptisms" of 84
    evangelical Christian 130
    experience of 67, 126–7
    GE's letters covering 113–14
    recognition of the reality of 25
    in *Romola* 147, 159
    uses of 113–16
    valued by GE 113–14, 118
supernatural, the 17, 35, 60–1, 157, 195
    see also miracles; myth
    rationalists vs. supernaturalists 36
    reading of Scripture 36, 73–4
superstition 74–5, 101, 148–50, 152, 155
    and folk religion 152
    primitive 196
    and religion 156–7
sympathy 77–8, 81–2, 89–90, 113–14, 117–18, 127
    divine vs. human 99–100
    lack of 88
    reverential 52

Talmud 197–9
  see also Judaism
Taylor, Charles 35, 176
Tennyson, Alfred Lord 72, 192
Theologico-Political Treatise (TTC)
  (Spinoza) 50, 72–5
theology 39, 86–7, 96–9
  afterlife 25
  and anthropology 59–61
  atonement 25
  of Butler 24–5
  Christian 98–9, 149–50, 162, 195–6
    Calvinism 25
    doctrine 102–3
    ignorance of 104
  faith 150
  of Feuerbach 59–61
  in Hebrew Bible 85–6
  in *Silas Marner* 151
  Strauss contrasted with English theologians 36
  traditional 151–2
Tracts for the Times of the Oxford Movement writers 5–6, 9
translations by GE 34–5, 38–40, 61, 146
  anonymous 50
  Essence of Christianity (Feuerbach) 17, 34, 59, 73, 78–9
  Ethics (Spinoza) 17, 64, 72–9, 81
  into and from German 35, 41
  good quality translation, GE on 38–9
  The Life of Jesus (Das Leben Jesu) (Strauss) 17, 20–2, 33–4, 38–40, 42, 59, 73
  of philosophy 11
  and teaching 17
  Tractatus Theologico Politicus (Spinoza) 50, 72–5
  translation period 40
  of works by Alexandre Rodolphe Vinet 26
Trinity Church, Coventry 19

Trollope, Anthony 192
Turgenev, Ivan 192
Turner, Frank M.
  Contesting Cultural Authority x

unmarried couples, comparative acceptance of 72
utterance 45–6

Vinet, Alexandre Rodolphe 26

Wallington, Mrs (boarding school, Nuneaton) 3–4
Ward, Henry 63 n.1
Watts, Francis 26, 28–9, 59
  GE's letters to 24–9, 42
Wesley, John 122–3, 132
The Westminster Review 33–4, 50–1, 53–4, 59, 61, 64, 66, 72–3, 76, 78, 110
  Belles-Lettres section 72, 94–5
  Contemporary Literature section 52
  elite readers 83
  Prospectus 52
  "Silly Novels by Lady Novelists" (1856) 82
Wilberforce, William 5–6, 165
Williams, John (Dissented missionary) 5–6
women 78–9, 170, 189–90
  French, contribution to literature 72
  sexual double standard for 65, 119
Woolf, Virginia 190
Wordsworth, William 20
working classes 41–2, 82–3, 101, 131, 151–2
  GE drawn to 87–8
  romanticizing, GE's objections to 84
  unrealistic portraits, GE's objections to 84

Yeoh, Paul 141–2, 144 n.11
Young, Edward 87–9

List of other titles in Spiritual Lives series

Ebenezer Howard
Inventor of the Garden City
Frances Knight

Walter Lippmann
American Skeptic, American Pastor
Mark Thomas Edwards

Mark Twain
Preacher, Prophet, and Social Philosopher
Gary Scott Smith

Benjamin Franklin
Cultural Protestant
D. G. Hart

Arthur Sullivan
A Life of Divine Emollient
Ian Bradley

Queen Victoria
This Thorny Crown
Michael Ledger-Lomas

Theodore Roosevelt
Preaching from the Bully Pulpit
Benjamin J. Wetzel

Margaret Mead
A Twentieth-Century Faith
Elesha J. Coffman

W. T. Stead
Nonconformist and Newspaper Prophet
Stewart J. Brown

Leonard Woolf
Bloomsbury Socialist
Fred Leventhal and Peter Stansky

John Stuart Mill
A Secular Life
Timothy Larsen

Christina Rossetti
Poetry, Ecology, Faith
Emma Mason

Woodrow Wilson
Ruling Elder, Spiritual President
Barry Hankins